Prince Edward Island

COLOURGUIDE

Sixth Edition

Edited by Jocelyne Lloyd

Formac Publishing Company Limited
Halifax

Contents

Formac Publishing Company Limited recognizes the support of the Province of Nova Scotia through the Department of Tourism, Culture and Heritage. We acknowledge the financial support of the Government of Canada through the Book Publishing Industry Development Program (BPIDP) for our publishing activities.

NOVA SCOTIA
Tourism, Culture and Heritage

Library and Archives Canada Cataloguing in Publication

The Prince Edward Island colourguide / editor, Jocelyne Lloyd. — 6th ed.

(Formac colourguides)
Includes index.
ISBN 978-0-88780-866-1
1. Prince Edward Island — Guidebooks.
I. Lloyd, Jocelyne

FC2607.P733 2009 917.1704'5 C2008-907947-7

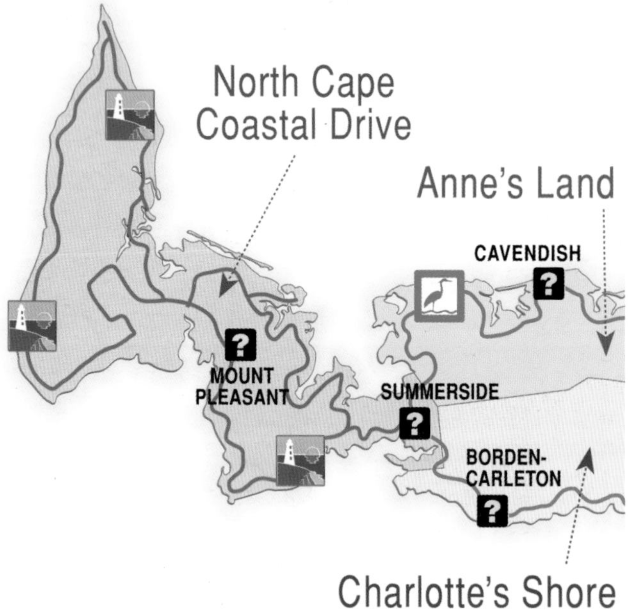
North Cape Coastal Drive
Anne's Land
CAVENDISH
MOUNT PLEASANT
SUMMERSIDE
BORDEN-CARLETON
Charlotte's Shore

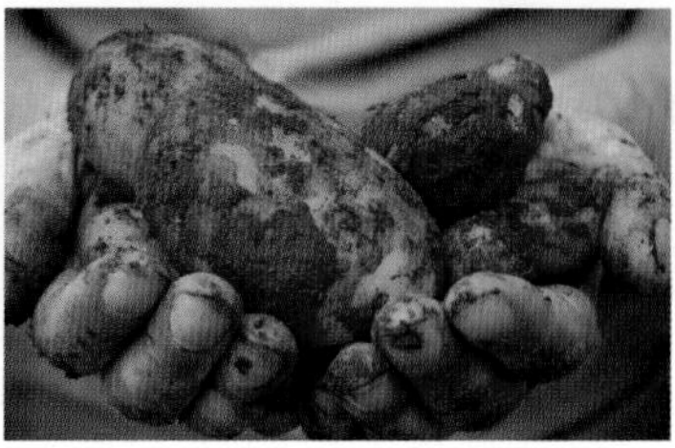

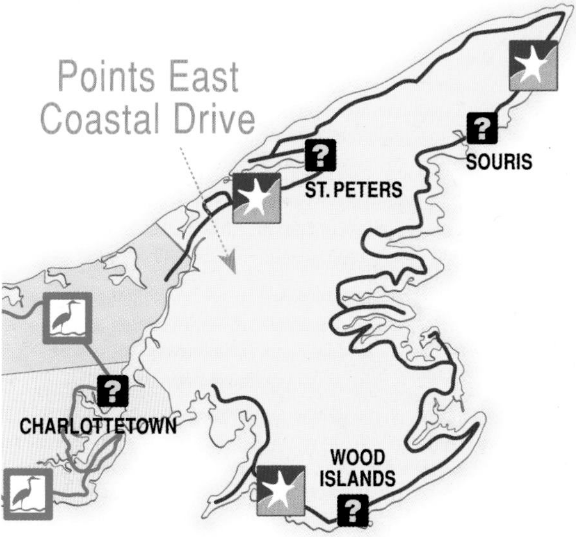
Points East
Coastal Drive
ST. PETERS
SOURIS
CHARLOTTETOWN
WOOD
ISLANDS

Welcome to Prince Edward Island!

This guide has been written to help you prepare a vacation in Canada's smallest province, giving you not only an introduction to the very best that Prince Edward Island has to offer but also detailed information on places to stay, where to eat and many other facilities.

The Island's Best section gives an overview of the landscape and cultural activities. It is followed by the Island Routes section, offering a tour of each of the four tourism regions. The final section of the guide contains listings, with practical information on everything you will want to do in Prince Edward Island: accommodations, restaurants, museums, parks and other attractions.

This book is an independent guide. Its editors and contributors have made their recommendations and suggestions based solely on what they believe to be the best, most interesting and most appealing places to visit. No payments or contributions of any kind are solicited or accepted by the creators or the publishers of this guide.

This book is the work of a team of talented writers, editors and photographers. You can read about them below:

COLLEEN ABDULLAH is a writer, visual communication designer and marketing consultant. She lives in Mahone Bay on Nova Scotia's beautiful South Shore.

LAURIE BRINKLOW is founder, owner and publisher of Acorn Press. She is publishing co-ordinator in the graphics department at the University of Prince Edward Island, where she is completing her Master of Arts in Island Studies.

STEPHEN BRUN is a reporter for the Eastern Graphic in Montague. He has worked for Golf PEI and at some of the provincial golf courses. His hobbies include watching/playing sports, creative writing and trying to get to know everyone on the Island.

KUMARI CAMPBELL owns and operates a consulting company, which primarily handles tourism marketing. She likes to write about travel and food and writes poetry in her spare time.

LOBIE DAUGHTON specializes in community-based economic development for the co-operative sector. He also works with a consulting business, "Healthy Community Partners," which focuses on personal and planetary health issues. Lobie lives in Mermaid, Prince Edward Island.

H. SHIRLEY HORNE, an award-winning freelance journalist, has written hundreds of articles over the past twenty years which have been published in most local, regional and some national and international newspapers and magazines. She is based in Charlottetown.

JOCELYNE LLOYD is an editor at the *Journal Pioneer* in Summerside and lives in Charlottetown with her husband and two young children. During her free time, she stays right on PEI, in hopes of a perfect beach day.

ANNA MACDONALD now works in the communications department at the University of Prince Edward Island, and was co-chair of the Anne 2008

Celebration Committee that helped organize events across PEI celebrating the 100th anniversary of *Anne of Green Gables*.

HUGH MACDONALD is a retired high-school teacher; author of a children's book, *Chung Lee Loves Lobsters*; four books of poetry, and a novel, *Murder at Mussel Cove*. He lives with his family in Brudenell.

WENDY MACGREGOR is a freelance writer, community activist and "born-again" Islander. She spends her winters in Halifax and summers in Cavendish with her husband, 3 children and skunk-chasing dog.

JOY BELL MACKENZIE is an avid cottager, having been a cottage renter and owner, mostly in the Cavendish area. She lives and works in Charlottetown.

WAYNE MACKINNON is a provincial government communications officer and a sessional lecturer in political studies at the University of Prince Edward Island. He is the author of a number of books and articles on Prince Edward Island history and politics.

IAN MACQUARRIE is a retired professor of biology at the University of Prince Edward Island. He is the author of *The Bonshaw Hills* (Institute of Island Studies).

RYAN VICTORIA MCADAM-YOUNG is an artist and entrepreneur. She lives and works in Mount Stewart with her husband, daughter and son. Ryan spends all her free time exploring the Maritimes in search of her latest and greatest back-country hike.

DAN MCASKILL is a naturalist, birder and writer who lives in Donagh. He's a leading expert on birding in Prince Edward Island, and is the Island's contact for the Audubon Society and Bird Studies Canada's seasonal bird counts.

ANNE MCCALLUM lives on a scenic 100-acre property in Hazel Grove, just west of Hunter River. She is the communications co-ordinator for the University of Prince Edward Island.

REG PORTER is an historical consultant and former lecturer in art history at the University of Prince Edward Island. He is retired and lives in Belle River.

FAYE POUND is the co-ordinator of the P.E.I. Senior's Federation. She has written on PEI heritage for the *Journal Pioneer*, helped establish the Wyatt Heritage Properties in Summerside and has received awards for her work in promoting Island heritage and architectural renovations.

NANCY RUSSELL juggles work at CBC Radio, writing books for young adults and playing chauffeur to her children. Her latest novel *So Long, Jackie Robinson* (Key Porter, 2007) was recently chosen by the Canadian Children's Book Centre as one of the Best Books for Kids & Teens.

JULIE V. WATSON is the author of more than 20 books and hundreds of periodical articles. She owns and operates Seacroft, a small publishing and marketing business, and conducts workshops on topics such as food and regional cuisine, travel, history and folklore and more.

CAMPBELL WEBSTER runs Campbell Webster Entertainment, as well as represents a number of well-known performers and speakers. He formerly led cycling tours of the Island and is now on the international board of humanitarian organization CUSO-VSO.

Introduction

Jocelyne Lloyd

Potato blossom

On a sunny, summer day on Prince Edward Island, there is literally something for you to do from sun-up to sun-down, and well into the night. There's no need to rush, though. Many visitors to PEI are content to start their day with a trip to the beach or the golf course and then spend the day just enjoying the beautiful vistas of dazzling water, red or white sands and blue sky. They may top off their day of "getting away from it all" with a heaping plate of seafood after hours of tasting the salt in the air.

Other Island guests may be more adventurous, though, and need a packed agenda to feel they haven't frittered away their holiday. They can be accommodated, too. the Island is small enough that you really can have it all.

A trip to the beach or the golf course is usually high on an island visitor's holiday to-do list, but seeking some surf or a hole-in-one doesn't have to take all day. In the summer, the sun is up by 6 am and — if you are, too — you can have your swim or play nine holes before breakfast.

Speaking of breakfast, if you're staying at one of PEI's numerous bed and breakfast establishments, you're in for a treat. Many of these accommodations, usually in heritage homes, pull out all the stops to make sure your day starts

with some hearty island fare. Baked goods, jams, meat and eggs are piled high on your plate — and you can probably see from your bedroom window the farm where the victuals first got their start.

Prince Edward Island is embracing its homegrown food like never before, with farmers' markets filled with hungry shoppers every Saturday morning. A section in the new Dining chapter in this 6th edition of the *Colourguide* explains more about the Buy PEI initiative and how it certainly will add some flavour to your holiday.

Also new to this edition — and related to the food theme — is information on the best restaurants in the province. The dining section in the listings also gives you a starting point for sampling island fare, but these are only recommendations. Feel free to dine wherever your stomach takes you. With a culinary school in Charlottetown, the Island always has new eating establishments opening up or changing chefs, and you may happen upon some brilliant cuisine not yet sampled by our writers.

The listings section at the back of the *Colourguide* includes the contact information for many of the hot spots picked by our writers, as well as some other handy facts for visitors. Some website and e-mail addresses weren't available at publication time because those ending in "isn.net" were changed recently. Phone for the address or

Enjoying an Island beach

Charlottetown Harbour

See the Golf chapter for where to tee-off

type the name of the operation into your Web browser to find the new URL.

The contributors to this book are experts on the topics they cover. They live, work, or spend considerable time in the area they've written about. They will guide you through the Island like a friend or relative would, showing you places and activities you may not want to miss. Their recommendations may not appear in the official PEI visitors' guide because they are not tourist operators and they are not gaining anything by having you eat or shop at a certain place. They just want you to enjoy yourself, whether you use your wallet or not.

In fact, many of the activities enjoyed by travellers to the Island are free or cost only a small fee. Hiking and

Pastoral scenery

cycling trails are well-maintained and free to use. Many museums and galleries in the province charge less than $5 a person or only ask that a donation be made to put towards operating costs. Go for a swim at an outdoor community pool or at a provincial beach for free while your children enjoy themselves on the playground equipment.

Golfing doesn't have to be pricey, either. While there are premium golf courses that are as expensive as they are challenging, there are still many family-friendly clubs with green fees of less than $30. For evening entertainment, there are always ceilidhs, concerts and other gatherings that are free of charge or just ask for a donation towards a worthy cause.

Browse through the chapters or the listings section for more ideas on how to spend your holiday, whether it's as cheaply as possible or by sparing no expense.

Potato field in bloom

Confederation bridge

Land and Sea

Ian MacQuarrie

Orby Head

Islands are different. Lack of physical contact with the mainland allows life to go its own way, to develop separate patterns and to foster uncommon relationships. With both plants and people, there is an island way of surviving.

Not that mainlands aren't important. Indeed, Prince Edward Island was once firmly joined to the continent; rising waters in Northumberland Strait effected a divorce comparatively recently, perhaps only 5,000 years ago, and signs of the old union are still quite evident. A few millennia earlier, glaciers thoroughly scoured the land, resetting the ecological clock. Much before that, erosion of ancient mountains provided material for the sedimentary bedrock on which the Island stands. These widely spaced historical occurrences have left a legacy of markers for the modern explorer.

Grand River estuary

Geology, geography, basic ecology

The Island rests upon part of a great plain of sedimentary rocks, formed in

Acadian Forest in Stanhope

Permocarboniferous times and now mostly submerged by the Gulf of St. Lawrence. Prince Edward Island and the Magdalen Islands (as well as parts of Nova Scotia and New Brunswick) are still above the tides, and bear witness to the character of this bedrock. The typical red colour of the bedrock is from its oxidized iron (rust) content. Informally called "redbeds," these rocks are younger than the granite, slate and quartzite so evident in neighbouring provinces. Redbeds are soft, and are easily broken and eroded or smoothed by water and ice action. Fossils are uncommon. Rocky outcrops are highly visible along the coastline, but inland a thin mantle of glacial debris (till) now hides most of this foundation.

The arrangement of bedrock controls general land form; the orientation of rivers, hills and valleys is as old as the rocks themselves. However, much more recently glaciers reorganized the landscape. The advance of the ice brought granite boulders from the mainland. These erratic visitors are common in the western part of the province. The huge weight of the glaciers crushed and scoured the terrain, smoothing the hills and actually pushing the land itself down. As the ice melted and retreated, beginning about 14,000 years ago, relationships between land and sea were quite changeable. Shell-encrusted beach terraces in western Prince Edward Island are now well above sea level; the land rebounded when released from its burden. Later, to the east, forests were drowned as the sea came surging back.

As glaciers retreated, plants and animals occupied the newly exposed ground. Some, following the ice closely, were able to reach the Island before the land bridge was inundated. Others never made it, or were forced to wait for thousands of years and catch a ride with humans. The

Farm near New London

Top: Erosion at East Point
Right: Covehead

Island flora and fauna contain no unique species, but the diversity and abundance are different from our neighbouring provinces. Later, the arrival of European settlers resulted in many rapid additions and deletions to the lists. Thus, disturbances hundreds to thousands of years ago brought about change that is still occurring; Island ecology still hasn't settled down.

At present, this is a small, crescent-shaped island, in area about 5,600 km, or one-tenth the size of Nova Scotia. The distance from tip to tip is about 230 km, with a highly variable width due to a much-indented coastline. No part of the Island is more than a few hours' walk from salt water, and this closeness to the sea profoundly affects all life. The sea is slowly claiming the land; coastal erosion may capture one metre per year (more in some places). The broad estuaries are drowned river valleys; rivers were longer when the sea level was lower. These productive estuaries, fertilized from the land and warmed by the sun,

Cavendish Cliffs

Sunset, Brackley Beach

are important in the lives of many species, including humans. Fishing and farming have been Island mainstays since settlement began.

The tidal range in this part of the Gulf is not great; high and low lines on a wharf are often only a couple of metres apart. However, the waters, particularly on the Strait shore, shoal so gently that even a short tide drop may expose a kilometre of sand bars. While the soft bedrock provides poor holding ground for marine algae (seaweeds), the bars and mud flats are good habitat for shellfish. There is no shortage of sand for beaches, often backed by dunes on the north and eastern shores. Seaward drainage may be blocked by the dunes, providing more rich coastal wetlands and ponds.

Inland, the topography is undulating and gentle: even the hills in central and eastern Prince Edward Island are seldom over a hundred metres high. The red soil looks deceptively fertile; it is really only a thin, fragile skin stretched over glacial rubble, with bedrock never far below the surface. The land is easily worked, but it requires lime and fertilizer for good crops. Farming has, perhaps only temporarily, shaped the surface and particularly the appearance of this land. The trees remain at the fringes, ever ready to return.

Walking through Acadian forest, Stanhope

Flora

While the Island, like its neighbours, belongs to the Acadian forest region, its isolation and profound degree of disturbance by European settlement result in a different array of species. As the glacial ice retreated, tundra-like vegetation followed closely; this, in turn, was displaced by spruce and pine, with the Acadian beech/sugar maple/yellow birch complex following later still. Indeed, many of the slower-migrating plants never got here at all. The aboriginal inhabitants would have known an excellent forest, with fine trees in both hardwood and softwood

Top: Purple Loosestrife at West Point
Right: Lupine

stands. This was the forest encountered by the Europeans, and they proceeded with great passion to cut, burn or clear almost all of it.

Forests today cover almost 50 per cent of the Island, but the composition is a shadow of the original; it is regrowth, with only scattered old trees remaining. Disease has decimated the beech. The mighty pine is mostly gone, as is the red oak, the Island's provincial tree. Many early settlers cleared, burned and then moved on; the land grew up into a new forest, dominated by white spruce, alder and, after a time, white birch. Short-lived species such as poplar and cherry are much more common now. It is good wildlife habitat, but contributes little to the provincial economy.

The settlers brought with them, by accident or design, many Eurasian plants; hundreds of these became successful in their new home. Almost one-third of the present vascular flora can be traced to such recent introductions. Many of our most troublesome weeds first crossed the Atlantic with the immigrants, and remained here after the more restless humans moved on to New England or western Canada. Daisy and hawk-weed are found now with the earlier-arrived goldenrod and wild strawberry; this multicultural mix is pleasing to the eye if not to the farmer's pocketbook.

Changing agricultural patterns also led to the contraction or expansion of species range. Lupines, troublesome weeds in pastures, were once strictly controlled by farmers. Now they riot for miles along roadsides; a weed has become a photo opportunity, its picture infesting the tourist literature. On the other hand, the opportunistic purple loosestrife of the marshes is widely condemned, although the rhetoric greatly exceeds any significant control measures. There are fashions in wild

Wildflower Meadow

plants, as well as in their garden relatives, and yesterday's enemy may become tomorrow's friend.

Fauna

Animal presence, or absence, has been controlled by the same factors: glaciation, land bridge and human settlement, with additions and deletions. Some common mainland animals never got here; the porcupine and white-tailed deer are conspicuous by their absence. Domestication of the native red fox brought about a short-lived bonanza for fur ranchers early in this century. Other non-native mammals

White Birch Trees

Top: Coyote
Centre: Squirrel
Bottom: Port-La-Joye — Fort Amherst

such as the raccoon and skunk were then brought in by optimistic ranchers. The market for such fur was not as strong as expected. Consequently, the animals were released and they happily spread over the entire Island.

When they became nuisances, larger animals such as the bobcat and black bear were easily exterminated, as was the beaver (since reintroduced). The latest addition is the coyote, first noted in the 1980s and now at home everywhere, including suburbia. The still-common red fox, once the Island's main mammalian predator, is now readjusting its life to this new rival, as are livestock farmers and pet-owners.

Relatively few amphibians and reptiles arrived before rising water cut off the land route. Only three species of snakes are present — inconspicuous ones at that — while there are no turtles

or tortoises at all. On the other hand, most of the expected mice, voles, chipmunks and squirrels, minks and weasels are fortunately present; they seem to cope with modern Prince Edward Island with little difficulty.

Below: Piping Plover
Bottom: Great Blue Heron

Settlement

The first recorded comment on the Island came from Jacques Cartier, in 1534. He wrote of its beauty, of its tall trees and of the potential for good farms. He also saw aboriginal people in canoes, who obviously had much earlier priority in discovery.

Archaeological digs have established the presence of humans at least 10,000 years ago. Shell mounds and tools are evidence that this Island provided a home for native populations for millennia. Their hunting economy would leave little mark on the landscape.

This was to change as the French arrived. Settlement began in the early decades of the 18th century, with the establishment of the first permanent Acadian communities. They were coast-dwellers; for a time their habit of using marshlands left much of the upland undisturbed. However, as the population grew, forest clearing, particularly burning, began in earnest. By 1755 perhaps 4,000 people were present, but the legacy from the old country included war, and the victory of the British led to the expulsion of the Acadians in 1758. A few escaped deportation and rebuilt their culture, but Île Saint-Jean became St. John's Island.

The British dealt with their new acquisition in a curious way. It was roughly surveyed and divided into 67 parcels of 20,000 acres each, more or less, which were then awarded to worthy supplicants through a lottery. Most of the winners became absentee landlords; their struggles with tenants (and each other) dominated the political life of the Island until after Confederation.

Farm on the North Shore

Thus was born the "Land Question" — who may own land and under what conditions — which remains an emotional issue today.

Now non-resident land ownership is discouraged. Exactly how many acres a farmer may own has been the subject of innumerable enquiries, commissions and regulations, not to mention sermons and letters to the editor. Some issues seem immortal.

In the 19th century, successive waves of land-hungry immigrants, mainly from the British Isles, reached the shores of Prince Edward Island. Irish and Scots put aside homeland differences in a new struggle. The forest was now the enemy, to be destroyed by any means. Thousands of small farms and hundreds of rural communities were established, many being quickly abandoned once the realities of agriculture in this climate became clear. A century ago the Island supported about 100,000 people, primarily on about 15,000 farms or in other rural trades. Today, the number of farms has shrunk to about 2,000; the present population of just under 140,000 is decidedly urban-oriented. While agriculture remains an important part of the economy, tourism is now becoming the major industry. Landscape beauty is more important than food production, and perhaps that's the way it should be.

Charlottetown from Victoria Park

Features

Confederation

Wayne MacKinnon

Province House, Charlottetown

To hear Islanders tell it, you'd think it was they who invented Canada. For years, the province has touted itself as "the Cradle of Confederation." Province House, where the Fathers of Confederation first met in 1864 and now the seat of the Island's legislature, is a national historic shrine, as is the street where the delegates walked from their ships to attend that celebrated Charlottetown Conference.

As proud as Islanders are of their role as Canada's birthplace, when they joined the rest of Canada in 1873 the Governor General was moved to remark that they were "quite under the impression that it is the Dominion that has been annexed to Prince Edward Island."

Truth is, the only reason Prince Edward Island became the Birthplace, or Cradle, of Confederation was that the Island delegates refused to attend any conference unless it was held on the Island. And when the people of Prince Edward Island finally decided to join the rest of Canada, their reasons were motivated more by pragmatism than by patriotism to their newly adopted country.

Established as a separate colony in 1769, the Island had long struggled against external domination. Its inhabitants fought to gain control of their own land against a system of absentee proprietorship. The need to gain autonomy was reflected in the long and sometimes bitter struggle for self-government. Islanders became solidly and strongly united behind the desire to win independence for themselves and their little country.

By the 1850s, Islanders had achieved a remarkable degree of progress on their "million-acre farm." The land was being steadily cleared and settled, and the neat pattern of farms and fields defined the nature of rural communities and the gently rolling countryside. Shipbuilding brought prosperity, and there was a flourishing local manufacturing industry. With a growing population and expanding economy came great optimism. Such was the level of confidence by Islanders in their independent status and outlook that they hosted a U.S. Congressional delegation in the 1860s to discuss free trade between Prince Edward Island and the United States.

Islanders had also developed a strong sense of their own identity. The constant tension with Great Britain over the land issue and the struggle for responsible government instilled a deep attachment to local institutions, and quickly led to their "coming of age." The farm, the school, the church and the local government became the centre of their world in "that little end of all creation."

This was not fertile ground for discussions of a union with neighbouring colonies, let alone with Upper and Lower Canada. When the idea of a Maritime Union was promoted in the early 1860s, largely by the British-appointed governors of the region, there was little support. The Island government grudgingly appointed delegates to attend a conference to discuss Maritime Union in 1864, but insisted the conference take place in Charlottetown. At the same time, the Canadian government was considering a broader union of all the British North American colonies. Led by John A. Macdonald, it inquired whether it could send delegates to discuss its proposals.

And so came about the Charlottetown Conference of 1864. For Islanders, the timing could not have been worse. The first circus in 21 years had come to Charlottetown, and there was no room for all the delegates in the capital's few small hotels. Only one member of the government was on hand to greet the Canadian delegates when their ship arrived in Charlottetown Harbour. Summoning as much dignity as was possible under the circumstances, he rowed out in a small oyster boat to welcome them.

But ever the gracious hosts, Islanders treated the Fathers of Confederation to a round of meetings, banquets and balls. George Brown, one of the Canadian delegates, said, "The ice became completely broken, the tongues of the delegates wagged merrily and the banns of matrimony between all the provinces of British North America formally proclaimed."

The idea of uniting the three Maritime provinces under a single government, which was not widely supported in any case, quickly died. The Canadian proposals, which would establish a federal union under which local governments

Lighthouse at Charlottetown Harbour

Fanningbank, the Lieutenant-Governor's residence

would retain some measure of control over their own affairs, were generally favoured by all delegates, including those from Prince Edward Island.

Although the Island delegation continued to participate in subsequent discussions, they had little interest in joining. They feared their individuality and identity would be lost forever and the interests of their small province subsumed by the larger union.

Confederation was also seen to be politically and economically disastrous to Prince Edward Island. The Island delegates were concerned that under the terms of union they would have little representation in a federal parliament and the role of their own legislature would be significantly reduced. Opponents said there would be little left for politicians to do but "legislate on the running about of dogs."

The result was predictable: Islanders and their government rejected Confederation outright. They were generally indifferent about the founding of the new nation on July 1, 1867, and regarded their neighbouring provinces, which had joined the union, with a mixture of smugness, piety and pity.

The Island's decision was a cause of consternation in both Canada and Great Britain. Eventually, the Canadian government, in a move to woo the Island into Confederation, came up with what it called "better terms." Following half-hearted discussions on the part of the Island government, the offer was rejected, and Prime Minister Macdonald felt he and his ministers had been "humbugged."

Confederation Bridge at Sunset

Finally, it was the spectre of economic ruin which brought the Island back to the table. In 1871, the Island government undertook construction of a railway with the promise of new prosperity. The contractors were to be paid by the mile and as a result the lines snaked their way across the province, pushing the project beyond the Island's limited financial capacity.

The Island government, finding it difficult to raise funds from lenders, was forced to reconsider. Representatives of the Island government went to Ottawa to see if the "better terms" offer was still on the table. Agreement was finally reached and put to the people in an election.

By now Islanders had generally recognized they had no choice. After extracting a few concessions, Prince Edward Island became Canada's smallest province on July 1, 1873.

Over the years Islanders have sought to reconcile their traditions of independence and self-reliance with their

Confederation Centre of the Arts

subordinate and dependent role within Confederation. It has not always been easy. Shortly after Confederation the Island economy went into decline. The shipbuilding industry, based on the construction of wooden vessels, all but disappeared. Thousands of Islanders left their homeland to go to the Boston States and other destinations.

Today, the railway is gone, the Confederation Bridge is open, and the Island's cultural traditions have faced the great challenge of mass communications. Yet Islanders remain committed to their way of life. In 1973, on the 100th anniversary of joining Confederation, a semi-satirical group was called into existence for the year to protest what it called the distortion of the Island's resistance to Confederation and to remind Islanders of their history of independent-mindedness. It was named the Brothers and Sisters of Cornelius Howatt, after one of the two politicians who voted against Confederation.

For a small geographical and political unit to maintain its distinct identity inside a vast country is a testament to the Island's strong traditions. As Lucy Maud Montgomery wrote in her autobiography, Islanders "may suspect that [the Island] isn't quite perfect, any more than any other spot on this planet, but you will not catch us admitting it."

Horse and carriage, downtown Charlottetown

Once Upon an Island Time

Wayne MacKinnon

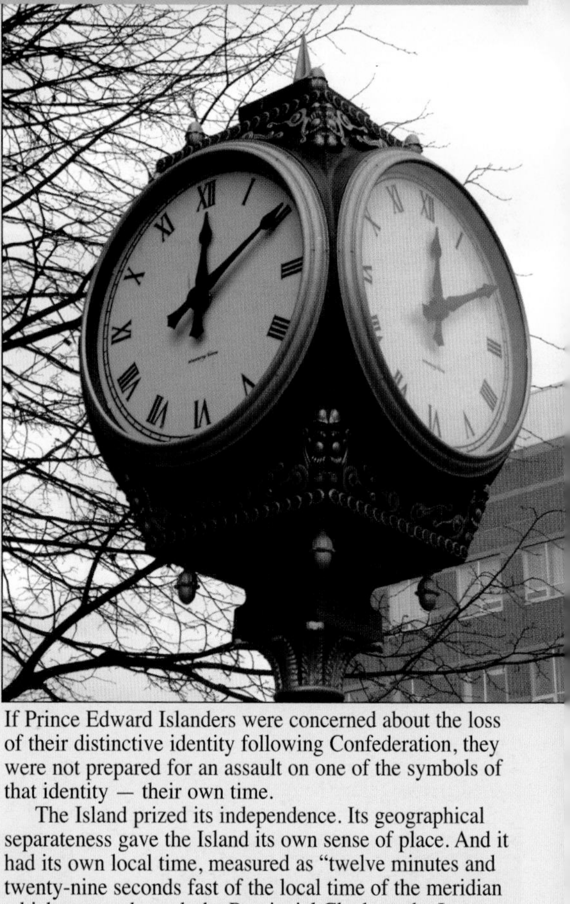

Clock in front of City Hall, Charlottetown

If Prince Edward Islanders were concerned about the loss of their distinctive identity following Confederation, they were not prepared for an assault on one of the symbols of that identity — their own time.

The Island prized its independence. Its geographical separateness gave the Island its own sense of place. And it had its own local time, measured as "twelve minutes and twenty-nine seconds fast of the local time of the meridian which passes through the Provincial Clock on the Law Courts Building in Charlottetown." With their own sense of time and place, Islanders considered themselves in complete harmony with the universe.

Islanders were therefore thunderstruck by the heretical proposal to adopt a new system called Standard Time. The concept of Standard Time was first introduced at a conference in Washington in 1884, where agreement was reached to arbitrarily divide the world into uniform time zones. A document circulated throughout Canada advocated the notion that time "is in no way influenced by matter, locality, distance or space," and went on to assert boldly that it was "essentially non-local." The view that time was "non-local" struck at the heart of one of Islanders' most cherished beliefs.

The campaign to introduce Standard Time was unrelenting. When Canada adopted it in 1884, Dominion Government offices on the Island switched to Atlantic

Standard Time, twelve minutes and twenty-nine seconds ahead of Island Time. The Island's railway switched to Eastern Standard Time to conform with the Dominion railway schedule. That was forty-seven minutes and thirty-one seconds behind Island Time. The result was confusion and annoyance. For example, to travel to Charlottetown to conduct business with the Dominion government, one would get up on Island Time, catch the train on Eastern Standard Time and make an appointment on Atlantic Standard Time.

The railways' switch to Eastern Standard Time was particularly galling. Islanders bitterly recalled that one of the conditions under which it was forced into Confederation involved giving up control over their own railway and they were unwilling to tolerate the further ignominy of the railway operating on "Upper Canadian" time.

Seizing on the confusion, proponents of Standard Time introduced a bill, *An Act to Alter the Present Method of Reckoning Time*, on April Fool's Day of 1889. They made it clear that the Island had little choice in the matter, pointing out that since Standard Time was generally adopted throughout North America, "No deviation of the rule will be permitted in this Island."

Opposition to this affront on the Island's right to self-determination was swift. A Mr. Sinclair rose in the legislature and denounced the bill. "I believe that Standard Time was adopted on the Dominion railways for the accommodation of strangers," he thundered. A Mr. Bell said the Dominion government had erred when it adopted Standard Time in the first place, and that Prince Edward Island should not further compound the mistake. Their remarks were greeted with loud applause from the public gallery.

Nonetheless, the bill passed, and the Island lost its own

Kensington railway station

time. A local paper reported on the adoption of Standard Time. "The minutes and the seconds are now the same everywhere," it lamented.

One dark night in May of 1889, three officials climbed the narrow stairs of the Law Courts Building and wrenched the hands of the Provincial Clock ahead by twelve minutes and twenty-nine seconds. The Island has never been the same since.

The Real Lucy Maud Montgomery

Anna MacDonald

Lucy Maud Montgomery and her birthplace

For most people, Prince Edward Island conjures up images of white sand beaches, red roads and Anne of Green Gables, the fictional red-headed orphan created by Island-born writer L. M. Montgomery. Anne's familiar face with its red braids and freckles forms the centre of a thriving industry here, appearing everywhere from gift shops and licence plates to theatre productions. But how well do people, Islanders and visitors alike, know Lucy Maud Montgomery, author of *Anne of Green Gables*?

L. M. Montgomery was born in Clifton (now New London), Prince Edward Island, on November 30, 1874, to Hugh John Montgomery and Clara Woolner Macneill. Shortly after Montgomery's birth, her mother developed tuberculosis. Clara became so ill that Hugh John moved her and their baby daughter to Cavendish to stay with Clara's parents, Alexander and Lucy Woolner Macneill. In 1876, Clara died, leaving behind her husband and 21-month-old Maud. With the death of his wife and the failure of his business in Clifton, Hugh John left his daughter with the Macneills and moved to Saskatchewan, where he eventually settled in Prince Albert and married Mary Ann McRae.

At the time of their daughter's death, Alexander and Lucy Woolner Macneill were in their mid-50s and had already raised six children. To be faced at this point in their lives with bringing up another child, especially one as lively, emotional and intelligent as Montgomery, must have been daunting for them. For emotional sustenance, Montgomery turned to nature, books, her imagination — and especially to writing.

Carriage ride at Park Corner

Montgomery did not lose touch with other members of her parents' families, particularly her paternal grandfather, Senator Donald Montgomery, and her Uncle John and Aunt Annie (her mother's sister) Campbell in Park Corner. There, she found the warm family atmosphere that was lacking in her Cavendish home. Her Grandfather Montgomery, who lived close to the Campbells, enjoyed her company, and her young Campbell cousins kept her well entertained. She developed a love for Park Corner that was to last a lifetime.

In 1880, at the age of six, she began attending school in Cavendish. In 1890, at age 15, she decided she wanted to live with her father in Prince Albert. While there, she wrote a poem and sent it to *The Patriot*, a newspaper in Charlottetown. To her great joy, *The Patriot* printed it.

She stayed in Prince Albert for a year, but

Lucy Maud Montgomery's Birthplace in New London

L. M. Montgomery Museum, Park Corner

homesickness and an unhappy relationship with her stepmother brought her back to Cavendish. She returned to school in 1892–93 to prepare for entrance exams to Prince of Wales College in Charlottetown, where she studied for a teacher's licence. She completed the two-year course in one year, finishing with honours.

In 1894, Montgomery began her teaching career in Bideford, a small community over 70 kilometres west of Cavendish. After teaching there for a year, she spent a year at Dalhousie University in Halifax, where she received her first payments for her writing by publishing poems and short stories in Canadian and American newspapers and magazines. She returned to Prince Edward Island in the spring of 1896 and in the fall took a teaching post in Belmont. She stayed there until July of 1897, continuing to write and becoming secretly — and soon unhappily — engaged to her second cousin, Edwin Simpson.

Her last teaching post was in Lower Bedeque, a community close to Summerside. While still engaged to Simpson she fell in love with a young farmer, Herman Leard, with whose parents she boarded. Although she loved Leard passionately, she did not pursue this romance because she knew she could never marry him. In June 1899, Herman Leard died of complications brought on by influenza.

Grandfather Macneill died suddenly on March 6, 1898, while Montgomery was teaching in Lower Bedeque. She returned to Cavendish to care for her grandmother, broke her engagement to Simpson, became assistant post-mistress and wrote when she could. With the exception of a nine-month stay in Halifax in 1901–02 when she worked as a

Parlour at Park Corner

proofreader for the *Daily Echo*, she remained in Cavendish for the next 13 years. In 1906, she became engaged — again secretly — to Reverend Ewan Macdonald, then the Presbyterian minister in Cavendish. When her grandmother died in 1911 she married him.

Garden at Green Gables

The years Montgomery spent in Cavendish with her grandmother were very productive. She sent off scores of poems, stories and serials to various Canadian, British and American magazines. In the spring of 1905, she wrote her first novel, *Anne of Green Gables*, published in 1908 by the Page Company of Boston after several other publishing companies had rejected it. Following its immediate success, she wrote three more bestsellers: *Anne of Avonlea* (1909), *Kilmeny of the Orchard* (1910), and *The Story Girl* (1911).

After Montgomery and Macdonald married in July 1911, they moved to Leaskdale, Ontario. Montgomery never lived on Prince Edward Island again. She kept in touch but returned to the Island only for visits.

Maud Montgomery Macdonald settled into life in Leaskdale. She raised two sons, Chester Cameron (born 1912) and Stuart (born 1915). Another son, Hugh, was stillborn in 1914. She led a busy life, but no matter how busy she was, she found time to write, maintaining a voluminous private correspondence, answering every fan letter personally, and making detailed entries in her journals. She always looked forward to her trips home.

In 1919, Montgomery discovered that her husband was afflicted with religious melancholia, a serious mental illness. This illness returned periodically and sent him into bouts of depression and insomnia. For the rest of their lives she did everything she could to keep his illness a secret and to help him through each debilitating episode.

Bideford Parsonage

Anne of the Island

Wayne MacKinnon

Anne at Green Gables

Imagine exploring one of the world's great islands with one of the world's most popular authors — someone who knows and loves the province well, and who will share her favourite haunts.

That guide is Lucy Maud Montgomery, author of the world-famous book *Anne of Green Gables*. Set in Cavendish, Prince Edward Island, this classic story was largely inspired by her deep attachment to the natural beauty that surrounded her. "Were it not for those Cavendish years, I do not think Anne of Green Gables would ever have been written," she recalled.

Those who want to follow Montgomery's path throughout the Island, see its natural beauty and way of life through her eyes, and explore her favourite "haunts" are invited to pick up an Anne of Green Gables Passport at tourism information centres. The passport can be stamped at many of the locations described in the following tour. Those who visit at least five of the 13 passport locations are eligible to win a bountiful basket of Prince Edward Island products.

Chronologically, your first stop is in New London (on the Blue Heron Drive, at the intersection of Routes 6 and 20) where Maud was born on November 30, 1874. This house, now open to the public, remains relatively unchanged and contains many treasured personal effects from Maud's life, including her wedding ensemble and personal scrapbooks.

Post office at Green Gables

When Maud was 21 months old, her mother died. As a result, she was sent to live with her maternal grandparents, Alexander and Lucy Macneill, in Cavendish. Quiet gardens surround the stone cellar where their farmhouse once stood (just east of the intersection of Routes 6 and 13.) This was the site of Maud's home from 1876 to 1911.

It was here that she wrote *Anne of Green Gables*. "I wrote it in the evenings after my regular day's work was done, wrote most of it at the window of the little gable room that had been mine for years."

L. M. Montgomery birthplace, New London

The tranquil heritage property has been passed down from father to son over four generations. John Macneill, a great-grandson of Alexander Macneill, and his family still live on the farm, and visitors are welcome to view the stone cellar and enjoy the grounds much as Maud must have done.

Close by, beside the Cavendish Church, a house similar to the original Macneill homestead has been relocated and restored as a postal museum.

One of the must-visits for Anne enthusiasts is the Green Gables homestead in Cavendish. Located just west of the intersection of Routes 6 and 13, Green Gables House was the setting for Maud's story of Anne. Her grandfather Macneill's cousins lived here and she spent many happy hours in their home. In 1937, Parks Canada restored the house, furnishing it as it would have been in Anne's day. For those who can't wait to see the interior, there's a virtual tour at www.gov.pe.ca/greengables. The grounds and outbuildings have been recreated to depict the Victorian setting described in the novel. The nearby Balsam Hollow and Haunted Wood trails reflect some of Maud's most precious woodland haunts.

After receiving her teacher's qualifications, Maud accepted a teaching position in Bideford. The young 19-year-old teacher boarded at the Anglican parsonage in Bideford, which is now open to the public (on Route 166.) Her room has been faithfully recreated and the museum also includes the actual cupboard that inspired the liniment cake story. In her journals, the young Maud recounted her days in Bideford, with skating on the ponds, community socials, and her experiences as a first-time teacher.

Following her first year in Bideford, Maud accepted a teaching position in nearby Belmont, overlooking Malpeque Bay. After a year's further study, Maud accepted a teaching position at a school in Lower Bedeque. It was in Lower Bedeque that it is said she first fell in love, but a future with the local farmer was not to be. The schoolhouse (located on Route 112, on the south side of the road) has been restored, and visitors are welcome.

In March 1898, her grandfather Macneill died and she returned to Cavendish to care for her aging grandmother. She spent the next 13 years there and, in 1908, *Anne of Green Gables* was finally published.

The one place on Prince Edward Island that Maud loved best was her uncle John Campbell's house at Park Corner on Route 20. The house, still owned by descendants, contains many artifacts relating to Maud's life, including rare first editions of her books. She spent summer holidays there as a girl, went there to live when her grandmother died, and was married in the parlour in 1911.

Maud described Park Corner as "a big white beautiful house smothered in orchards that was the wonder castle of my childhood. Here, in other days, there was a trio of merry cousins to rush out and drag me in with greetings and laughter. The very walls of that house must have been permeated by the essence of good times."

Many of Maud's stories were inspired by the house at Park Corner. "If I ever could build a house I would change nothing," she said. "It would be exactly like this old home." The enchanted bookcase described in *Anne of Green Gables* may be found at the museum, and the pond on the Campbell farm became her "Lake of Shining Waters."

The Montgomery Manor, also in Park Corner, is the heritage homestead built by Senator Montgomery, Maud's grandfather. Still owned by the Montgomery family, the house is open to the public during the summer months, and the china dog Magog, of Gog and Magog fame, is on proud display, along with other artifacts in the parlour.

Lucy Maud Montgomery died in 1942. She lay in state at Green Gables and was buried in the Cavendish Cemetery in a plot on the crest of a hill she had selected herself because "it overlooks the spots I always loved, the pond, the shore, the sand dunes, the harbour." The cemetery is at the intersection of Routes 6 and 13.

The author's original manuscripts, scrapbooks and other personal items can be viewed at the Confederation Centre Art Gallery and Museum in Charlottetown.

Kindred Spirits is a unique quarterly publication developed on Prince Edward Island by Montgomery's descendants. As of late 2008, the publication is available exclusively online at www.annesociety.org, a treasure trove of Anne lore. L. M. Montgomery and Anne enthusiasts may receive more information by calling 800-665-2663 or writing to: *Kindred Spirits*, Avonlea, PE, C0B 1M0 Canada. As Anne herself said, "Kindred spirits are not so scarce as I used to think. It's splendid to find out there are so many of them in the world."

Lucy Maud Montgomery's wedding dress at her birthplace in New London

And, every year, the L. M. Montgomery Festival (www.lmmontgomeryfestival.com) is held near Cavendish, bringing together people from around the world to recognize and celebrate the creator of Anne of the Island with music and stories, fun and friendship and, of course, ice cream. Montgomery's life and career has led to the establishment of the L. M. Montgomery Institute (www.lmmontgomery.ca) at the University of Prince Edward Island. The Institute, with an international scope, is a centre for research on Montgomery's life, her work and her Island. It hosts events and projects to bring together those who wish to learn more about the many facets of Prince Edward Island's most illustrious writer.

In 2008, Montgomery enthusiasts from around the world gathered to celebrate the 100th anniversary of the publication of *Anne of Green Gables*. Prince Edward Island declared 2008 the "Year of Anne." The year-long celebrations featured writing contests, Anne parties, festivals of art and theatres, and many other special activities to mark what has been described as a world classic novel.

L. M. Montgomery Museum, Park Corner

All the while, she continued to write, publishing six more novels based on Anne and creating other popular heroines, including Emily (*Emily of New Moon*, *Emily Climbs*, *Emily's Quest*). She also published two novels she called "adult": *The Blue Castle* and *A Tangled Web*.

In 1926, the Macdonalds moved to Norval, Ontario, where they remained until Macdonald retired from the ministry in 1935. They then went to Toronto where they bought a house Montgomery aptly named "Journey's End." There Maud Montgomery Macdonald lived until her death on April 24, 1942. She was buried in the Cavendish cemetery, close to the fields, woods and sea she had known and loved since childhood. Her husband died in November of 1943 and was buried beside her.

A prolific author, Montgomery wrote some 500 short stories, 500 poems and 20 novels, 19 of which were set on Prince Edward Island. She also left behind an invaluable legacy of journals, letters and scrapbooks in which she recorded her thoughts on virtually every topic from gardening and cats to religious philosophy and current events. Her fictional and non-fictional works are now prized as social records of late 19th- and early 20th-century Canadian life. Her novels have been published in over 30 languages, including Japanese, Polish, Swedish, Norwegian and French.

Perhaps the best way to get to know Montgomery is through her own words. Several decades after her death, her son, Dr. Stuart Macdonald, placed her journals at the University of Guelph. In 1985, Drs. Elizabeth Waterston and Mary Rubio published *The Selected Journals of L. M. Montgomery, Volume 1: 1889–1910* (Toronto, Oxford University Press). Four more volumes have since been published (1987, 1992, 1998 and 2004).

Particularly in her journals, Montgomery reveals the depths of her emotional, sensitive nature. Like the heroines of her books, the emotions she felt — whether painful or joyful — affected her very deeply. She suffered greatly

Green Gables

over unhappy events that affected her personally and the world in general. Her journal entries reflect the anguish she felt over certain events in her life, but they also disclose her sense of humour, her intense love of beauty and nature, her deep attachment to Prince Edward Island, her intelligent and creative mind, and her passionate need to write.

The fame Montgomery achieved during her lifetime and posthumously did not earn her high praise from academics nor from all reviewers and critics. Academics tended to dismiss her as a writer of little importance who wrote charming stories mainly for girls and women. But this evaluation has changed over the past two decades. Canadian and international scholars now study Montgomery as a novelist, journal and letter-writer, social commentator, autobiographer, photographer, poet and short story writer. Articles on various aspects of her life and works are published in numerous scholarly publications, and in popular media such as books, magazines, newsletters, videos, television, movies and newspapers.

Bedroom at Park Corner

Established in 1993 at the University of Prince Edward Island, the L. M. Montgomery Institute celebrates Montgomery, her works and her Island home. The Institute holds biennial international conferences on Montgomery, and it hosts an electronic discussion list about Montgomery, with subscribers from around the world. It has co-produced an award-winning CD-ROM entitled *The Bend in the Road: An Invitation to the World and Work of L. M. Montgomery* and played a lead role in creating a virtual exhibition about Montgomery, hosted by the Confederation Centre Art Gallery.

Park Corner

The year 2008 marked the 100th anniversary of the publication of *Anne of Green Gables*, Montgomery's first and most famous novel. A year-long celebration of the anniversary included entertainment and educational events and activities focused on the novel and its creator. The L. M. Montgomery Institute's eighth international conference, held in late June, focused on Anne of Green Gables and her creator; over 200 people attended presentations by over 50 presenters from ten countries, including Iran, Turkey, Italy, Sweden, Australia, Finland, the United States and Canada. Local community groups and organizations hosted celebratory events for people of all ages. As well, commemorative items, including a 100th anniversary edition of the novel, a book about Montgomery's scrapbooks, stamps in Canada and Japan, and a Canadian coin, were created in honour of the anniversary. Nova Scotia writer Budge Wilson wrote a prequel, entitled *Before Green Gables*, to Montgomery's novel. Published by Penguin Books in 2008, Wilson's book tells the story of Anne's life before she came to Prince Edward Island.

Garden at Green Gables

Cottage Life

Wendy MacGregor and Joy Bell Mackenzie

Cottage life in Prince Edward Island offers a perfect summer escape, whether one is looking for a quiet hideaway or a launch pad into playland. Bring the whole family, come and go as you please, barbecue fresh fish or read a book on your deck as the sun goes down over the Gulf. These are only some of the benefits of renting a cottage for your vacation in Prince Edward Island — and there are plenty of cottages to choose from (www.canadaselect.com; www.cottagesincanada.com).

First, consider the area in which you want to stay. The wide, white sand dunes at Cavendish Beach are well-known to many families and, of course, Cavendish is also the home of Anne of Green Gables. Here, the cottages that are close to the water and well-maintained with full services are generally booked a year in advance, so don't leave this until the last minute. That said, it is always worth checking at the beginning of the season to see if there have been cancellations at any of the most popular settings.

If the Cavendish area of the PEI National Park is your destination of choice, but you cannot find anything appropriate, do try the neighbouring areas of North and South Rustico, Stanley Bridge and New London. All these locations are close to the north shore and boast many attractions — from music to antiquing to nature trails and biking. The Acadian flavour of the Rusticos appeals to many.

At the eastern end of the National Park,

Clamming, Oyster Bed Bridge

Brackley Beach and Stanhope have fewer cottages on the water, but many that are a short walk from the beach. There are also scenic boat tours and deep-sea fishing off Covehead Wharf. There is nothing better than a feed of fried clams right on the dock. There are interpretive tours in the National Park and two self-guided trails — Long Pond Loop and Bubbling Springs/Farmlands Trail. From the park it is a short trip into Charlottetown for those much-sought-after souvenirs.

Travelling west from Cavendish toward Summerside, cottages are available in the nearby Hebrides cottage development or at Clinton or New London. French River's dramatic views take visitors a little off the beaten path. The Darnley and Seaview areas offer beautiful white sand beaches that are not in the National Park. A lot more privacy comes with a little more distance from the amusements, and many travellers are attracted to the rustic cottages right on the sand at Malpeque, home of the famous oysters and Penderosa Beach.

For a quiet getaway steeped in protected dunelands and marshes, consider the serenity of Greenwich and St. Peters, 40 kilometres east of Charlottetown, or even further east to the "singing sands" of Fortune Bay and Souris. This area is renowned for its unspoiled scenic beauty, and the Trans Canada Trail runs right through it. The spectacular Greenwich Beach, the newest addition to PEI National

French River

Top: Cabot Beach Provincial Park, near Malpeque
Above: Inn at St. Peters

Park, and the top-rated Links at Crowbush Cove golf course are found here.

There are inns and bed and breakfasts along the route, and private cottages at Lakeside, Red Head, Greenwich and Fortune. Restaurants are neither frequent nor lavish, but there are more every year. If you plan ahead, you could book a room and enjoy gourmet dining at the Inn at St. Peters, a few kilometres before the entrance to Greenwich, or at the Inn at Bay Fortune, former home of George C. Scott and Colleen Dewhurst.

On the south shore, Victoria is another charmingly picturesque destination. This flourishing artistic community boasts delightful galleries, rental cottages, B&Bs, good food and local theatre. The south shore tends to have warm shallow water and red sand beaches, perfect for playing, clamming or leisurely walks at low tide on the hard-packed flats. Check tide times though, because the small tidal pools at low tide give way to high tides where the water actually reaches the bank — then it's time for a raft!

Visitors to Prince Edward Island often have a preference for either the north or south shores, but both have their merits. Coming from Charlottetown, toward Victoria, there are many cottages for rent in nearby Augustine Cove, Rice and Rocky Points, and further west past Borden-Carleton at Chelton Beach and in the Bedeque area.

On the eastern shore at Brudenell River Resort, guests can relax in cabins on the premises or take golf lessons at the Island Golf Academy — fun and learning for the whole family. The nearby town of Montague offers amenities, cottages on the Brudenell River and a lovely restaurant called Windows on the Water Café.

At the west end of the Island, private cottages and B&Bs are available at Tyne Valley and Alberton. A new inn and restaurant have been built at Northport and, at West Point, a lighthouse is outfitted as an inn and restaurant. The resort at Mill River offers challenging golf and a fun park for children. It is a great family destination in winter because of its skating rink, tubing hill and cross-country skiing facilities.

If cost is no object and you are looking for privacy and comfort, you may want to consider some of PEI's new luxury cottage rentals (www.peiluxuryrentals.com;

Victoria Wharf

www.ppbo.com). A handful of four-and-a-half and even a few five-star cottages, with spectacular views and lots of amenities, can now be found. The most impressive may be those situated on the Gulf of St. Lawrence in Sea View (www.beautifulpei.com). These spacious retreats offer peace and privacy, breath-taking scenery, gourmet kitchens, and in some cases even a private swimming pool and hot tub, but of course this will all come at high-end prices. (www.beautifulpei.com; www.stonehedgebysea.ca) In the northeast near Souris, there's scenic solitude at the Chateau Bayfield (www.panmurebeachhouse.com; www.chateaubayfield.com). Such accommodations are extremely limited, however, so if you have specific travel dates in mind it's necessary to book early.

In trying to choose between PEI's many wonderful cottage options, you need to establish whether your personal priority is the beach, swimming, golf, amusement parks, fishing, cuisine or some other interest so you can stay close to the attractions you plan to visit.

The Canada Select rating system awards stars based on the facilities that are offered, providing an objective standard by which to compare cottages. Be aware of cottage operators' cancellation policies. Many cottages have their own websites giving prospective renters sneak previews. Because business is competitive, and the season is so short, prices are generally consistent. You will pay a little more to be in Cavendish, or to be right on the water. And if you come in the shoulder- or off-season, you can generally get a better rate.

Remember, one of the great things about PEI is that even if your kids force you to book by the beach when you want to be by the golf course, nothing is ever that far away.

Artist's Studio, Victoria

Chateau Bayfield

The Island for Kids

Nancy L. M. Russell

Avonlea — Village of Anne of Green Gables

My kids are tickled pink that a million people a year come to visit "their Island." My sons marvel at the traffic jams on University Avenue on days when it clouds over. And they delight in spotting licence plates from across North America. Much to their surprise, "our Island" is really popular — especially when the sun is warm and the ocean waters even warmer. Where are all these visitors in the middle of February, we wonder?

I asked my youngest son why so many people come to PEI. His answer: Because PEI is cool! How cool? Well, you're going to find out.

We live on an island, so the beaches are a great source of entertainment. PEI beaches are ideal for children of all ages to scour for pieces of polished glass, crab shells, driftwood and other treasures. For older kids, the beaches are a place to bodysurf in the waves or snuggle in the sand for that first-ever summer romance. One word of caution: beware the rip-currents on the Island's north shore. Stick to beaches with lifeguards, particularly when the surf is up.

Exploring tidal pools

Everyone on PEI has a "favourite" beach. Most of my friends consider Basin Head the best. You are not supposed to jump off the bridge there, but ... well, you'll see. Basin Head is also home to the famous "singing sands" and a

Old Home Week, Charlottetown

fisheries museum. A short drive away, you'll want to take lots of photos of the wonderful lighthouse at East Point. Still in the neighborhood, we don't have trains, but if you head to Elmira, there's a railway museum, including a working miniature train.

Another popular beach can be found at Greenwich, near St. Peters, part of the PEI National Park. Greenwich is home to a breathtaking parabolic dune system. It's all protected now but there are boardwalk trails that wind through the park. The view is worth the walk! There's also a great interpretive centre. And before you leave the eastern part of the province, you may want to travel back in time at Roma at Three Rivers, near Montague. Guides in period clothing help you explore a 1700s French settlement established by Jean Pierre Roma.

Sticking with eastern PEI, if you have younger children, don't miss Kings Castle Provincial Park, near Murray River. It's a popular spot for Grade one field trips. This is a great place to picnic, and catch your breath while the kids run around. Best of all, it's free!

The size of Prince Edward Island makes it a perfect spot for day-tripping, which is what we locals like to do. For example, we love to fish for trout at Ben's Lake, about half an hour east of Charlottetown. The deep-sea fishing expeditions are also a big hit with kids. The Bearded Skipper is their favourite guide for the two-hour fishing trip out of North Rustico Harbour. There are also great kayaking adventures at several locations around the Island.

My eldest son likes "old-fashioned" things. At Orwell Corner Historic Village and the Agricultural Museum,

Orwell Corner Historic Village

Shining Waters Family Fun Park

halfway between Charlottetown and Wood Islands, kids can see how a farm was run in the late 1800s. The Village also has a blacksmith shop, country store, church, and school. Nearby, Macphail Woods has an interpretive centre perfect for kids who love nature, as well as some great trails.

If you're around Orwell in the evening, there are ceilidhs during the summer. (Don't forget the mosquito spray!) You can hear fiddle music and local tunes, performed by a mix of seasoned musicians and up-and-coming young stars. In fact, there are ceilidhs across the Island. And, if it's music you like, be sure to take your children to hear the bagpipes played beautifully at the College of Piping in Summerside.

Cabot Beach Provincial Park in Malpeque is a short drive away from Summerside. Be sure to take the local roads to experience driving on authentic PEI clay, unless it's spring or fall and impassable. A visit to the car wash aside, it's worth it!

Cavendish is, of course, a mecca for kids. You have to

Wax World of the Stars

put aside your adult restraint and relish in the sheer silliness of Ripley's Believe It or Not and The Wax World of the Stars. Shining Waters Family Fun Park opened in 2006, replacing the legendary Rainbow Valley. The Fun Park features 30 acres of rides and other attractions, including — yo, ho, ho — Buccaneer Bay. Sandspit has more heart-pounding rides to appeal to a slightly older crowd. There are also lovely bike trails around the former Rainbow Valley site.

Old Home Week, Charlottetown

For the more historically minded, Avonlea Village warrants a stop, with its re-creation of a rural community in the late 1800s. How can you go wrong with making ice cream and drinking raspberry cordial, to say nothing of the lively entertainment and a visit to Lucy Maud's classroom? Fans of *Anne of Green Gables* recommend a tour of all the local Montgomery sites and for those who have read all the books, it's a pilgrimage worth making. For those who prefer *Arthur the Aardvark*, the beaches of Cavendish are blissfully white of sand and soft on the feet.

My children are disappointed that PEI no longer has any trains, but the former railway tracks have been turned into trails that are great for mountain bikes. I often see families touring from one small community to another, particularly from Mount Stewart to St. Peters.

My children and I are determined to someday visit all the lighthouses on the Island. One of the most-photographed is at Cape Tryon, on the North Shore. We also like West Point, where we climbed to the top and had to shield our eyes from the working light. There's a museum there and you can even stay overnight in the West Point Lighthouse.

Also, up west, as they say, you'll find the Mill River Fun Park — not quite Disney, but good clean fun. And for spud fans, there is the PEI Potato Museum.

At Avonlea Village

A ten-minute drive past Tignish is North Cape. It's described as "Nature and Technology in Perfect Harmony." And it really is! Your jaw will drop as the wind turbines appear in front of you. If the tides are right, you can see the spot where the waters of the Gulf of St. Lawrence meet the Northumberland Strait. You can also observe the longest natural rock reef in North America as you walk the Black Marsh Nature Trail. At the Wind Interpretive Centre, you can see inside a giant turbine and take a spin at generating electricity.

On your way back from North Cape, you can learn about Acadian history on PEI at the Acadian Museum in Miscouche. A great stop if you have kids

Old Home Week, Charlottetown

in French immersion!

A lot of wildlife can be seen on Prince Edward Island, if you look hard enough. The largest mammal is a coyote — rarely seen. Foxes, on the other hand, are regular visitors to our neighbourhood, even climbing into our backyard. The crows and foxes will regularly pillage for golf balls at local courses. The great blue herons stand like sentinels at dusk, searching for fish. Another local favourite is the piping plover. We love to catch a glimpse of the lithe bird, but we always heed the "keep away" signs on the local beaches when the tiny plover eggs are hatching.

The Island has two drive-in movie theatres, one in Brackley Beach and the other in Cascumpec. Charlottetown and Summerside have multiplex movie theatres, which are particularly crowded on rainy days during the summer. The malls carry the latest trends for teens who like to shop, and even bargain brand names at the factory outlet stores in North River, on the outskirts of Charlottetown. Digging through the bins at Froggies, a second-hand clothing nirvana in Charlottetown, is a true authentic Island adventure.

Harbour Hippo

For more highbrow entertainment, the Confederation Centre of the Arts has a great library and programs for kids. Check out the family musical entertainment performed by the Charlottetown Festival's outdoor amphitheatre. For the historically minded kids, the Parks Canada film at Province House is interesting enough that by age seven both of my sons could sit through it with no squirming at all. Be sure to keep an eye out for the Fathers (and Ladies) of Confederation strolling the streets of the capital.

Kids seem to get a kick out of the Harbour Hippo, an

Mini golf at Sandspit

amphibious vehicle that takes visitors on a land-and-water tour of Charlottetown. And, speaking of water, the CARI aquatics facility in Charlottetown features diving boards, a rope swing, and a water slide with an impressive G-force rating — at least when the parents use it. Summerside also has a great pool facility, and bowling at the Credit Union Place.

Every summer, we play a few rounds of mini-golf and make a few visits to the go-kart track, both popular pastimes for visitors. My children also love to visit the Charlottetown Driving Park to watch the horses race. It's harness racing — with standardbred horses pulling sulkies, or bikes as they're called. Think chariot racing, as one friend described it to her kids. There are also lovely local harness tracks — my favourite is Pinette, featuring unforgettable community race nights.

During the summer, local community festivals are really the heart and soul of what makes this Island a great place for kids. The biggest are the Lobster Carnival in Summerside and Old Home Week in Charlottetown. Many Islanders look forward to taking their kids to one of several powwows held every summer across the

Slide at Sandspit

Island. You can also visit the Mi'kmaq Cultural Centre at Lennox Island, where you can try traditional foods.

Speaking of eating, Prince Edward Island has great food for children. Every kid has to climb on the giant cow at Cows for a photo opportunity, eating ice cream, of course. The Wowie Cowie flavour is a family fave. Frosty Treat in Kensington and the Richmond Dairy Bar have wonderful ice cream and "fries with the works" (not the time for a lesson in nutrition!), and then there's the seafood. My kids love lobster, mussels and even oysters. Our favourite place to eat is the Farmer's Market in Charlottetown. Be sure to say we sent you!

You can work off all those calories by taking the kids for a walk on the boardwalks in Charlottetown or Summerside. Kids will also love climbing and swinging at the Eliot River Dream Park, a community-designed wooden playground for all ages in Cornwall. The new Boundless Playground at Glen Stewart School in Stratford is accessible to children of all abilities and has become a destination point for many families. Both communities are a short drive from downtown Charlottetown.

When you're arriving or leaving the Island, be sure to make the most of the coming and going — you haven't really visited the Island unless you've tried to keep a toddler entertained in the ferry line-up at Woods Harbour. You can get great photos of the Confederation Bridge down on the rocks just past Gateway Village in Borden-Carleton, and minivans give you a fantastic view going over the bridge.

For years, a favourite Prince Edward Island tourism slogan was "Come Play on Our Island." You have your pick of beaches for a sandbox, the Gulf of St. Lawrence for a swimming pool, and more adventures than the latest episode of The Doodlebops or Hannah Montana. Prince Edward Island is a place all kids will love. So come play on our Island — and bring the kids!

Confederation Bridge

Lobster Suppers

Julie V. Watson

Lobster traps and buoys

The lobster has long been recognized as part of the tradition of Prince Edward Island, and nowhere is it enjoyed more than at the community suppers that have become an integral part of every summer.

Community suppers began many decades ago as a joint celebration honouring the arrival of the lobster season and warm weather. They were held in community halls, church basements and even on lawns. Members of the community would traditionally offer lobster, chowder, potato salad and probably some slaw, with pie, squares and strawberry shortcake for dessert. Homemade bread and pickles rounded out the feast.

The logic behind the menu was simple — it consisted of whatever was available. Local fishers would donate the lobsters. Potatoes for the salad and the chowder would come from someone's cold storage, as would the cabbage and carrots for the coleslaw. Strawberries were usually a good bet, as the season usually coincided with the lobster harvest. Biscuits, bread, pies and squares were made by local women and donated, along with jars of their own pickles.

These suppers were quickly recognized by "townies" and locals alike as being both delicious and a great bargain. Tourists, having already displayed superior intelligence by choosing Prince Edward Island as a vacation destination, were quick to sniff out these terrific experiences. The word quickly spread.

Now fundraisers have extended these events from one-day affairs to a full season of suppers. The labour would be supplied by the people of the community and all the profits would go into the coffers of the church or organization

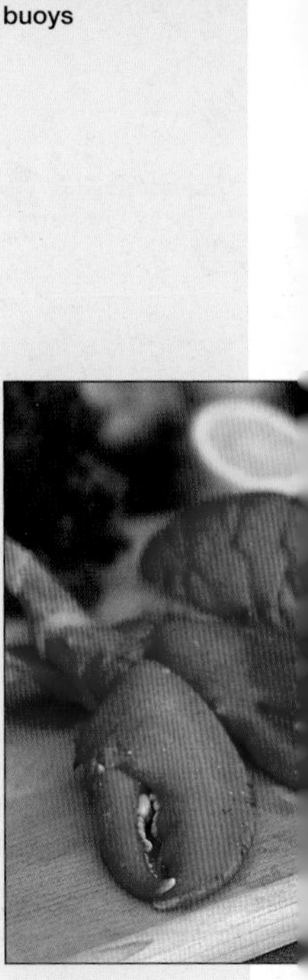

holding the event. Just as the profits were important for the good of the community, so were the opportunities for employment. That is why so many of the suppers are found in rural villages. Many a student has paid for his or her education by serving up lobster dinners.

As time passed, more and more lobster suppers were added until most of them became privately owned businesses. Each has a distinctive personality, and one supper can't be said to be better than the rest. Islanders, after all, do know how to cook their lobster. Some suppers have down-home entertainment or sing-alongs, and some are licensed for alcoholic beverages; these all help determine a personal favourite. No matter which you choose, the atmosphere will be casual, even homey. You could be seated next to someone from the other side of the village, or from the other side of the world.

So successful have the suppers become that tour buses now make them a regular stop. The informal celebration of the province's premier seafood harvest has become part of the Island experience that summer visitors seldom miss. Few other establishments offer up such an accurate representation of a down-home celebration in yesteryear's style.

Today, more than 35 years after the first formalized suppers began, menus have changed just a little. Another Island seafood, the blue mussel, is often added to the typical fare of chowder, lobster, salads, homemade rolls and desserts. Grown in Island waters, the mussel is plump and delicious — and often offered up for repeats. Some locations offer a garden salad instead of coleslaw, or perhaps a baked potato instead of the salad. But the important ingredient — the traditional lobster of Prince Edward Island — is always there.

Charlottetown

Delicious lobster, served hot or cold according to your preference, is the star of the meal. For some years, several establishments offered all-you-can-eat lobster for a set price, but these are pretty much a thing of the past. Instead, there's the option of buying a second or even a third or fourth lobster, if desired. Second helpings are often offered of other items such as chowder, mussels, rolls, salads and even desserts. Some establishments offer all you can eat of these items, or a salad bar.

In recognition that some people (admittedly very few) actually don't like lobster, there are always alternatives. Ham, scallops, steak, pork chops, salmon or sole are examples. Children's menus are always available. The suppers are still prepared and served by locals, most of them trained by professionals to offer the best service

Cardigan Lobster Suppers

possible. Staff are friendly, and generally impart a sincere Island welcome.

Credited with starting it all, St. Ann's, PEI's Original Church Lobster Supper (www.lobstersuppers.com), located between Stanley Bridge and New Glasgow off Route 224, is still very popular. Held in the church hall, it gained fame not only for the superb food, but also because the parish priest entertained with the organ, leading a sing-song of old and new favourites. There is no guarantee of such entertainment today. After all, a priest has to save some voice for the Sunday sermon. But you can count on a delightful time with dinner music and a satisfyingly full feeling to send you on your way.

New Glasgow Lobster Suppers (www.peilobstersuppers.com) are another great favourite. Evening after evening, tour bus after tour bus rolls in. Amazingly, its two dining rooms accommodate everyone without ever seeming to be overcrowded. On the contrary, the crowds add a feeling of gaiety to the occasion. New Glasgow's policy of unlimited rolls, chowder, mussels, salad, dessert and beverages ensures that they are busy, not to mention the fact that they have a legion of excellent cooks in the kitchen. Situated on the banks of a lovely river in a small village, this supper is one of the best.

You can also get lobster in the village. The Prince Edward Island Preserve Company, just down the road, will serve lobster rolls and lobster quiche for lunch as long as you phone ahead. While there, check out the beautiful New Glasgow Country Gardens.

Cardigan Lobster Suppers, served at the historic Old Store heritage building in the small village of Cardigan near Montague, took the tradition to the eastern end of the province. It's a grand spot, with two decks and the dining room overlooking the Cardigan marina and harbour. The five-course supper is a little different because it comes with hot veggies and a baked potato.

Fisherman's Wharf (www.fishermanswharf.ca) in North Rustico is a good place for abundant food. The gigantic salad bar, lobster

MacKinnon's Lobster Pound, Charlottetown

right from its own holding tanks, and a general party atmosphere with lots of chatter to accompany the meal add up to an experience like no other. Those who don't like lobster can fill up on the salad bar for a discounted price while their seafood-loving friends chow down.

"Up west," as Islanders like to say, the Centre Expo-Festival Centre in Abram-Village serves up a touch of Acadian culture with their lobster suppers. At West Point Lighthouse Inn, supper can be enjoyed on a patio beside the sea or in the dining room. The folks at West Point have even been known to arrange a lobster boil on the beach (with prior notice). It's a wonderful experience to sit with a bonfire crackling, sucking out every morsel of tender lobster meat as the sun sets over the sea. West Point is a magical sort of place, a country inn located in an operating lighthouse, which carries on the community tradition.

Picnic at the wharf at North Rustico

Festivals are held during the summer and fall, and many of them feature a lobster supper, particularly the Northumberland Fisheries Festival in Murray River (www.exhibitions-festivalspeiae.com.murrayrivercomm.pe.ca), the Tyne Valley Oyster Festival and the Summerside Lobster Carnival. The folks at the visitor information centres can help track down what is available.

Then, of course, there are the die-hard lobster lovers who simply want a "scoff" without the trimmings. In this case, it's do as the Islanders do, which is to head down to a wharf, such as those at Rustico, Stanley Bridge, Covehead, Charlottetown, Summerside or Wood Islands. Here, the seafood outlets offer fresh-from-the-sea lobster — either cooked on the spot or ready for your own pot. Find a picnic table overlooking the sea, or head back to your cottage or cabin, for you have the makings of a feast fit for royalty.

Rustico fishing boats

Fun, indeed, but it doesn't quite compare to experiencing the suppers. The advice we Islanders offer is to check them out, call to see when they are the least busy, and make a reservation. For a list of lobster suppers check under Travel and Vacation at www.gov.pe.ca/infopei then type lobster suppers in the search box. Whichever lobster supper you choose, go with an empty stomach and a desire for good food, good fun and a rare ambience.

Best Beaches

Jocelyne Lloyd

Cavendish Beach

With over 500 kilometres of coastline, Prince Edward Island offers seemingly endless opportunities for every beach lover. Whether for relaxing under an umbrella, walking for hours along the water's edge, splashing around with the kids or hunting for interesting rocks and marine life, PEI has a beach for everyone.

All supervised beaches, and those falling under the jurisdictions of the provincial and national parks systems, are marked on Tourism PEI's highway maps. Many of these beaches have changing facilities, picnic areas and playgrounds. Supervised beaches usually employ lifeguards from Canada Day weekend to Labour Day. For those looking for more secluded areas to swim and sunbathe, there is often a beach to be found at the end of a dead-end road or near a lighthouse — but residents appreciate respect for "No Trespassing" and "Private Property" signs.

The Island's most famous beaches — the white sand beaches, bordered by grassy dunes, that stretch for miles — are found on the north shore in

Cavendish Beach

Prince Edward Island National Park. You have to buy a pass to enter the park and its beaches, but you can save money by buying family and season passes, or by purchasing an early-bird pass by late June. Cavendish is the most popular beach for tourists as it's close to shopping, golf, Green Gables House and many other attractions. In recent years Brackley, Stanhope and Dalvay beaches have become increasingly popular. Stanhope Beach is good for small children as it is supervised and has a small playground, picnic facilities and a canteen. Foxes and hares are becoming tamer by the season, resulting in more frequent sightings, but Park officials advise you not to feed them. An unsupervised part of the National Park, and therefore a much less crowded area, is Robinson's Island, which can be found by coming through the gates at Brackley Beach and taking the first left past the entrance to the parking lot.

Basin Head

Rip currents are common on the north shore, so it is important to always swim with a friend and stay close to the shore, especially on unsupervised beaches. If a rip current pulls you away from the shore, you can usually get out of it by staying calm and swimming parallel to the beach.

The recently developed Greenwich adjunct to the PEI National Park boasts pristine white sand beaches and magnificent dunes. Three walking trails criss-cross the peninsula, letting visitors experience the dunes, marshes and wildlife close up. The path from the parking lot all the way around to the supervised area of the beach is also a beautiful route. The St. Peters Bay side offers shallower, warmer water, ideal for snorkelling, or you may prefer a nice, secluded spot tucked near a dune on the north side of the peninsula. The whole walk can take hours though, and you'll need to carry water with you on hot days.

Surf Conditions

Other beaches that offer white sand and magnificent dunes, but do not have an admission charge, are Panmure Island Provincial Park near Montague at the eastern end of PEI, and Cabot Beach Provincial Park near Malpeque in the northwest. Both these parks have overnight camping facilities. Blooming Point Beach is one of the more beautiful beaches on the Island, and it is rumoured that there has been a "clothing optional" area further down the beach. Access to Blooming Point is via a narrow road, and it can be difficult to get in and out on a sunny Saturday or Sunday.

A unique beach offering something for nearly everyone is Basin Head. Near the northeast tip of the Island, Basin Head has a surfguard station, picnic area, canteen and ice cream stand. There are also washroom and changing facilities. The beach is at the end of a short boardwalk from gift shops and the Basin Head Fisheries Museum. You can leap into the rushing river, letting it carry you to the beach, dive off the footbridge, swim in a more shallow area or go for a walk on the "singing sands." The polished sands of this beach squeak when you walk on them.

The south shore is the preferred destination for some — the water is considerably warmer, and parents with small children like these beaches because they tend to be shallower. Snails, minnows, hermit crabs and the like abound in the tidal pools. It's important to check the tide schedule in the daily papers, though, or one could end up

walking halfway to Nova Scotia before the water is deep enough for swimming. Another downside to south shore beaches is the seaweed, which is smelly when the tide is out and sometimes a considerable barrier to clear water when the tide is in. Others find the red sands of the south shore to be not as appealing as the white sands of the Gulf of St. Lawrence.

Tea Hill Beach is a terrific spot to take the kids for a swim and a picnic. About a ten-minute drive east of Charlottetown, Tea Hill has a decent-sized playground and picnic tables nestled under pine trees. Besides being pretty, the trees have the added bonus of keeping the blazing afternoon sun at bay. The water is bath-water warm by the end of June, and when the tide is in it gets deep (but not too deep) quickly.

Top: Brackley Beach
Above: Low tide, Victoria Beach

Other family-friendly south shore beaches are Chelton Beach Provincial Park, near the Confederation Bridge, and Argyle Shore Provincial Park, halfway between the bridge and Charlottetown. Victoria-by-the-Sea on the Argyle Shore is a lovely little village for poking around in, and offers a relaxing picnic spot and beach as well.

Cedar Dunes Provincial Park, at the western end of the province, is ideal for a long walk along the beach. More open waters here have created white sands and dunes reminiscent of the north shore. The West Point lighthouse has a magnificent view.

Although dangerous for swimming, the waters of the Gulf of St. Lawrence and the Northumberland Strait converging over Canada's longest natural rock reef at North Cape is fun to watch. At low tide, a stroll along the reef may reveal marine life, shore birds and seals, or Irish moss harvesters might be there using horses to haul what they have gathered from the beach.

Although agricultural run-off and private property make many of the Island's river beaches unusable or inaccessible, there are a few inviting places to swim, walk and canoe. At the western end of the province, Mill River and Green Park provincial parks have large campgrounds with river beach facilities. The Rodd Mill River Resort has a marina where canoes, kayaks and pedal boats can be rented for an afternoon of fun on the river. In the east, at

Brudenell River Provincial Park, there is another river beach with a marina nearby. Pinette Provincial Park, just past Point Prim when coming from Charlottetown, is a good choice for a quiet day at the river.

Above: Waterskiing at Souris Beach
Middle: Westpoint Lighthouse
Bottom: Driftwood

The best months for swimming at the beach are July and August, when the air and water temperatures are both warm enough. It's also good to know that later in the summer there are fewer jellyfish. These jellyfish aren't as toxic as some varieties — their stings feel like being slapped with a wet towel, and rubbing a handful of sand on sore skin will usually lessen the sting — but sometimes the pure proliferation of them keeps people out of the water.

If you can stand the air temperature when you exit the water, September can be a wonderful time for swimming. There are fewer people at the beach and the water is often as warm as it was in August.

If a day at the beach does not include swimming, but just a leisurely stroll or an exploration of tidal pools, you can set out as soon as the snow melts and the dirt roads have firmed up, or until the first big snowstorm in the fall or winter. And if you're dressed for it, walking on a beach strewn with ice floes can be the perfect sunny afternoon adventure in winter.

Birding

Dan McAskill

Birders at lookout in Stanhope

The diversity of habitats in short distances combined with a wide variety of birds makes birding on Prince Edward Island a wonderful experience. Some of the many species that may be seen throughout the seasons are the northern gannet, great cormorant, brant, Barrow's goldeneye, bald eagle, peregrine falcon, piping plover, whimbrel, lesser black-backed gull, Iceland gull, Caspian tern, black guillemot, barred owl, brown creeper, Cape May warbler, black-throated blue warbler, Blackburnian warbler and Nelson's sharp-tailed sparrow. From late May to early autumn, a day's outing can yield 100 species or more, and birders can record over 40 species in a single day in mid-winter.

Over 353 species of birds have been recorded on the Island. Four of the hottest woodland birding sites are the Macphail Woods (Orwell), the Brookvale Nordic Ski trails in the spring and summer, the Valleyfield Demonstration Woodlot (near Montague) and the New Harmony Demonstration Woodlot (near Souris). The softwood, mixed-wood, hardwood and shrub areas in these woodlots host a variety of breeding birds. A birder can often find mourning warblers, black-throated blue warblers and Blackburnian warblers, and hear the songs of the winter wren and brown creeper at these sites. In early spring and autumn, hundreds of warblers pass through the woodlands in various parts of the Island, particularly at migration points such as East Point, North Cape and Cape Bear.

Juvenile Black-Backed Gull

Three species of owls, namely great horned, barred and northern saw-whet, are widespread on the Island. Late-spring to early-summer birders on a night excursion can usually hear their calls on near-windless nights in areas with fairly extensive woodlands. With really good luck, long-eared, short-eared, screech or boreal owls might be heard, and sightings of snowy owls are common some winters.

The salt marshes adjacent to the sand flats at Tracadie Harbour, Covehead Harbour and the Souris Causeway are excellent for shorebirding during the spring migration period and from late July to early October. Pick a time when the tide is mid-tide and rising so that the birds are pushed towards the shore. One might even encounter rarities such as the western sandpiper or a stilt sandpiper. Along sand spits or near the entrance to barachois ponds during spring and summer, there may be protective fencing for the piping plover. This is the Island's only nesting endangered species and it is struggling to survive. Birders should move quickly away from these sites. Guided viewing opportunities for piping plovers are sometimes available through naturalists in PEI National Park. During some years at Covehead Harbour, you can safely view one of the breeding areas from the bridge or parking lot. In addition, the Covehead salt marsh is a good spot for viewing Nelson's sharp-tailed sparrows and willets, but road changes have eliminated the roadside parking

Macphail Woods ground hemlock

Endangered dunes on the North Shore

that once afforded easy access.

Coastal and wetland birding opportunities abound on the Island. From spring through autumn, one can often see northern gannets, great cormorants, common eiders, black, surf and white-winged scoters and long-tailed ducks from coastal viewing points such as East Point, North Cape, Cape Tryon, West Point and Cape Bear. On windy days, East Point and sometimes the other coastal viewing points offer opportunities for spotting pelagic birds such as razorbills, common murres, shearwaters and phalaropes through a telescope. In northeastern Prince Edward Island in particular, there have been autumn sightings of black-headed, lesser black-backed, Iceland and glaucous gulls. The Pigot's Trail at Mount Stewart and the Bubbling Springs Trail in the PEI National Park offer good trails for sighting freshwater marsh birds.

Piping Plover

The principal birding events on the Island are co-ordinated by the Natural History Society. The Bain Bird Count is held on the last Saturday in May and there are four Christmas bird counts. The Neil Bennett Autumn Birding Classic fundraiser which is held in late September to early October welcomes visiting birders. Contact the Society at PO Box 2346, Charlottetown, PE, C1A 8C1, or search its website.

A birding centre is located at the Hillsborough River

Eco-Centre at Mount Stewart. Starting in 2007, the eco-centre began celebrating an Eagle Festival that features opportunities to view bald eagles, which concentrate on the Hillsborough because of the presence of large numbers of gaspereaux spawning in the river. This festival includes presentations on bald eagles and other topics. Information on the festival is available online at www.hrec.mountstewartpei.ca.

Bald Eagles

Great Blue Heron

Copies of the *Field Checklist of Birds* are available online at www.peiplay.com or search its website and at visitor information centres. There is a listserv for birders through the University of Prince Edward Island and the details for subscribing to it are on the Natural History Society's website. The checklists feature sighting frequency by season and the breeding status of each species. Some of the Island's birding hot spots are featured in Jeffrey Domm's Formac *Pocket Guide to Prince Edward Island Birds* and Geoff Hogan's *Familiar Birds of Prince Edward Island.*

Golf

Colleen Abdullah and Stephen Brun

New Green Gables Golf Course

From the scratch player to the high handicapper, there's no disputing Prince Edward Island has something to offer every golfer. There's nothing like getting out the clubs that first fine Saturday in spring, with fresh breezes blowing off the Gulf, and enjoying life outdoors amidst scenery usually found on postcards. Depending on the kindness of the spring, enthusiasts have been known to tee off as early as mid-April. Golfing in the fall has become more popular, as courses are less crowded and the weather remains beautiful into September and much of October. The gorgeous fall foliage is a bonus.

With Prince Edward Island's numerous links, friendly clubs and first-class amenities, golfers of every skill level can find a place to either hone their game or simply unwind with a friendly — yet challenging — round. With prices ranging from less than $20 for 9-hole courses to around $100 for high-end 18-hole championship courses, it's also affordable. Another attraction is that the courses are all close to major centres, as well as to each other.

The Island is most famous for its hospitality, its agriculture and Anne of Green Gables, but in recent years PEI has also become known as a fantastic golf destination. Leading golf course designers have been inspired by the scenic beauty and seaside setting of PEI to create new golf courses that have become internationally acclaimed. In 2003 *SCOREGolf* magazine, recognized as the most reputable publication for the sport in Canada, named PEI as Canada's #1 Golf Destination for the second time running. In 2005 *SCOREGolf* awarded PEI the Best Golf Destination in Atlantic Canada. This country's golfing public agrees – the *Toronto Sun* voted PEI the Best Golf and Travel Destination in North America for the last two years. Given the size of PEI, these are enormous endorsements.

The individual courses have also received a disproportionate number of accolades. There are some 30 golf courses on the Island, and of those *The Globe and Mail* has placed nine in the top 100 courses in Canada. In the 2005 golfers' choice awards conducted by *SCOREGolf* magazine, The Links at Crowbush Cove was voted the course having the best scenery and best condition.

From a provincial perspective, the Island's government-owned courses are more than holding their own. Dundarave, the red-sandstone 18-hole championship golf course designed by architects Dr. Michael Hurzdan and Dana Fry and opened in July 1999, has been awarded a four-and-a-half star rating by *Golf Digest*. *SCOREGolf* magazine rated Dundarave, which is part of the Brudenell River Resort, in the top six best golf resorts in Canada. It is significant to note that there are at least six (soon to be more) PEI courses awarded the four-star designation by *Golf Digest*: Mill River, Fox Meadow, Brudenell, Crowbush Cove, Dundarave and Glasgow Hills.

On the links at Dundarave

PEI has hosted its share of professional and amateur championships. The Canadian Professional Golf Tour used Brudenell as a regular stop for a number of years. In 1996, Mill River hosted the first du Maurier Team Challenge, a format that had the top Canadians from the LPGA tour paired with the du Maurier Series in a team skins format. Crowbush was the site of the 1997 Canadian Amateur Golf Championship and the 1998 Export "A" Skins Game. The golfing, and non-golfing, public were drawn to the course, hoping to get a glimpse of golfing greatness – Mike Weir, Fred Couples, Mark O'Meara and John Daly. A celebrity golf event in 2006, Legends of Golf, saw life-long rivals Jack Nicklaus and Tom Watson tee off at Dundarave to a huge gallery and extensive international media coverage. In 2007, Weir and fellow PGA Tour pro Vijay Singh also played the Legends of Golf event at Crowbush Cove.

A suggestion for anyone not familiar with the Island: what many consider three of the most majestic courses in Canada – Brudenell River, the Links at Crowbush Cove

Glasgow Hills

and Dundarave — are located in the Eastern end of the province. There are also some fine 9-hole courses in that part of the province, including Eagle's View, a newer championship course nestled in Murray River. Eagle's View has carved out its own little niche, featuring an interpretive centre that focuses on the region's history. The course surrounds MacLure's Pond, the Island's largest body of fresh water.

At the other end of the Island, in the North Cape region, the multi-award-winning Mill River is a golfer's dream — all one could ask for in a game with 18 distinctly different and memorable holes. In Summerside, the province's second-largest centre, and near the Confederation Bridge, is the *Golf Digest* three-star Summerside Golf and Country Club. This club has hosted the Canadian Senior Ladies Championship. The 9-hole St. Felix Golf and Country Club, designed by Graham Cooke and Associates, rounds out the golf experience in this part of the province.

Fox Meadow

There are four 18-hole courses in Cavendish, all within

Mill River

five minutes of one another, including Glasgow Hills, designed by Les Furber, and the relatively new Graham Cooke-designed gems, Eagles Glenn and Anderson's Creek. The fourth is the lovely Green Gables Golf Course, for many synonymous with PEI. This awesome foursome makes the Cavendish area a golfer's paradise.

Recent extensive renovations to Green Gables have made it a championship-level track. Course architect Thomas McBroom, best known on the Island for designing Crowbush Cove, blended his own concepts with Stanley Thompson's original 1939 design. Between them, McBroom and Thompson boast the designs of 31 of Canada's top 50 courses. The $5-million renovation in 2008 sees improvements to virtually every aspect of the course from tee to green, and also includes a makeover for the clubhouse. The course was lengthened from about 6,500 yards to more than 7,000, and will look to host some big events in future golf seasons. Stanhope Golf and Country Club, another award-winning course, designed by Robbie Robinson, is close to both Charlottetown and the beaches. Stanhope and Rustico Resort are the granddaddies of golf in PEI and have been favourites with golf vacationers for generations. There are several 9-hole courses in this vicinity too. A 9-hole course can provide a challenging and satisfying game — Red Sands is a fine example — and for those who want to sharpen their skills, have limited time or want to give the whole family a taste of golf, the park-like setting of Forest Hills might be a good and affordable choice.

There are a half-dozen golf courses within 15 minutes of Charlottetown, the capital city. The championship Fox Meadow Club at Stratford is a masterpiece. The golf, the service and the surroundings are all remarkable. The Belvedere Golf Club, on the edge of Charlottetown, is the home club of LPGA star Lorie Kane and should be part of a well-rounded golf tour. Classic golf at very

Anne Chouinard from the Canadian Golf Academy

Glen Afton

reasonable rates can be had at Glen Afton, and Dog River Golf Course at Clyde River offers a course that is really fun to play. When time is at a premium, Countryview is a handy but challenging 9-hole course.

Teaching the game has become a specialty service on the Island, offered by the Canadian Golf Academy at Fox Meadow Golf and Country Club. Widely known as one of the top teaching facilities in the country, its director is Anne Chouinard, whose prize pupil is Lorie Kane. The professional faculty addresses all aspects of the game, from one-hour private lessons to three-day workshops for groups to a three-year program in course management in affiliation with Holland College. The Academy also conducts private lessons and clinics at Brudenell, Crowbush Cove and Dundarave.

The Cavendish area pioneered online booking in Canada. Today golfers can book tee times at most Island courses in real time online. Check the golf listings in the back of this book for golf course details and websites.

Golf Prince Edward Island has taken that convenience

New Green Gables Golf Course

one step further — an entire golf vacation can be booked through its website at www.golfpei.ca. Golf PEI began in 1989 with only six clubs, and today has 21 member clubs; its rapid growth attests to the importance of the sport to the Island. Of its many good golf offerings, everyone has a favourite; for some it's Brudenell, partly because of its layout, and partly because it's both forgiving and challenging at the same time. Many are enthralled by the undulating fairways and challenging greens of the Links at Crowbush Cove, recognized by *Golf Digest* as Canada's Best New Course in 1994. Families return year after year to Rustico Resort for an all-in-one laid-back vacation with comfy cottages on the beach and grand ocean views from every hole on the course. Some golfers prefer a traditional layout like Belvedere or the classic Glen Afton, which makes for a good walk; others go for high-tech layouts like Anderson's Creek or Eagles Glenn with its cutting-edge practice facility. A combination of traditional and modern is offered at Dundarave.

Many hotels, motels and resorts offer golf packages; details are available in the *Prince Edward Island Destination and Golf Guide* and at www.peiplay.com/packages. If you feel like a kid in a candy shop with all the great golf choices PEI has to offer, a counsellor at Golf PEI (866-465-3734) will help custom-design a golf vacation package, and even book dinner reservations and theatre tickets.

A golf vacation in PEI can be a great value with all the resort packages available, reasonable B&B, inn and cottage accommodations and affordable green fees. Proximity to beaches, theatre, shopping and outdoor activities means there is always plenty to keep the whole family (even the non-golfers) happily entertained for the duration of a great PEI golf getaway.

The Links at Crowbush Cove

Cycling

Campbell Webster

Cycling the Confederation Trail at Mount Stewart

Cycling Prince Edward Island has gained such popularity in recent years that the premiere international women's cycling event has become the Tour de PEI. The trend has not gone unnoticed by the provincial government, either, which now puts out cycling guides for those who wish to explore Prince Edward Island's coast on two wheels. For trails and information, visit the provincial website at www.gov.pe.ca. For cycling-related events on PEI, see www.cpei.ca.

The conversion of 350 kilometres of rail beds to walking and cycling trails has ensured a path that's never too steep, a result of the gradual incline required for trains. The Confederation Trail stretches 279 km from tip to tip of the island. There are four spur trails connecting Borden, Charlottetown, Montague and Souris that together add 78 km. Most of the trail has been upgraded with a fine gravel surface for smooth cycling.

PEI is ideally suited to the day ride or multiple-day continuous touring. The day ride is a personal favourite. When I find time to cycle in the summer and early fall, I typically take out my map of PEI and pick out a circular route that is between 60 and 80 kilometres long. While I have favourite routes, even after years of cycling I often find new round trips that include roads and communities that I have yet to visit. The day-ride approach is recommended to tourists

Tandem riders in Charlottetown

who want to include cycling as part of their vacation, but don't plan to spend their entire time on a bicycle.

A cyclist can usually tell from just looking at the Tourism PEI map and consulting the very detailed *Visitors' Guide* (both available from visitor information centres and the Department of Tourism at no charge) what will be an interesting ride. To set out on a day ride, all that's needed is to pick a circular route, choose a starting point, drive to that point (I have never had trouble finding a parking spot anywhere when heading out on a day ride), lock the car and begin the trip.

One favourite day route of mine starts at the West Point lighthouse and heads north on Route 14 towards Skinners Pond. The first 20 kilometres of this ride affords the cyclist a rare continuous cliff-edge ride along the ocean, passing numerous harbours and historic churches set against the bluffs of the Northumberland Strait. There is ample

Confederation Trail

West Point Lighthouse

opportunity to stop and go swimming, as well as a variety of communities to visit along the way. When you get to Campbellton, you head east towards Alberton and the north shore (it is only about a one-hour ride from the south shore to the north shore on this part of the Island). You can get to Alberton via Route 145 or Route 150 or by hooking up with the Confederation Trail off Route 145. Once in Alberton, there are a number of routes back to West Point. Taking an alternate route is often a positive experience for cyclists on PEI.

Another route, and one that I usually ride alone, provides long stretches of interior roads that offer distant horizons and extensive views of woods and farmlands. This route begins at the corner of Routes 2 and 8 in Summerfield. There is a small church on the corner. Follow Route 8 south towards Bedeque and enjoy the view. The Village Store in Bedeque is a great place to stop for lunch and chat with community members who use this store as an informal meeting place. From Bedeque, there's a variety of ways to return to Summerfield — simply pick one from your map. All the return routes are interesting and have very little car traffic on them.

Confederation Trail

The same approach can be applied to picking multiple-day continuous rides. The advantage of planning a bike

Cyclists at West Point

tour on PEI is that virtually all of the roads and all of the Confederation Trail are rewarding rides. With the exception of the highways (Routes 1–4, 6, 7, 13, 15 and 16), almost all of the roads have light traffic.

So when planning multiple-day rides, you can construct your own routes based on what you'd like to see and do — go to the beach, deep-sea fishing, the theatre or a lobster supper.

Three of the most important concerns of the cyclist are the topography of their cycling destination, the traffic and the quality of the roads. PEI is unique in all these areas and it is important to take these factors into consideration before you begin. If you were playing a word association game and the word "island" came up you might, being a devout cyclist, respond with the word "flat." While it is true that there aren't any snow-capped mountain ranges on the Island, you mustn't expect it to be one long countertop. It is generally quite flat along the shores, but also considerably more windy. Most inland routes have some hills, and although very few Island hills should take you more than ten minutes to cycle, they tend to come in rapid succession. If the most feared words of the cyclist are "Lunch is just over that mountain," then the most-often-heard words of the Island cyclist are

Road near Irishtown

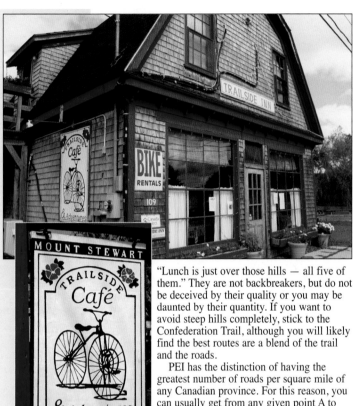

Trailside Café

"Lunch is just over those hills — all five of them." They are not backbreakers, but do not be deceived by their quality or you may be daunted by their quantity. If you want to avoid steep hills completely, stick to the Confederation Trail, although you will likely find the best routes are a blend of the trail and the roads.

PEI has the distinction of having the greatest number of roads per square mile of any Canadian province. For this reason, you can usually get from any given point A to any given point B in a number of ways. This is ideal for cyclists who want to avoid busy routes and still cycle to the most popular areas. If you are setting out to one of these popular destinations, you might try the following method in selecting quieter roads: on your Visitor's Map select the direct route to your destination. These routes, particularly in Queens County, will have a fair amount of traffic. Then choose the route you will take; you should have no trouble finding a secondary road or part of the Confederation Trail beside, or near, the main route. These secondary roads are usually quite narrow and have little or no shoulder, but owing to the extremely light traffic this is usually not a problem. Generally, you will find the most traffic in Queens County, some traffic in Kings County, and very little in Prince County. In early spring and fall almost anywhere on the Island is lightly travelled with the exception of Routes 1 and 2.

Keeping these tour-planning facts in mind, and opening yourself to the abundance of choice and community that is PEI, you are bound to have an excellent cycling vacation on the Island.

Walking & Hiking Trails

Dan McAskill

Trail at Green Gables

With the many hues of green from the crops and the deciduous and coniferous forests, interspersed with the vivid reds of our soils, the vistas on the island are often breathtaking. A simple turn in a trail can bring one to fields of wildflowers rippling in the breeze, shaded forest glades alive with the calls of birds or ponds dappled with autumn leaves. There is something here for everyone — from those who enjoy the boardwalk and waterfront trails of Charlottetown to those who wish to see the Island much as it was when the first Europeans first visited these shores.

Short Hikes

For walking enthusiasts, the Island features more than 60 short trails scattered throughout the province. The vast majority are designed for a brief exposure to our natural habitats and range from one to three kilometres long. The gentle topography of the Island means that usually these trails can be walked by most people, with usually only short slopes of a grade up to 15 percent.

Should you be visiting Charlottetown and wish a short walk or series of hikes, there are several good options. A walking trail and boardwalk by the Hillsborough River, Canada's 17th designated Canadian Heritage River, lead from Victoria Park to Joseph Ghiz Memorial Park. It goes past some of the historic homes, including Beaconsfield and Government House, Fort Edward, the Hillsborough Canadian Heritage River Monument and Confederation Landing Park. Another part of Charlottetown's Routes for Nature and Health extends from the western edge of Charlottetown to follow a freshwater stream and pond. For part of its length, it runs beside the Ellen's Creek Wildlife

Management Area, where thousands of waterfowl may be seen in autumn. This trail can be accessed from North River Road or Beach Grove Road. The Royalty Oaks Natural Area trail on the eastern side of Charlottetown offers an interpretive walk through a four-hectare hardwood woodlot that features some very large specimens of our provincial tree, the red oak. Also on the eastern side of Charlottetown, the East Royalty Nature Pathway passes through woodland beside Wight's Creek while the Hillsborough River Walkway, adjacent to the Queen Elizabeth Hospital, runs along the bank of the historic Hillsborough River and through old hardwoods.

The Town of Stratford lies across the Hillsborough River from Charlottetown. Stratford offers a one-kilometre trail at the Robert Cotton Park as well as a series of trails with connecting sidewalks. The six demonstration woodlot trails in the provincial forest, which are marked on Tourism PEI's map of the Island, offer an opportunity to look at various forest management choices. There are two trails in each county, located at New Harmony (near Souris), Valleyfield (near Montague), Auburn (25 kilometres northeast of Charlottetown), Brookvale (in south-central PEI), Wellington (near Summerside), and Foxley River (near Portage). Each woodlot features self-guided trails with interpretive brochures and signage describing various practical forest management options available to private landowners. These options focus on forest stewardship for timber, wildlife or other forest values. At the other end of the forest-management spectrum, the three trails at Macphail Woods near Orwell focus on nature interpretation and forest management treatments geared to ecological forestry. While at Macphail Woods a visit to the nature centre, Sir Andrew Macphail House, or Orwell Village will add to the experience. These sites are near the Trans Canada Highway, about 32 kilometres east of Charlottetown.

For those who wish to experience some of the Island's oldest remaining forests, the trail at Townshend Woodlot north of Souris on the Souris Line Road (Route 305) offers the opportunity to see a remnant portion of the Acadian hardwood forest, which dates back to the mid-1800s. In

Watershed at Hillsborough River

southeastern Prince Edward Island, the Eagle's View Golf Course and Interpretive Centre's trails bring you through a stand of magnificent red and white pine along the side of MacLure's Pond at Murray River. Both these sites form part of the island's natural areas system, designed to conserve representative biological reserves in the province.

Pigot's Trail on the Allisary Creek Impoundment, located 20 kilometres east of Charlottetown in Mount Stewart, features a freshwater Ducks Unlimited marsh. This trail can be accessed off the Confederation Trail just south of the Hillsborough River Eco-Centre or via Main Street. The trails at the Harvey Moore Wildlife Management Area (Route 4 south of Montague) meanderaround ponds that are teeming with waterfowl, especially during the migration season.

Goose

Great Blue Heron

Prince Edward Island National Park occupies the central north shore of the province. Here walkers can venture along wooded pathways, across marshlands and ponds, through old fields, and across dunes to the beach. The area has many attractions, and some visitors may golf, shop for crafts or go to an amusement park while others hike. The trails in Cavendish offer the walkers and hikers of the group a variety of choices. There are the Balsam Hollow and Haunted Woods Trails at Anne of Green Gables House (note: there is a small additional access charge at this site), or the longer, double-loop Homestead Trail through coastal marsh, old fields and woodlands. On the eastern side of the National Park in Dalvay and Stanhope, the Bubbling Springs, Farmlands, Reeds and Rushes, and Woodlands Trails will bring you through wooded old fields, past barachois ponds and through dunes.

Lying still further east and separate from the main Park, the Greenwich adjunct to the PEI National Park is located on the north side of St. Peters Bay. This magnificent area features one short and two longer interpretive trails. The 4.5-kilometre Greenwich Dunes Trail travels through old fields, woodlands, a pond via a floating boardwalk, dunes and the shore, leading the walker to a spectacular viewpoint over the Greenwich sand dunes. Steps and short steep slopes make this trail inaccessible to those in wheelchairs. The 1.2-kilometre Havre St. Pierre Trail explores the Acadian period of our history, while the 4.7-kilometre Tlaqatik Trail takes visitors through archeological sites dating back 10,000 years.

Family picnic on St. Peters Bay

In the western part of the

Boardwalk at Greenwich

Island, the Fairy Trails at Cedar Dunes Provincial Park offer an opportunity to explore lowland forests of spruce, balsam fir and cedar. The adjacent sand beach allows you to cool off after the hike. The Black Marsh Nature Trail in the extreme northwestern part of the province wanders along coastal cliffs and via a boardwalk through a bog near the Atlantic Wind Test Site. Seals can often be seen in the coastal waters. On Route 2 near Coleman Corner, the Trout River Trail winds along the historic river after which it is named. North of Summerside, tucked in the northwest corner of Malpeque Bay, lies the Path of Our Forefathers Trail with its two loops (three kilometres and seven kilometres). These trails allow the hiker to explore the Mi'kmaq culture and their use of plants amidst the Lennox Island landscape.

In the south-central area just east of Bonshaw, the Strathgartney Nature Trail runs through the woodlands overlooking the historic West River. To the north of this site, the Nordic Ski Trails in the Brookvale Provincial Forest have over ten kilometres of walking trails. In addition, this is a great woodland birding site.

A stop at the local visitor information centre or PEI National Park offices will provide brochures for some of the better trails. The city of Charlottetown and the town of Stratford have good maps of the their trail systems. A *Trail and Nature Map* is available from the Island Nature Trust and other outlets. Some of the trails in the PEI National Park, in Charlottetown and at other sites such as Lennox Island are designed for mobility-challenged individuals.

Excursions

Confederation Trail

The pre-eminent trail system on Prince Edward Island for those desiring true excursion hiking or cycling is the Confederation Trail. This low-slope trail runs 350 kilometres along the abandoned railway beds that transect the Island, and grows longer every year. The main Confederation Trail now spans the Island tip to tip, a distance of 279 kilometres. It passes through woodlands and rich fields, along some of our magnificent harbours and bays and through many of the communities that played a key role in the development of Canada's smallest province. The compacted stone-dust surface provides excellent footing.

Cedar Dunes Provincial Park

Besides the main line, branch

Trail at Bonshaw, Fall

lines provide hiking routes from Emerald to Borden-Carleton (18.5 kilometres), Royalty Junction to Charlottetown (nine kilometres), Mount Stewart to Georgetown (39.5 kilometres), Montague Junction to Montague (ten kilometres) and Harmony Junction to Souris (8.2 kilometres), and a section of trail in the southeast runs from Murray River to Murray Harbour. Another part of Charlottetown's Routes for Nature and Health extends from the western edge of Charlottetown to follow a freshwater stream and pond. For part of its length; it runs beside the Ellen's Creek Wildlife Management Area, where thousands of waterfowl may be seen in autumn. This trail can be accessed from North River Road or Beach Grove Road. The Royalty Oaks Natural Area trail on the eastern side of Charlottetown offers an interpretive walk through a four-hectare hardwood woodlot that features some very large specimens of our provincial tree, the red oak. Also on the eastern side of Charlottetown, the East Royalty Nature Pathway passes through woodland beside Wight's Creek while the Hillsborough River Walkway, adjacent to the Queen Elizabeth Hospital, runs along the bank of the historic Hillsborough River and through old hardwoods.

The town of Stratford lies across the Hillsborough River from Charlottetown. Stratford offers a one-kilometre trail at the Robert Cotton Park as well as a series of trails with connecting sidewalks.

The six demonstration woodlot trails in the provincial forest, which are marked on Tourism PEI's map of the Island, offer an opportunity to look at various forest management choices. There are two trails in each county, located at New Harmony (near Souris), Valleyfield (near Montague), Auburn (25 kilometres northeast of Charlottetown), Brookvale (in south-central PEI), Wellington (near Summerside), and Foxley River (near Portage). Each woodlot features self-guided trails with interpretive brochures and signage describing various practical forest management options available to private landowners. These options focus on forest stewardship for timber, wildlife or other forest values. At the other end of the forest-management spectrum, the three trails at Macphail Woods near Orwell focus on nature interpretation and forest management treatments geared to ecological forestry. While at Macphail Woods a visit to the nature centre, Sir Andrew Macphail House or Orwell Village

Atlantic Wind Test Site

will add to the experience. These sites are near the Trans Canada Highway, about 32 kilometres east of Charlottetown.

For those who wish to experience some of the Island's oldest remaining forests, the trail at Townshend Woodlot north of Souris on the Souris Line Road (Route 305) offers the opportunity to see a remnant portion of the Acadian hardwood forest, which dates back to the mid-1800s. In southeastern Prince Edward Island, the Eagle's View Golf Course and Interpretive Centre's trails bring you through a stand of magnificent red and white pine along the side of MacLure's Pond at Murray River. Both these sites form part of the Island's natural areas system, designed to conserve representative biological reserves in the province.

Top: Wood Islands Provincial Park
Above: Scenic trail beside the Hillsborough River

Pigot's Trail on the Allisary Creek Impoundment, located 20 kilometres east of Charlottetown in Mount Stewart, features a freshwater Ducks Unlimited marsh. This trail can be accessed off the Confederation Trail just south of the Hillsborough River Eco-Centre or via Main Street. The trails at the Harvey Moore Wildlife Park has been expanded to connect these areas to Wood Islands.

Agriculture was not the only thing that moulded this landscape over the centuries. The need for shipping access points along the train route led to frequent stops in many small communities. Today this has yielded a trail system on which hikers have many options — from a few kilometres to as much as one can cover. Communities scattered along the trail offer resting places and shopping sites. In some of these communities, shorter trails allow one to explore various landscapes and cultures.

Fields at St. Ann

Two of the Confederation Trail segments follow historically important waterways. The route eastward from Charlottetown follows the Hillsborough, a Canadian Heritage River. Here, hundreds of sailing ships were built along the tidal estuary that stretches over 30 kilometres upriver from Charlottetown. The Mi'kmaq, French, Scottish and Irish all used this water corridor to access the interior of the Island. In the east, the branch lines between Georgetown, Cardigan and Montague join the major communities along the Three Rivers, designated a heritage river in 2004.

In the northeast the termination point of the Trail is in Elmira. Here one of the branch museums of the Prince Edward Island Museum and Heritage Foundation celebrates the Island's railroad history. From Elmira, roadways allow the hiker to continue the excursion to the eastern terminus of the Island at East Point.

The western section of Confederation Trail extends from Charlottetown to Tignish (actually mile "0"). This 180-kilometre section of trail leads through the central uplands region, providing spectacular views, particularly during the autumn when the hardwood and mixed forests provide a dazzling display of colour. From Kensington westward, the topography is relatively flat. Amidst the agricultural landscape, small woodlots, wetlands and streams abound. The wetter soils in this area yield some different plants for those exploring the trailside botany.

Further information and maps are available from Island Trails, PO Box 265, Charlottetown, PE, CIA 7K4, or from InfoPEI at www.peiplay.com. Confederation Trail brochures are provided at visitor information centres.

Provincial Forests

In 2000, the provincial government designated a system of 22 provincial forest areas and 187 satellite provincial forests scattered throughout the Island. These properties have over 270 kilometres of forest roads that are accessible to the public. The forest road and highway junctions are marked by a sign with a green diamond-shaped symbol on which there's a gold image of an acorn with a leaf/conifer on top of the acorn. In addition to these public properties, there are also wildlife management areas, natural areas and impoundments.

Scenic Heritage Roads

A campaign by concerned Islanders and the Island Nature Trust led to the creation of a protected system of Scenic Heritage Roads in 1987. This allows visitors and Islanders alike to carefully drive or walk on sections of tree-canopied and open roads that have outstanding beauty. These narrow, low-maintenance roads are designated on the PEI highway map, and a brochure highlighting them is available at the Island Nature Trust.

Scenic Trail near Souris

Architectural Treasures

Reg Porter

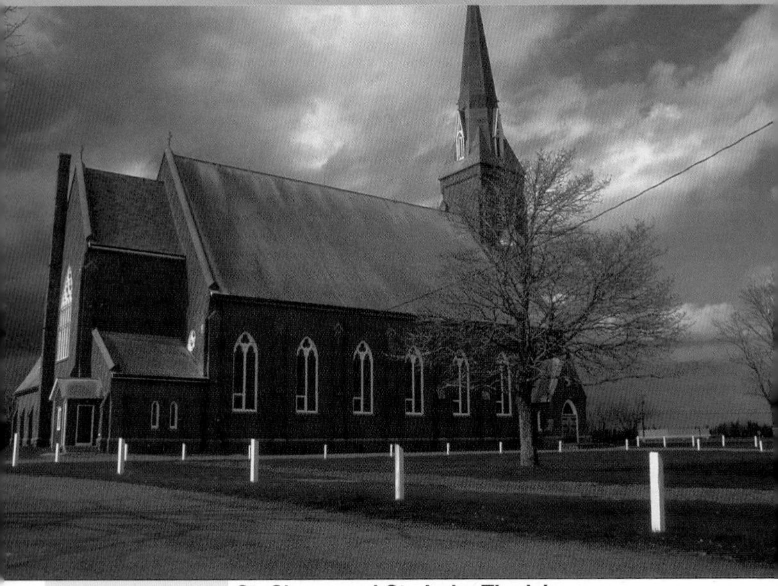

St. Simon and St. Jude Church

St. Simon and St. Jude, Tignish

The Church of St. Simon and St. Jude at Tignish was built by its first resident pastor, Peter McIntyre, an energetic man who, in 1860, the year of the church's completion, would become the Island's third Roman Catholic bishop. McIntyre obtained a design from the New York architect Patrick Keilly, an Irish follower of Augustus Welby Pugin, one of the greatest of 19th-century proponents of the Gothic style as suitable for Christian worship. The church is immense and built entirely out of locally made brick, most of which still covers the building.

The interior, once decorated to resemble stone blocks, was repainted in 1888 by a Montreal painter and decorator, Frans-Xavier Meloche. He and his students painted life-size statues of the twelve apostles on the walls between the large stained glass windows. The chancel has two huge murals representing the Assumption of the Virgin into heaven and the Transfiguration.

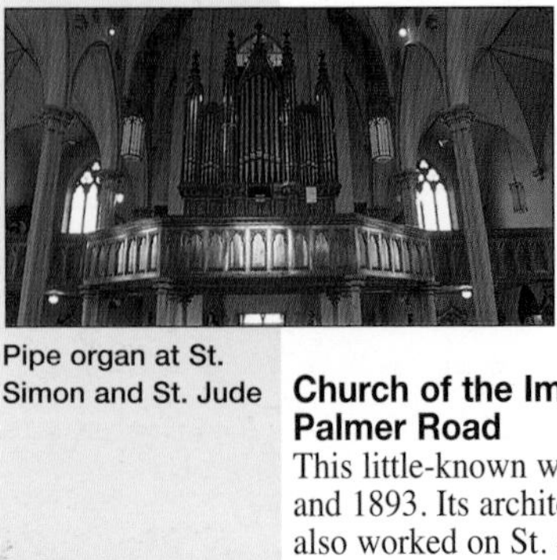

Pipe organ at St. Simon and St. Jude

Church of the Immaculate Conception, Palmer Road

This little-known wooden church was built between 1891 and 1893. Its architect was Frans-Xavier Meloche, who also worked on St. Simon and St. Jude Church.

The church is in the Gothic style and covered entirely in elaborate designs of shaped wooden shingles, typical of building practices of the time. The three altars, built by Island craftsman Bernard Creamer, have survived in perfect condition and give visitors an accurate impression of the original appearance of the structure. The elaborate wooden trusses that support the vault and the patterned wood create a rich interior.

One extraordinary addition to the building is a complete stained glass cycle designed by P. John Burden and executed by Blaine Hrabi, both Island artists, to replace the original clear glass of the church's many windows. Begun in 1985, the windows are striking, especially the great rose window in the façade of the church, which combines traditional Christian symbolism with exceptionally fine contemporary design.

Church of the Immaculate Conception, façade and rose window

McLean House, Southwest Lot 16

The Queen Anne Revival style (c. 1885–1900) is characterized by a large central core topped with a hipped roof decorated with classical motifs of an earlier age, and a tall corner tower with a high conical roof. The McLean House at Southwest Lot 16 is one of the finest examples of this style on the Island.

The house was designed around 1912 for J. G. McLean by Percy Tanton, a self-taught Summerside architect. An unusual feature of this Queen Anne house is the fact that the great corner tower was left open, providing two large balconies overlooking the splendid vista of Grand River with the tall profile of the gothic church of St. Patrick's in

McLean House

the distance. The effect this creates is far more harmonious than in most surviving houses of the period on the Island.

Yeo House, Green Park Provincial Park, Port Hill

James Yeo was an entrepreneur and shipbuilder from North Cornwall near Bideford, England, who had settled in the area of Port Hill by the early 1820s. A rough and driven man, he eventually founded a mercantile and shipbuilding empire in the area of Port Hill. In 1866 he decided to build a new home overlooking his shipyard.

Above and Below: Yeo House

This house, the culmination of an earlier Romantic trend of centre gable decorated with elaborate barge boards

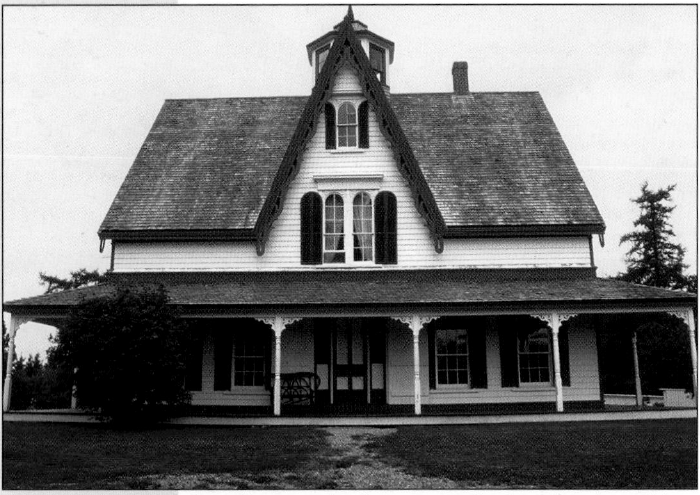

along the eaves, has been restored to its original condition by the Prince Edward Island Museum and Heritage Foundation. The interior has formal parlours, a dining room and a study flanking a centre hall which runs the length of the main house into the kitchen wing.

At this isolated site, more than any other, visitors may feel a powerful affinity with the past.

St. Mary's Church, Indian River

In 1896 the old church at Indian River was struck by lightning and burned to the ground. By October 1902 the present building, designed by Charlottetown architect William Critchlow Harris, was consecrated. An imposing structure on high ground, it can be seen for miles.

St. Mary's Church

In recent years, the fate of this church was in doubt because there was no longer a congregation to support a parish. Its renewed life is due to the efforts of passionately dedicated local

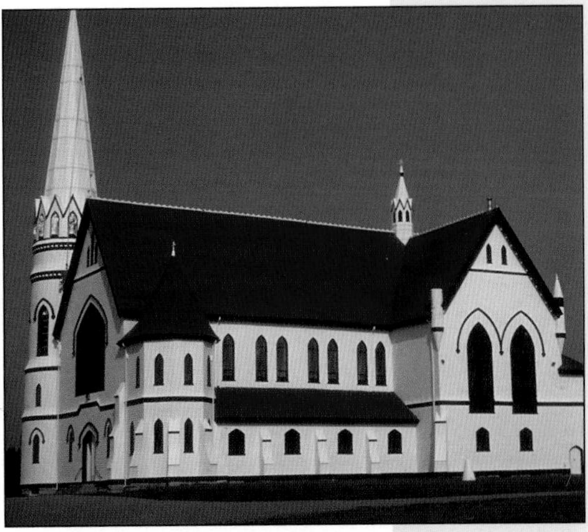

St. Mary's Church

individuals who raised funds, with Island-wide support, for its restoration and repair. Now concerts of various kinds are held there every summer and the fame of this exceptionally well-designed church is spreading.

The exterior of the church is typical of the Shingle style developed in the United States before the turn of the century: shingles literally wrap around everything, even the smallest turrets. The chancel and altar are particularly fine, representing Harris's design at its best.

The Farmers' Bank, Anglo Rustico

The Farmers' Bank in Rustico was built in the 1860s by Father Georges-Antoine Belcourt, a priest with years of missionary experience in western Canada who was sent to take over the administration of this mostly French-speaking parish.

It is constructed out of local sandstone that was quarried and shaped by local masons. The marks of their chisels on the stones remain as testimony to their individuality and skill. The style chosen for this building was English Georgian, at that time the supreme style of the reigning establishment. The function of this bank was far from the ordinary concept of banks in the country. Prefiguring the co-operative movement in Prince Edward Island, the bank served as an organization for local farmers, providing security in the form of low-interest loans in times of need. The bank even printed its own paper currency, now incredibly rare and known only through a few surviving examples. It served the local population from 1864 to 1894. Today this structure has undergone a major restoration and houses the local historical museum.

The Farmers' Bank

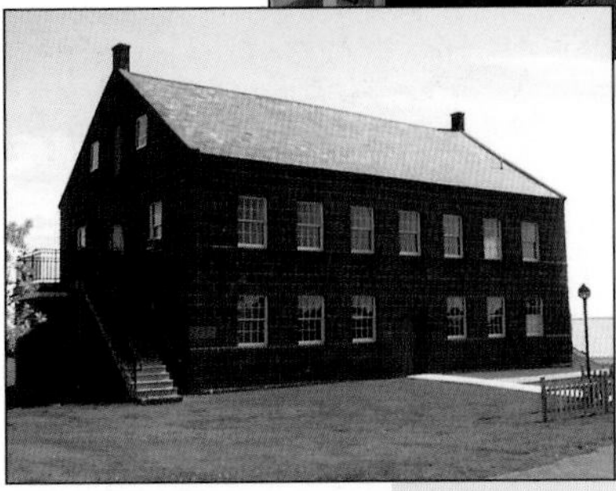

Strathgartney Homestead, Strathgartney

In 1875, Robert Bruce Stewart, the largest landed proprietor in Prince Edward Island and master of Strathgartney, was forced to sell most of his

67,000 acres of land to the Island government. This was the end of a long and bitter struggle against British absentee landlords that had been going on for a century.

Although the house has undergone many changes over the years, including the addition of a larger "new house" to the original homestead, the feeling of a grand home surrounded by unbounded acres of timber and agricultural land is still to be encountered in this spot. The oldest part of the house is the smaller centre gable structure, which retains much of its character as a building of the pre-Confederation period. The larger, later addition looks over the remains of a terraced garden, which, to gauge from its remnants and stray perennials, must have been of extraordinary beauty.

Strathgartney

Nearby is Strathgartney Provincial Park, where visitors may explore one of the last great stretches of upland forest left on the Island.

The Atwell Stone House, Clyde River

During the 1830s and 1840s a fair number of local red sandstone houses were built in the style popular at that time, consisting of a central plan with one or two bays and a centre gable or dormer above the front door. Today only a handful of these precious houses remain as witnesses to the determination of British settlers to build in the style and materials they knew best at home. By the 1850s, such houses were no longer built because the framed timber house was cheaper and better adapted to PEI's climate. At the same time, the Island's brick-making industry began to overshadow sandstone in popularity.

The Atwell House, built in 1842, always attracts a great deal of attention because of its peculiar hooded gable, the only one of its kind in the province.

The exterior of the house is well-preserved and demonstrates clearly the style of most of these stone houses. Windows and doors were framed in a similar manner. The rest of the wall area was carefully filled in with rubble construction. The contrast between the smoothly finished major blocks and this rubble infill creates a dramatic texture that is particularly visible when the sun shines obliquely on any of its wall surfaces.

All Saints Church, Cardigan

This picturesquely situated church, built in 1874, is in the neo-Gothic style. It was later enlarged by the addition of a transept.

All Saints Church

The high altar of this church is of particular interest. It was built by William Lewis, a native of Dumfries in Scotland. Lewis was a stonemason whose work is to be found in cemeteries all across the Island. The architectural framework for the altar is carved out of a grey-green Nova Scotia sandstone. All the panels of the altar table and arches are filled with a white marble with pale grey veining, upon which are carved various sacred symbols. The design can be called primitive, but its execution is flawless and the general effect is magnificent.

The building is bright and cheerful and is one of the best surviving examples of a pre-Vatican II Council church where all the statues of saints and two fine carved-wood side altars have been preserved.

The Beaton/Leard House, Souris

This small elegant neo-classical house was built around 1854 by Donald Beaton, an important fish merchant and politician. He chose the centre-plan Georgian country villa style, popular on the Island in the early years of the 19th century, with a centre hall and staircase leading to pairs of rooms on either side.

In the 1950s, the house came into the possession of the Leard family and they renovated it very sympathetically in a New England Colonial Revival style. Although the original details of the house were all replaced with new cladding, the earlier style and proportions were entirely compatible with the new shell.

This building demonstrates, perhaps more than any other structure on the Island, the persistence of the neo-classical styles on the Island, even though the period between 1850 and the First World War was marked by a tremendous flowering of all the late Victorian eclectic styles that imitated Gothic, Italian Renaissance, a non-existent Queen Anne, Romanesque and, finally, a return to the classical values of another age.

Point Prim Lighthouse, Point Prim

To the east of Charlottetown is a long splinter of hard sandstone that forms a spearhead-like peninsula of land, which the French and Acadian settlers of the 18th century called Pointe Prime. From earliest times, the point and the dangerous rocky shallows in its vicinity proved a hazard to navigation. In 1845 a decision was made to build a permanent structure to aid navigation through these treacherous waters.

Isaac Smith, a Yorkshireman who immigrated to the Island in 1817 at the age of 22, built Point Prim Lighthouse

while he was in the middle of constructing the Colonial Building, now called Province House, in Charlottetown. Smith also built the Lieutenant-Governor's residence (1834), an insane asylum and the Central Academy, which was to become Prince of Wales College.

This circular 18.5-metre shingled tower was built of brick over a massive timber core, which can still be seen by visitors. The polygonal lantern is the original, and although it is now run by electricity, all original elements remain.

The Macphail House, Orwell Corner

Sir Andrew Macphail (1864–1938), a pathologist at McGill University in Montreal, was a writer, doctor, organizer of the Canadian Field Ambulance in the First World War and an agriculturalist. Through his research on lobster canning, he became the saviour of the Island lobster industry which, at the time, was suffering from spoiled stock resulting from improper sanitary conditions during packing.

Sir Andrew, who liked to spend his summers at the family farm at Orwell, loved the good things of life. Around 1911 he had a baronial dining hall built on the site of the kitchen wing so he could entertain his friends, a veritable who's who of the day.

Point Prim Lighthouse

Macphail House

Today the Macphail estate is owned by a foundation dedicated to keeping alive the memory of Sir Andrew and his times. The house has become a tea room and conference centre, and the remains of the extensive estate feature a nature trail and experimental woodlot.

The Church of Christ, Montague

Travellers entering Montague are often surprised by a small, very attractive brick church with a tower capped by an enigmatic pagoda-like roof. The Church of Christ was built of locally made brick in 1876, probably to the designs of a very energetic and talented builder named John McLellan (1820–1887). In 1856, a Rev. George Bowler in Roxbury, Massachusetts, had published a richly illustrated book called *Chapel and Church Architecture*. John McLellan owned a copy of this book and he seems to have combined two of Bowler's designs into one! The first was in the Italianate style with the typical round-headed window, which gave its shape to the building. But the pagoda-like tower roof came from an entirely different design. The two have been combined to produce this extraordinarily attractive structure. Recent additions have been discreetly built so as not to detract from the church's soaring profile.

The Church of Christ's pagoda-like roof

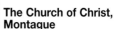

Festivals & Celebrations

Julie V. Watson

Old Home Week in Charlottetown

Prince Edward Islanders have demonstrated their love of celebrations and festivities since the days when the Fathers of Confederation arrived in 1864 for the Charlottetown Conference, which led to the founding of our nation. While meetings and great debates were going on among politicians, Island citizens gathered from far and wide to have some fun. It didn't take long for those visiting dignitaries to realize they were missing out. Grand balls and parties on board ships and in the governor's mansion, and spectacular dinners were quickly organized to celebrate their coming together in fine Island style.

The celebrations have changed in nature. Things are more casual today. We tend to party on shore instead of on ships, but Islanders still celebrate both their heritage and all that is great about Island life in this more modern time.

The Charlottetown Festival sets the tone of summer entertainment in the capital city, with free outdoor performances whose young performers gain a loyal following, as well as mainstage productions all summer long. Its venue, the Confederation Centre of the Arts in the heart of downtown Charlottetown, is home to the original

Fireworks

stage show *Anne of Green Gables — The Musical*™ , Canada's longest-running musical, and offers a variety of on-stage performances.

Festivities around the city are topped by the Festival of Lights centred around July 1, Canada Day. The several-day event bills itself as Canada's biggest birthday bash east of Ottawa. The city comes alive with nightly concerts, buskers, a food fair, carnival and midway, all topped by a fireworks display over Charlottetown Harbour.

The city waterfront is also the place to be at the other end of the summer season. A huge tent rocks with the PEI International Shellfish Festival held in mid-September. This celebration of PEI shellfish features oysters, lobster,

PEI International Shellfish Festival

mussels and clams — those same delicacies enjoyed by the "Fathers" so many years ago. Great fiddlers with toe-tapping Maritime-style entertainment in a kitchen party atmosphere, the PEI/World Oyster Shucking Championships, the PEI/International Chowder Championships and much more make for a simply great weekend.

This is just a sampling of dozens of PEI festivals. You can be sure Islanders celebrate their heritage, and just about anything else, given the opportunity. The prime festival time runs from May through September. Summer events range from professional productions that span the season to small one- or two-day affairs, which many consider to be tiny jewels in the festive calendar.

There is no doubt that music is the backbone for many

of the Island's best gatherings. While traditional offerings are the heart and soul of our festivals and events, they represent just a portion of what is available. From classical to Celtic, from production song-and-dance numbers to humorous one-man acts, our festivals are renowned for their on-stage performances.

Bluegrass and old-time band enthusiasts can get a double whammy with back-to-back toe-tapping weekend festivals held in Rollo Bay and Abram-Village each July.

On the other end of the musical spectrum, organizers of the Indian River Festival decided to add a little romance to their fine music series. Here, lovers of chamber music, jazz and choral concerts may surrender their senses to the breathtaking acoustics of the century-old St. Mary's Church in Indian River. This festival of "music you can hear with your heart" is year-round, including a very fine Christmas concert, and in the summer, gourmet coffee and treats can be enjoyed on the lawn.

New to the music festival scene is the PEI Jazz and Blues Festival, which debuted in July 2006 with big names and big crowds under a big tent in downtown Charlottetown. Watch for this blockbuster event to become even bigger and hotter.

As much as they love music, Prince Edward Islanders also love to celebrate their roots, and do so through Acadian, Irish and Celtic festivals, concerts and games. These gatherings focus on things traditional — after all, descendants can trace their families back to the pioneers who arrived from across the Atlantic as early as the 1600s.

The College of Piping in Summerside is home to a Celtic Festival, Highland Storm, which kicks off in late June at the Summerside Highland Gathering with competitions and celebrations of the Highland arts of piping, dancing, drumming and all things Scottish. In

PEI Jazz and Blues Festival
Hilario Duran Trio featuring Hilario Duran, Mark Kelso (drums) and Roberto Occhipinti (bass)

August, the Caledonia Club of PEI hosts an annual Highland Games at Lord Selkirk Provincial Park in Eldon, adding traditional athletic competitions and a kilted golf tournament to the usual concert, piping and dancing.

L'Exposition Agricole et le Festival Acadien de la Region Évangeline celebrates all things Acadian with entertainment, a parade, lobster suppers, horse pulls, pole climbing, strongman competitions and much more.

The Fiddlers and Followers weekend adds barbecues, lobster parties and old-fashioned picnics to their music festival held in North Rustico. The Ceilidh at the Irish Hall in Charlottetown celebrates traditional Irish music and dance mid-May to mid-September, bringing together some of the best East Coast talent. Emerald Junction promotes Irish heritage and community spirit with its Summerfest in late July, as does Tignish with its Irish Folk Festival in August.

Islanders celebrate their harvests and fine foods, particularly seafood, with great gusto. The Tyne Valley Oyster Festival is a down-home rural party complete with a parade and, as one jolly fellow said, "great grub."

Members of the College of Piping and Drumming

The Summerside Lobster Carnival has been going on since the 1950s. It features lobster, of course, and also great harness racing, dinners, talent shows, street sales, a fiddling contest and a spelling bee, along with a midway and local entertainment. There is a Wild Blueberry Festival in St. Peters in August, a Potato Blossom Festival in O'Leary in July and a new Wine Festival in Summerside, also in July. Later that month, they celebrate seaweed at the Irish Moss Festival in Tignish.

Highland Games

Lovers of things that move — cars, boats and motorcycles — are not left out. July is highlighted by the annual PEI Street Rod Association Show in Summerside, one of the oldest and largest outdoor car shows in Eastern Canada with street rods, antiques, special interest and classic cars. British Car Days Across the Bridge, in Charlottetown and Cymbria, attracts more enthusiasts from the US and Eastern Canada each year, as well as a good

Acadian Flag, Mont-Carmel

crowd of enthusiastic admirers. The Island Rally, now more than 20 years young, lures hundreds of motorcyclists to the Brackley Beach area each Labour Day weekend for a family-oriented gathering that includes motorcycle games. The Souris Sea Fest includes sporting events, traditional boat races, a beauty pageant and live entertainment.

For a real Maritime experience, the Northumberland Provincial Fisheries Festival in Murray River has activities ranging from provincial dory races to dances to a poultry show. For a similar experience, there's also the West Point Lighthouse Festival and Boat Races.

And then there are the celebrations that focus on the agricultural lifestyle enjoyed by so many Islanders. Many of them have new events that make for great spectator enjoyment. Noting the loyal following garnered by traditional horse pulls, some folks decided to add their own twist to the competitions, which prove both noisy and exciting. They like to "pull" with just about anything mechanized — tractors, three- and four-wheelers and lawnmowers. Whether four-footed or four-wheeled, the demonstrations of horsepower are great fun.

Horse shows with draft horses, English and Western riding and now miniature horses are ever-popular. The tiny equines in particular are attracting a growing audience that delights in their antics.

Of course, the agricultural exhibitions still include livestock, home arts and crafts, and many more

British car days

Peake's Wharf, Charlottetown

traditional components. You'll find woodsmen's competitions, meals, midways, antique engines, exhibits and displays, trade shows, all manner of competitions and just plain old-fashioned good, neighbourly visiting going on.

Old Home Week in Charlottetown draws folks back to the Island from far and wide to take in the PEI Provincial Exhibition. The longest and largest of the exhibitions, it has 15 cards of top-notch harness racing held over ten days in August. It also includes a huge parade through Charlottetown with floats and bands luring folks streetside. In fact, the capital shuts down for this popular forerunner to the Gold Cup and Saucer Race. Gold Cup Night fairly vibrates with excitement as one of the region's most prestigious harness races brings the best horses to the gate.

Other great exhibitions to take in include the Crapaud Exhibition in late July, Alberton's Prince County Exhibition in mid-summer, and L'Exposition Agricole et le Festival Acadien in Abram-Village in late August.

While many festivals are rooted in the past, the traditional spirit of joy extends to more recently established traditions. Capture PEI, for example, invites writers and photographers to expand their creative horizons. The Gay and Lesbian Pride Festival is fun-filled and colourful. The Studio Tour Weekend around the Island in late September or early October celebrates local crafts, both ancient and modern.

The spirit is infectious, so watch out — you may catch the festival bug and have a blissful time recovering from a heavy dose of PEI music, excitement, laughter and good fellowship.

Old Home Week, Charlottetown

Theatre

Campbell Webster

Anne of Green Gables —The Musical™ with Natalie Daradich as Diana Barry, Amy Wallis as Anne Shirley, Catherine O'Brien as Mrs. MacPherson, Hank Stinson as the Minister, Charlotte Moore as Rachel Lynde and Sophie Hunter as Mrs. Pye.

While all things tourism in PEI may not lead back to *Anne of Green Gables*, a great deal of it does. The influence of the Anne novels is considerable and has had the happy effect of introducing a vibrant summer theatre scene, both Anne-related and otherwise. PEI is unique among the Maritime provinces in having a play as a pillar of its tourist industry, and attending *Anne of Green Gables — The Musical™* is a common part of many PEI vacations.

The musical's popularity has always presented Island theatre professionals with a peculiar challenge: how to inspire tourists to see theatre other than *Anne.*

One answer may simply be Anne. A new play, also based on the Anne books, gives Anne-lovers a chance to see a new musical about the courtship of Anne of Green Gables. Entitled *Anne and Gilbert,* this definitive Island romance has become so popular, it plays throughout the summer at Summerside's Harbourfront Jubilee Theatre (www.jubileetheatre.com).

For a theatre experience that complements your Anne-centred vacation, a visit to the Montgomery Theatre in Cavendish would be in order. The new theatre, on the site of Avonlea Village, stages plays that Anne Shirley or L. M. Montgomery might have gone to, such as Oscar Wilde's *The Importance of Being Earnest.* See www.themontgomerytheatre.com to find out what's

Victoria Playhouse, Victoria

planned during your vacation.

Back at the Charlottetown Festival, the Confederation Centre of the Arts offers more than just Anne, including performances in its more intimate Studio and MacKenzie theatres, and presentations by the Confederation Centre Young Company in the outdoor amphitheatre. Check the festival listings to find out more about their season, which

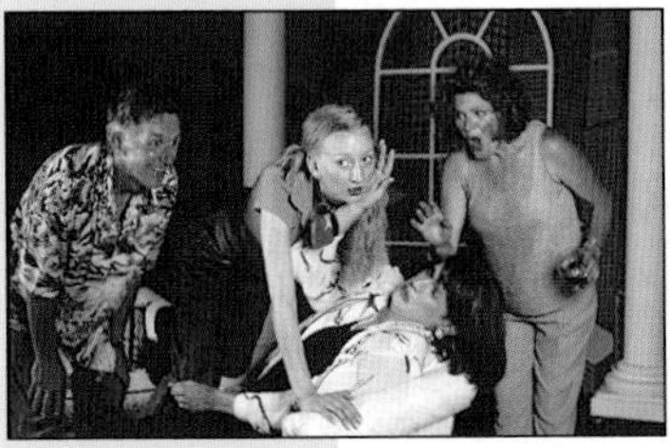

includes a concert series as well. Visit www.confederationcentre.com for ticket information and show times.

Over the years, concerted efforts of a variety of groups to build regular theatre audiences has produced some great amateur and professional theatre, whose quality often exceeds what you would expect of a small community. ACT, an amateur association which promotes theatre within the province, has a very informative website, www.actpei.ca.

The oldest of the other theatres is the Victoria Playhouse, now in its third decade. It runs a full season of live theatre, a Monday-night concert series and regular storytelling shows by artistic director Erskine Smith. You might begin your Victoria theatre experience with dinner at the fantastic Landmark Café, run by the Island's number one extrovert, Eugene Sauvé, giving you the makings of a memorable Island evening.

Many smaller venues across the Island feature storytellers, ceilidhs and other forms of true Island

The Drawer Boy, Victoria Playhouse, l-r: Erskine Smith and Ben Raynor

entertainment. The summer of 2008 saw the birth of the Festival of Small Halls. Check out www.smallhalls.com to see what's lined up for this season.

The Indian River Festival, set in the majestic St. Mary's Church, has become increasingly popular in recent years. The church was designed by famed Island architect William Critchlow Harris, who had a gift for architectural acoustic design. Programming is a range of shows from across Canada and around the world, and includes diverse acts from world music to classical and popular concerts.

Harbourfront Jubilee Theatre, Summerside

This impressive lineup features new shows a few times each week. The schedule is announced in the spring. Visit www.indianriverfestival.com.

The Guild in Charlottetown (www.theguildpei.com) is a popular and active theatre space. Its programming is eclectic, ranging from the energetic productions of aspiring young performers to plays by the finest Island writers. It is also often the site of performances by the Island's sketch comedy groups. The best and most memorable production in recent years has been *Sketch 22*, the visceral and hilarious attack on all things Prince Edward Island and beyond.

Mélanie LeBlanc as Anne, Peter Deiwick as Gilbert, in *Anne and Gilbert*, the Island Love Story

To get off the beaten track check out the Festivals and Events page of the Prince Edward Island government website at www.gov.pe.ca, the monthly Arts & Entertainment publication *The Buzz* and the local newspapers. These resources provide a very complete listing of almost every public performance at community centres and theatres, churches and museums. There are real finds in these listings, such as the Basin Head Fisheries Museum speaker series or the weekly ceilidhs at Malpeque Community Centre. In recent years more and more of these smaller shows are appearing, proving that Island culture may start with Anne, but it does not end there.

Crafts

Colleen Abdullah and Ryan Victoria McAdam-Young

Island crafts on display

Craft shop in Rustico

The sea, sky and lush greenness of Prince Edward Island has inspired the creation of arts and crafts since human habitation began here over 10,000 years ago. Today's citizens are no different. Artists and craftspeople can be found on every part of the Island working in just about every medium imaginable. Some are traditionalists who are keeping long-established crafting techniques alive while others are creating modern ways of paying tribute to their Island home. The artisans outlined here are just a sampling of the thriving arts community on PEI. While exploring our Island's four regions you will undoubtedly discover many "gems" of your own!

Points East Coastal Drive

Arriving on Prince Edward Island via the Wood Islands Ferry puts you in the heart of eastern PEI. For your first taste of Island crafting, head west to Melville and Koleszar Pottery. Hedwig Koleszar creates delicate porcelain forms that are meant for everyday use. She offers demonstrations and studio tours on Fridays from 3 to 5 p.m.

Doubling back past the ferry terminal will bring you to Little Sands home of the Rossignol Estate Winery. While there you can visit their vineyard, farm and art

Mi'kmaq craft

gallery. Murray Harbour is next and home to a variety of crafters and shops, including Miss Elly's Genteel Gifts & Stuff, where all manner of collectables and crafts can be found. After taking in a weaving demonstration, head back on the road and visit Murray River. This quaint village's Old General Store showcases an array of crafts in an old-fashioned setting.

Make your next stop Panmure Island, which has a rich Mi'kmaq history and boasts the oldest wooden lighthouse in Prince Edward Island. Keep an eye out for traditional native crafts and visit the lighthouse gift shop. Continuing on your northeastern journey will bring you to Montague, one of the Island's fastest-growing communities. Enjoy a day spent exploring little streets, visiting craft shops and dining at a variety of restaurants. At the Serendipity Boutique, mixed media artist Ruth VanDuiven creates jewelry, *objets d'art* and handcrafted souvenirs.

Prince Edward Island's eastern shore offers beautiful views and many points of natural and cultural interest, not to mention some fabulous craft-hunting opportunities. The charming bayside community of Cardigan is home to one of the Island's most exciting artisan organizations, the Cardigan Craft Centre. This art co-operative features paintings, pottery, textile arts, sculpting and woodworking. While on-site, you can meet artists at work and learn more about their inspiration and use of materials. In nearby Georgetown, visit Shoreline Designs and artist Peter Llewellyn in his working studio. Peter's creations include jewelry, Island sandstone carvings, pottery and ceramic pieces.

During your drive to Souris, watch for in-home craft shops, as many craftspeople will advertise their wares with front yard signs that simply say "Quilts for Sale" or "Woodworking." Souris is the location of the Magdalen Islands Ferry Terminal and the commercial centre of eastern Kings County. While in town, make sure you stop at Log Cabin Arts and Crafts, where everything is handcrafted locally, and Naturally Yours, a garden centre that also sells paintings, crafts and souvenirs.

East Point, as the name suggests, is the Island's easternmost tip. Prepare for a fantastic view when you climb to the top of the lighthouse, and don't forget to stop in at their craft shop. They have a wide array of local books, music and crafts.

Once you have rounded the eastern tip of the Island you will pass through many north shore villages. St. Peters has added numerous businesses over the last several years, many of which sell local arts and crafts. The shops of St. Peter's Landing include Glenroy Gallery, Chez Charley Gift Boutique, Salt Water Rose Gifts and the Turret Bell

Books & Art. Down the street you will find the St. Peters Bay Craft & Giftware Shop. This shop specializes in pewter jewelry made on-site. You can even watch a demonstration of molten pewter being cast into a mould and the casted metal buffed and finished.

The Points East Coastal Drive winds its way to an end in historic Mount Stewart. Once a centre of railway and shipbuilding on the Island, the village is now a popular stop because of its wonderful trails, protected wetlands and Eco-Centre. My own shop, Ginger Snaps, is located in the Eco-Centre, where I offer sea glass jewelry, local wool fashions, hand-painted baby clothes and 3-D works of art made from beachcombed materials. We also sell local pottery, handmade soap and hand-stitched teddy bears. Make sure you stop in and say hello!

Darren Matheson, Trout River Pottery

Anne's Land

Prince Edward Island's north shore is home to our most famous fictional resident, Anne of Green Gables. Over the years the area has become filled to the brim with restaurants, amusement parks, novelty entertainment attractions and, of course, craft shops. Drive in any direction for a few kilometres and you are sure to find something of interest. Don't forget your map, though, because some of your best adventures in Anne's Land are sure to be off the beaten path.

Entering the area via Route 6 will bring you to Brackley Beach. This is a beautiful community to explore and home to Peter Jansons' The Dunes Studio Gallery. The Dunes is one of the Island's best known and most distinctive art and craft stores. Don't let its modern roadside appearance fool you — the back wall is almost completely made of windows that overlook complex water gardens and distant rolling dunes. Works of over 50 contributing artists are displayed for sale and include

The Dunes Studio Gallery

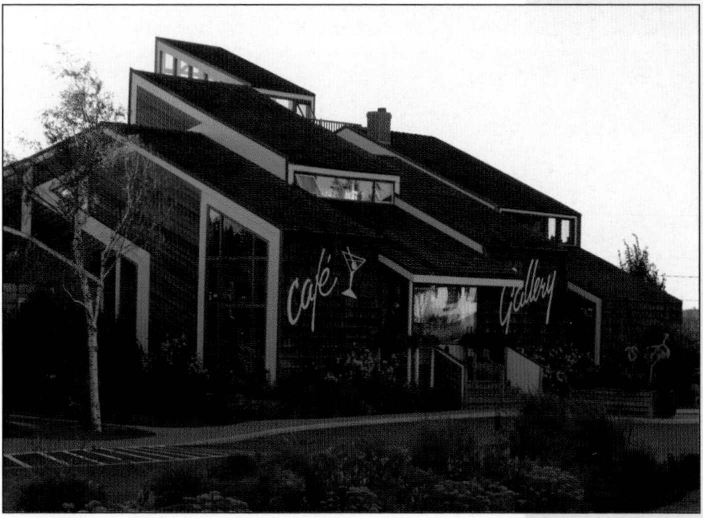

pottery, paintings, prints, photos, sculptures, fashion and garden art. You can even enjoy fine dining in their café.

Travelling west will take you to the Rustico area. This colourful part of the Island has a distinctive Acadian flair. North Shore Island Traditions Past & Present Rug Shop (Rustico Road) offers demonstrations and teaches visitors about traditional Maritime rug hooking. Gaudreau Fine Woodworking (Route 242) displays the work of PEI's premier woodworkers and potters. Call ahead if you are interested in participating in any of their seasonal Studio Events. From here a short drive will bring you to New Glasgow. Known for their lobster suppers, the community is also the location of the New Glasgow Mercantile and the Prince Edward Island Preserve Company, as well as The Toy Factory, where you can see a variety of wooden toys being made.

The Dunes Gardens

Your westward journey will soon bring you to Cavendish, Stanley Bridge and New London. Craft and gift shops abound in this area. Cavendish is sure to keep even the most exuberant craft hunter busy for hours, if not days! For a small taste of what it has to offer, visit the shops at the Cavendish Boardwalk. Those looking for a more peaceful experience will enjoy Village Pottery in New London, Trout River Pottery in Millvale and Stanley Bridge Antiques, Gifts and Gallery in — you guessed it —

Leards Range Front Lighthouse, Victoria

Stanley Bridge. You might also want to check out Stanley Bridge School and Stanley Bridge Studio while in the area.

Memories Gift Shop, New London

South Shore

If you have come to the Island via the Confederation Bridge you will find yourself in the South Shore Region. Craft-hunting opportunities begin just metres from the bridge at Gateway Village, home to more than 20 shops and services. Travelling southeast along the Blue Heron Coastal Drive will take you through one of the Island's most beautiful areas, where rolling hills meet the waves. One of the prettiest seaside villages is Victoria-by-the-Sea, where you can visit several shops and sample handmade chocolates at the Island Chocolates Company.

Denise Reiser's Legend of the Mi'kmaq at the Gateway Village Interpretive Centre

Charlottetown and its outlying areas have an abundance of galleries, studios and shops. The Charlottetown Farmer's Market is a great place to start. The Market, full of local foods and crafts, is a favourite gathering place for local artists, musicians and craftspeople. Located on Belvedere Avenue, it is open Saturdays from 9 a.m. to 2 p.m. and also on Wednesdays during July and August. Just around the corner on University Avenue is the new Best of PEI Market. This market offers local food and

a wide selection of crafts and other items for sale, all of which are made in PEI.

In the downtown, take a walk through Victoria Row, Lower Queen Street, Lower University Avenue, Water Street and Peaks Quay. This lively downtown core is full of shops and cafés. Be sure to stop at Moonsnail Soaps (Water Street), where you can view the soap-making process and purchase some deliciously scented items, and The Green Man (University Avenue), where you can buy Island-designed and made fashions and accessories.

If you are in the mood for a country drive, head inland to Breadalbane on Route 246. Here you will find the Stanley Pottery & Weaving Studio and Shop. This enchanting stop features the work of Malcolm and Christine Stanley and has been featured in *National Geographic* and *Craftsman's Way*. From their studios nestled in the woods, these artists create breathtaking works of art in clay, alpaca, cashmere and silk. You can watch them at work and even sign up for courses and workshops. This stop is not to be missed!

North Cape Coastal Drive

Called "Up West" by Islanders, this naturally pristine and secluded area of the Island celebrates the rich Acadian and Mi'kmaq cultures. Enter the region via Route 2 and visit Malpeque Fine Iron Works on the Barbara Weit Road in Lower New Annan. Here you will find blacksmith Eric Schurman and his artist wife Dianne creating whimsical iron products and recycled metal art for your home and garden. Next, make your way to Summerside. This thriving seaside city is the economic center of western PEI and home to the College of Piping. Be sure to visit their Celtic Gift Shop. While in the city spend an afternoon at Spinnakers' Landing. This tiny waterfront shopping area features craft shops, dining and free Maritime entertainment.

Baskets at Lennox Island

Lennox Island, northwest of Summerside, is PEI's largest First Nations community. Learn about the Mi'kmaq people and stop at the Indian Art & Craft of North America Shop. This interesting store features both traditional and non-traditional native art; it specializes in split-ash baskets and Micmac Productions earthenware pottery and figurines.

Next travel southwest of Summerside to PEI's Acadian shore. Here, another cultural craft experience awaits you in La Region Évangeline. The Abram-Village Handcraft Co-op has some of the best traditional and contemporary Acadian art the Island has to offer. The shop features weavings, quilts, rugs and a mini museum. While in the

Acadian Flag Hooked Rug

area, visit Boutique-à-Point in Mont Carmel and the Acadian Museum in Miscouche.

Continuing on Route 2 west will bring you to the Island's most westerly tip. This area is one of the Island's least travelled and is known for its spectacular sunsets. At West Point you will find our tallest functioning lighthouse. It has been converted and now houses a museum, restaurant, inn and craft shop. Continue north to Bloomfield and the MacAusland Woollen Mills where blankets of 100% virgin wool are created. In Lauretta on Route 151, be sure to visit Kerras Jeffery at Back Road Folk Art. He will introduce you to his many folk-art friends and show you the world's largest hand-held eggbeater! In Tignish you can tour the production studio at Tignish Treasures Gift Shop & Holiday Island Productions. This business produces collectable Island souvenirs and makes body and bath products with seaweed and Irish moss.

When "Up West" be sure you make it to North Cape. From this interesting environmentally rich community you can watch the waters of the Gulf of St. Lawrence and the Northumberland Strait collide, see seals and watch windmills. If you are interested in learning more about wind energy visit the interpretive centre. Its gift shop also has a huge assortment of Island-made items.

For more information on Island crafts swing by any PEI visitors centre and pick up a copy of the Prince Edward Island Craft, Art and Giftware Directory and the PEI Studio Tour Map or visit www.gentleisland.com. Enjoy your Island treasures and happy collecting!

Spinnakers' Landing

Lighthouses

Wayne MacKinnon

Covehead Lighthouse

Carrying out their centuries-old vigils of the sea, lighthouses hold a unique fascination for people. They occupy a treasured place, particularly on an island. Prince Edward Island's earliest lighthouse was built at Point Prim in 1846. It is still among the island's most interesting, one of the few round brick lighthouses in Canada. Soaring to a height of over 18 metres, it is easily visible from the Charlottetown waterfront and along the south shore.

The first colonial lighthouses were octagonal in shape, in contrast to the square towers with sloping sides built after 1873. And they were built to last. Exposed to some of the most extreme weather conditions on Prince Edward Island, the fact that these structures remain basically unchanged is testament to traditional craftsmanship.

The lights themselves, known as lanterns, were originally fuelled with cod-liver oil and the light was projected by an elaborate arrangement of mirrors. Later on, higher intensities were achieved with lenses, a significant improvement over the reflector arrangements which had to be protected from the sun to prevent fires. With electricity came the present mercury-vapour lights.

Lightkeepers faced a demanding and unremitting task. Fuel had to be carried up the three or four flights of stairs to the top of the tower, and the clockwork mechanisms had to be wound. Dwellings were often attached to the lighthouses, which meant constant vigilance of the light could be carried out with relative ease.

Lighthouses were vulnerable to the elements. During a heavy gale in 1879, the New London lighthouse was literally lifted from its position and carried 200 metres westward, destroying the lantern. Hazards of a different kind encroached on the Panmure Island lighthouse — in 1861 a fence was erected to prevent pigs from rooting away the sandstone foundation.

The East Point lighthouse occupies a unique place in Canadian history: it has been relocated twice. In 1882, when the British warship *Phoenix* was wrecked, the disaster was blamed partly on the lighthouse being located too far from the cliffs. It was jacked up and moved closer, and a fog horn was installed. By 1908, however, erosion was threatening the foundation, so it was jacked up again and moved 60 metres inland to its present location.

Battery Point

West Point, the tallest of the square wooden towers, is 17.5 metres high. Painted in broad horizontal bands of black and white, the tower itself supplements the light as an aid to navigation. Interpretive displays in the tower recall the life and times of its keepers — there were only two in all the 87 years the light was manually operated. West Point also offers accommodation and a restaurant — the only inn in Canada to operate in a functioning lighthouse.

There are more than 50 lighthouses in PEI, many of which are accessible. On the whole the lighthouses are well preserved and maintained. Several lighthouses across the Island are operated by community groups and are open to the public. A few offer tours and incorporate museums. A complete list of PEI lighthouses and a downloadable lighthouse map are available at http://www.gov.pe.ca/infopei/index.php3?number=66290. A brochure, *Lighthouses of PEI*, is available from the PEI Lighthouse Society, RR#2 O'Leary, PE, C0B 1V0; 902-859-3117.

North Rustico Harbour at dusk

Automation has brought the era of lightkeepers to an end. The structures remain, however, solitary and serene — symbols of steadfastness in a world of infinite change.

Museums & Galleries

Faye Pound

Avonlea Village

Islanders have a deep attachment to their province. They go out in the world across the water, and when they come back it's as though they're baseball players rounding third base and heading for home.

This strong sense of pride in place makes the telling of the Island story important to Islanders. And nowhere is this better told than in the Island's museums. The Island has more than its fair share of those special places where story is told in photographs, maps and artifacts — as well as through the people, the keepers of these stories.

L. M. Montgomery put the Island on the world map with her international bestseller, *Anne of Green Gables*. Her popularity has led many a history buff or local volunteer organization to celebrate her accomplishments by establishing museums across the province. The PEI National Park in Cavendish has even centred its operations around Green Gables House, which served as inspiration for her novel. Other museums include the Lucy Maud Montgomery Birthplace museum in New London, the Anne of Green Gables Museum at Silver Bush in Park Corner and, across the road, the Lucy Maud Montgomery Heritage Museum in her grandfather Senator Montgomery's old homestead. All provide fabulous opportunities for experiencing an up-close-and-personal glimpse into some of the Island's typical Victorian interiors — and a look into the old rural order of

Anne of Green Gables Museum, Park Corner

Montgomery's PEI, before electricity and pavement changed it all.

Heading west from Park Corner you will come upon the Keir Memorial Museum in Malpeque, which is housed in an old Presbyterian Church. Here the local people have poured their hearts into gathering artifacts that interpret life along the north shore, from the time of the Mi'kmaq through the Acadian era to the settlement by the Scots and Irish in the late 1700s, to farming and fishing before the 1950s. William Pound's 1887 horse-drawn hearse, Dr. William Keir's collection of 19th-century medical instruments and a country store display are some highlights in the story of early Malpeque life. Hand-forged oyster tongs and wooden hand rakes from the mid-1880s interpret "men's work," while an entire wing is dedicated to the womanly arts of butter-making, mat-hooking, spinning and weaving. Volunteers teach the old crafts with a hands-on approach using vintage spinning wheels and looms.

Train enthusiasts will enjoy the Kensington Train Station, which provides a tour of the Island's railroad

Kensington Train Station

heritage. The early 20th-century stone station is the site Montgomery had in mind when she wrote the scene where Matthew Cuthbert meets Anne at the train station.

It's a short drive to Summerside and its cultural treasures, including the Wyatt Heritage Properties, the culture and heritage division of the city of Summerside and the J. E. Wyatt House, a restored Confederation era house left to posterity by his daughter. Across the street is the MacNaught History Centre and Archives, perfect for delving into a bit of research on genealogy or local history. Their Master Name Index provides genealogists with a broad research tool on microfilm, providing an excellent way to search hundreds of thousands of entries organized by name. Transcripts of all PEI cemeteries are on hand, as well as the church records of Prince County and a collection of fine art interpreting Summerside history. For $3 you can buy the booklet *Heritage Walking Tour*, a self-guided walking guide to city architecture featuring 40 properties.

The International Fox Museum is only a short walk

away and takes you into the glory days of the "Fox Years," when this area was a world headquarters for the industry. The museum is housed in "The Homestead," the splendid 1853 house of R. T. Holman, one of the founding merchants of the city. The Holman garden is one of oldest gardens in North America. A walk down to the harbour leads to the Eptek Art and Culture Centre with its ever-changing exhibits. Eptek, a Mi'kmaq word for "hot place," presents exhibitions on fine art, history, visual arts and crafts, and programming to interpret local and Canadian cultural heritage. A bookstore supplies some of the best titles of Island interest, and a small research holding of microfilm of local papers from the 1860s to 1950, census and business directories are also on hand. The south hall has local heritage on display in maps and photographs.

The drive west on Route 2 takes the traveller to the crossroads of Miscouche and the Acadian Museum, which tells the vibrant heritage of our Acadian community. A well-stocked genealogy room helps visitors find their ancestors. Exhibits explain the culture and lifestyle of the Island's first European settlers from 1720 to the present.

A drive around Malpeque Bay (the Mi'kmaq word for "great big bay") to Green Park Shipbuilding Museum and Historic Yeo House ends in a magical experience: ascending the stair to the cupola or "Widow's Walk" to look over the surrounding fields and the bay where James Yeo, Sr., launched his ships for England. Understanding the importance of shipbuilding gives a broad understanding of the pattern of settlement and the development of the province in coastal trading times.

The Green Park Shipbuilding Museum

The Bideford Parsonage Museum up the coast gives another view inside a community museum that interprets the golden age of sail and documents the times when L. M. Montgomery lived in the house and taught at the local school. A few minutes' drive away is the Ellerslie Shellfish Museum, which tells the story of the Malpeque oyster. Lennox Island is home to much of the Island's Mi'kmaq population, and the Lennox Island Mi'kmaq Cultural Centre houses displays about Mi'kmaq heritage. The "Walk of Our Forefathers" takes you through the woods along three to ten kilometres of trail with interpretive murals explaining the culture of our First Nations people.

The Alberton Museum is one of the province's finest community museums, a place for the traveller to gain a well-rounded understanding of life in Prince Edward Island. It is possible to lose oneself to time travel in their extensive photograph collection of local farming and fishing, military history and community life. The old

Acadian Museum

courthouse has a comprehensive collection of compiled genealogies, scrapbooks and local church records. Nowhere is there more hands-on help and information with a personal touch.

Wind power enthusiasts will find there is much to learn at the North Cape Interpretive Centre. Established in 2001, eight gigantic white windmills form the first commercial "wind farm" in Atlantic Canada and produce three percent of PEI's energy. The centre has an extensive display on the technology of wind power, a marine aquarium and a section devoted to local heritage, with documents explaining the geology of the area, its fishery, and the Acadian and Irish population who work on some of the most dangerous fishing grounds in the province. The North Cape lighthouse provides a fabulous view of the sunset or the meeting of the tides off the long rock reef.

Along the coastal drive, huge horses haul Irish moss off the beaches and boats come and go with their loads of lobster traps. Down the coast is Miminegash, the centre of the Irish moss harvest. This plentiful seaweed (*Chondrus crispus*) became a financially viable crop during the Second World War, when research developed new uses for the moss and its carrageenan as a gelling/stabilizing agent in the production of ice cream, toothpaste, cosmetics and medicine. In 1942 about 750 tons were shipped, resulting in a new harvest the locals called "easy money" — though its harvesting is back-breaking labour.

In O'Leary is the Prince Edward Island Potato Museum, home to "the world's largest potato." The museum celebrates the monumental contribution the lowly potato has made to the Island. For lighthouse enthusiasts, the West Point Lighthouse houses a charming exhibit on the history of all the lighthouses on PEI. They serve up some of the finest in local seafood and provide accommodations in what used to be the lightkeeper's bedroom, located directly below the lantern room.

Charlottetown is a beautiful city at the edge of a splendid harbour, with some good walks for stretching your legs while appreciating the 19th-century architecture. Throughout the summer months, the Confederation Players tour the downtown in their lavish 1860s costumes.

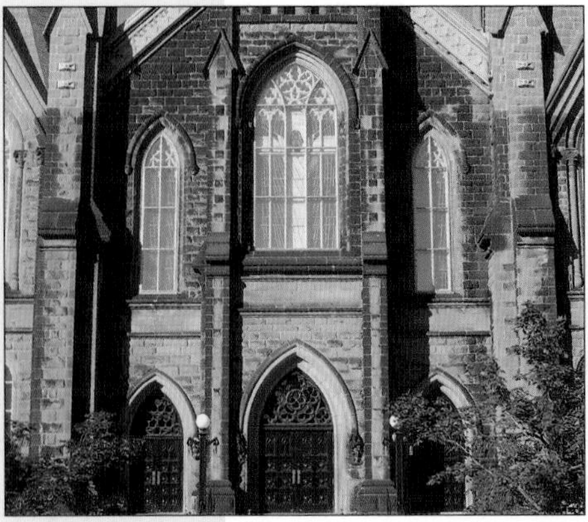

St. Dunstan's Basilica, Charlottetown

Well-informed on Charlottetown's buildings and their historical significance, these young people are master interpreters of "olden times," and are especially good at inspiring children toward a love of history. Their street theatre serves up the story of the town during the Charlottetown Conference in 1864 in an engaging way, full of the colour of the day when a visiting circus stole local attention away from the first meeting to establish a Dominion of Canada. Actors take the roles of the Fathers of Confederation — Sir John A. Macdonald, George Étienne Cartier and W. H. Pope, to name a few — as well as local folk, some opposed to Confederation, others lamenting the land troubles of Islanders or interpreting Mi'kmaq heritage. Actors stage vignettes in front of Province House and engage in impromptu debates on street corners for the amusement and education of all.

Founders' Hall tells the story of the Confederation of Canada in a hi-tech way that is sure to engage children. A walk up Great George Street to Province House National Historic Site offers up the real thing. Confederation Centre Library is next door, and it's the best stop for books on local heritage. The Public Archives on the fourth floor of the Coles Building is open for those interested in a more scholarly dig.

Beaconsfield Historic House is a beautifully restored 1877 shipbuilder's mansion on the Charlottetown Harbour. A climb to the cupola will take you back in time, and Beaconsfield's well-stocked bookstore is open for browsing. A leisurely walk around the boardwalk through Victoria Park passes Fanningbank, the historic residence of the Lieutenant-Governor, which offers daily summer tours. Across Charlottetown Harbour is the Port-la-Joye–Fort Amherst Historic Site at Rocky Point.

Beaconsfield interior

The drive east across the Hillsborough Bridge takes the traveller through some of the prettiest countryside, particularly if one dallies along the shore roads to Orwell Corner Historic Village. The clock stopped round about 1890 in this country village of 19th-century buildings. The Prince Edward Island Museum and Heritage Foundation began restoring the abandoned buildings in the 1970s and recently opened a new agricultural museum. A three-minute drive leads to the 1850 Sir Andrew Macphail Homestead, the 12-room house in which his classic book, *The Master's Wife*, is set.

Orwell Corner Historic Village

Skirting the coast, one can make a wonderful lighthouse tour with stops at Point Prim, Cape Bear, Wood Islands and Panmure Island. These lighthouses have exhibits outlining local history and tours of their interiors. The Point Prim lighthouse, the Island's first, was built of local brick in 1845 to a design by English architect Isaac Smith, who immigrated to the Island at the age of 22. It's a steep climb to the lantern room in a polygonal cupola 25 metres above sea level. The mercury-vapour light penetrates 27 kilometres across the Northumberland Strait on a clear night. Run by two local Women's Institutes, tours explain the evolution of lighthouse technology from the days of seal oil-burning in the 1840s to electricity and eventually to automation in 1969.

Founder's Hall and Visitor Information Centre, Charlottetown

The picturesque town of Montague is home to the Garden of the Gulf Museum, a lovely sandstone building by the river. The museum's director, Donna Collings, is helpful and knowledgeable when it comes to interpreting the Island's past. A highlight of their collection is a volunteer militia coat of Captain John MacDonald of Tracadie — one of the oldest garments in existence on PEI, dated by its buttons that read "Island of St. John," the Island's name before 1799. An extensive photograph collection of Montague and area from 1867 to 1967 is the cornerstone of their offering. For the hunter of genealogy in Kings County, there is no better place to begin than here. Local

historians give the best directions, so there's no need to reinvent the wheel or become frustrated.

No trip to Kings County is complete without a visit to Basin Head Fisheries Museum. Their interpretive displays provide details on the different methods of lobster fishing and canning. Basin Head is a part of the provincial museum system. From the bridge that spans the "Run," it's easy to imagine the lobster boats plying this fast stretch of water to an artificial harbour dredged in the early 20th century.

Elmira Station

The East Point Lighthouse is close by, as is the Elmira Railway Museum on what is now the Confederation Trail. This is a restored 1912 wooden station, the end of the line for the "friendly little railroad" that connected the Island with a meandering iron rail.

A stop at one of the wharves at North Lake, Naufrage or Red Head is a good idea to round out one's understanding of the Island's fishery. The Rustico Harbour Fisheries Museum on the wharf in North Rustico is centred around understanding fishing in the good old days. Their exhibit is colourful and has a down-home appeal with a sense of humour. The wooden building on the wharf has the smell of the sea — a perfect backdrop to perusing the exhibits and photos relating the story of the local fishery. A wonderful little film brings to life the oral tradition of fishermen, telling about the back-breaking days of lobster fishing with wind and manpower while showing how large gas and diesel engines and hydraulic gear changed everything. A quote from an old fisherman, Long Vincent Gallant of Rustico, says it all: "You had to be rugged, boy, then. You had to take it. Couldn't go in the cabin like you can today. You had to take everything that nature chucked at you. But times were good. Lots of fish!"

To understand Prince Edward Islanders, it's important to stand on the beaches and wharves with the Island's sun and salt breeze — but it's equally helpful to mix it in with a tour of the Island's museums. Only then will the visitor truly be carried into the heritage and culture of Prince Edward Island.

Basin Head Fisheries Museum

Dining

Lobie Daughton & Wayne MacKinnon

Dunes Seafood Chowder with Lobster

You're in for a real treat as a culinary explorer on Prince Edward Island. Eateries have evolved over the past decade, with the best getting better and overall quality ratcheting up. Much of the improvement can be traced to the growing influence of the Culinary Institute of Canada. Keen youngsters come to Charlottetown to train as chefs, and then they tend to stick around to pollinate the various cafés and inns. It is well worth making a reservation at the Lucy Maud Room for a meal prepared and served by some of the Institute's top students in a lovely setting that overlooks Charlottetown Harbour.

Many of the better places to eat are seasonal, so you'll find a much greater choice of restaurants in the summer, whether for fine dining or for roadside fish and chips. One of the best seasonal locations is The Dunes in Brackley Beach. The garden setting is exquisite and you can shop for fine art, crafts and furnishings that the owners acquire on their travels in the off-season. There are always interesting drinks on the menu, such as the "rhubarbtini," and they make the best tomato-based seafood chowder that I've ever

Shaw's Hotel

had. The menu offers selections from vegetarian pad thai to thoroughly meaty choices. Desserts are wonderful and the coffee strong.

In fact, the Brackley Beach area is easy to build a day of food around. Shaw's Hotel has a good dining room that does a stellar breakfast. A few miles westward at Oyster Bed Bridge, Dayboat serves sophisticated fare under the guidance of the Shapiros. You can enjoy the best crab cakes on the Island while you watch ospreys hunting fish in the bay from Dayboat's large deck. In mentioning the wonderful crab cakes, I should insert a word of caution that applies to all of the Island's fine restaurants. No matter where you choose to eat, great food requires great preparation. Chefs come and go as their careers develop, so be aware that last year's restaurant review may be heaping praises on kitchen staff who are long gone. It's worth comparing notes with other visitors to find out which places they particularly like this year, as a single-skilled chef can transform a restaurant.

Of course, certain universal truths of supply-and-demand apply. Charlottetown is packed with places to eat, while at the Island's extremities, there are fewer choices. Way up west, there's the Wind and Reef at North Cape. In the east, one excellent novelty that has appeared in Souris is La Belle Cloche, a small operation started by a bored visitor from Singapore. The authentic Asian tastes and the family atmosphere combine

Inn at Bay Fortune

Dalvay-by-the-Sea

for a fun and friendly food experience in an area of the Island that is not known for its cosmopolitan cuisine. Working one's way back from east to west, there's gourmet food at the justifiably renowned Inn at Bay Fortune, but there's also good eating — and bilingual service — at Rick's Fish & Chips in St. Peters. Stop off for a swim in the National Park at Dalvay and you can build up an appetite for the dignified dining room at the Dalvay-by-the-Sea hotel (one of the few places to offer a good afternoon tea). Dinner at Dalvay is well worth making time for, and they have one of the best port selections on the Island — ideal for sipping beside the massive fireplace late in the season.

Gahan House

You can't talk about eastern PEI without a tip of the hat to the many golf courses, all of which serve at least some kind of food. Quality varies from year to year, but it is worth keeping an ear open for intelligence on what they are serving in the clubhouse dining rooms. Both Crowbush and Brudenell have had decent menus in the past, so don't rule them out if you are nearby when hunger strikes.

Islanders have had a love affair with fast food that has resulted in some of the best-performing franchises in the country. The phenomenal success of the ubiquitous Tim Horton's chain underpins the growth of the Murphy Group's more diverse culinary ventures. Beginning with the Gahan House brew-pub, the Murphys have branched out into restaurants that range from Fishbones (cheapest oysters in town at happy hour) and the neighbouring

Castello's (decent Italian/Sicilian) to Sim's Steakhouse & Oyster Bar (not the cheapest oysters!). All of the Murphy dining rooms serve the excellent micro-brew beers from the Gahan House; the Sydney Street Stout and the Iron Horse Brown Ale are almost meals in themselves.

Speaking of micro-brew, the Delta Prince Edward hotel also has Murphy beer on tap, and the Delta's Selkirk Room restaurant should not be overlooked as a great place to eat. Good service and comfy wingback chairs complement an interesting menu that works hard to incorporate local and organic ingredients, but without making a big deal about it.

Just behind the Delta, the Shapiros (remember Dayboat) have opened Flex Mussels, an informal and outdoorsy eatery with a good selection of oysters, both raw and cooked, and featuring the best rendition of French-style "frites" east of Montreal, as well as their many, many, many signature mussel dishes. Non-seafood eaters can also find plenty of meat on the menu, but it wouldn't be my favourite spot to take a vegan.

Flex Mussels, Charlottetown

Until fairly recently, vegetarian and vegan options were much more limited on the Island. You still don't find the kind of omnipresent vegetarian choices that are common in Europe, but an influx of Chinese immigrants has bolstered the existing ethnic food establishments to unprecedented levels. There are even two wholly vegetarian and mostly non-dairy "tea houses" in Charlottetown at which you can eat full meals. At the Tai Chi Garden on Pownal Street, indoor diners must remove their outdoor footwear and don the slippers provided. Those more wary of their hosiery can always eat at one of the outside tables in the lovingly tended garden. The menu is limited, but good — I recommend the hot and sour soup. A few blocks to the northeast, the Formosa Tearoom has a more varied menu and welcomes a shod clientele. It is a particular favourite with young people, and you can admire the latest piercings and fashions while eating an assortment of yummy foods that includes a few vegan oddities such as fake ham and fake (or insert your own term) chicken. The Formosa's owners also import arts and crafts that are on sale along with the food. You will not find any Anne memorabilia, but there are plenty of charming tea-sets, laughing Buddhas and the like.

No overview of Charlottetown dining would be complete without mention of the many Lebanese food establishments. When Islanders elected Canada's first non-Anglo-Saxon Premier in the person of Joe Ghiz, it was an

Lebanese Mezze

acknowledgement of the major influence that Lebanese settlement had on PEI during the 20th century. Charlottetown's business landscape was transformed by Lebanese entrepreneurs and their influence was most noticeable in the restaurant scene. For decades, the only commercially available "alternative" food on PEI consisted of the falafel, kibbee, hummus, tabouleh, etc., from Lebanese cooks. Cedars Eatery remains a favourite with many Islanders and visitors, especially given the late-night indie music venue upstairs, Baba's Lounge, that showcases many of Canada's best bands. Shaddy's Restaurant is just a block away on the other side of University Avenue, and they also pride themselves on authentic Lebanese dishes. Right next door is Charlottetown's first craft bakery & café, Leonhard's, where you can try authentic German foods. Matthew and Marilla wouldn't know the place these days!

If you want to keep it simple, the best fish and chips in Charlottetown can be found across the Avenue at Brit's Fish & Chips or at the Water-Prince Corner Shop seafood market down near Founders' Hall. There are plenty of other eating places to pick from, whether Thai or pub, hotel or drive-through, but my recommendations would certainly include Just Us Girls on Queen Street, a quirky, pink, fun-fest of gal-themed eats, drinks, clothing and knick-knacks. Their crab cakes came very close to being the best of the summer, and their menu is

Lot 30 Lobster

always interesting. Talented chef, Gordon Bailey, has opened up Lot 30 (evenings only) in the heart of downtown, and he is also a key player in the Urban Eatery complex at the Confederation Court mall that has raised the term "food court" to a new level. Half the places in Charlottetown seem to have "confederation" in the name, so beware of confusion. However, if you wander into Mavor's by mistake (in the Confederation Centre of the Arts), it's safe to sit down and order. For olive lovers, their salmon nicoise is a good bet. Most Chinese food on PEI has a distinctly western tinge, but if you get side-tracked until really late and you're still hungry, the China Garden is open later than almost everywhere else and their chow hoy sin sure hits the spot at 2 a.m.

Charlottetown has the usual chains, such as Cora's and Boston Pizza, but it also has a healthy diversity of small coffee shops, juice bars and so on. A few years back, finding an espresso was a day's work, but the machines are almost everywhere these days. The same cannot be said of Summerside, the self-styled "western capital," where both coffee and dining choices are much more limited. The Brothers Two is always popular, and the misleadingly named Loyalist Lakeview Resort (it neither has a view of a

The Pearl

Lobster Supper

lake, nor is it a resort) has a pretty dining room with good choices. If you're heading further west and you're good at planning ahead, The Doctor's Inn in Tyne Valley will do dinners by appointment using ingredients that are mostly harvested from their own organic market garden or from the sea. Their eggs are PEI's best, but you'll need to stay over at their B&B to eat those!

While on the subject of eggs, best brunch I've found is at The Pearl near Rustico. Maxine and her staff have done a great job of creating a welcoming space full of thoughtful touches. The Pearl is a good place to eat at any time of day and they sometimes have live music in the evenings. The Rustico area abounds with lobster suppers if you want to try one. Everyone has an opinion about their personal favourite, so I'll just say that it's worth braving the whole "tourist trap" thing in order to enjoy a scoff from the focused menu. You'll always get really fresh lobster and chowder, as well as all of the usual accompaniments.

Some of the best places to eat on PEI are not just seasonal, they're only open weekly or on special occasions. These hidden gems include Farmers Markets where you can enjoy African and Indian meals, construct a picnic of locally smoked eel and handmade lemon meringue pie, or buy the freshest ingredients to create your own meals with the inspiration you've garnered from your foodie explorations around Canada's smallest province. Be alert, too, for announcements of community suppers, special events, fundraising benefits, and other opportunities to sample meals that are not regularly available. You could be in for a very agreeable surprise.

Top: Lobster Supper
Above: Malpeque Oysters

Island Culinary Delights

More and more people are discovering the joys of local foods. Prince Edward Island, long renowned for its famous potatoes and Malpeque oysters, provides a cornucopia of fresh and delicious foods to explore and enjoy. What better way to experience the Island and its people than to partake in its many and varied culinary delights harvested from the bounty of land and sea.

Culinary tourism is a relatively new phenomenon, where visitors can learn more about local cultures and traditions. Sitting down to a lobster supper in a local church hall, shopping at a local farmers' market or attending one of the many festivals and exhibitions celebrating foods from blueberries to oysters to potatoes is a way of taking in not only Island hospitality, but some of the best food to be found anywhere in the world. Island food, served in the traditional Island way, provides nourishment both for the body and the soul.

Discovering the delights of Island food is easier than ever before. Prince Edward Island kitchens are making it more of a point to feature local delicacies. Chefs are increasingly seeking out fresh fish, herbs, fruits and vegetables, seafood and other products which they proudly

feature on their menus. There's even a new annual award called Taste our Island that acknowledges the special efforts made by chefs and restaurants across the province who work with local producers to create the best meals ever. There's a six-day dining tour for discerning palates that will usher you to a table in some of the Island's most distinctive and charming restaurants (www.gentleisland.com /food). And just around every bend in the road, there are new culinary experiences to be enjoyed, from clams to ice cream cones.

Top: Salt Cod Fishcakes
Above: Fresh Strawberries

Every summer on the Island, people await the arrival of fresh fruits and vegetables. Whether it's the eagerly awaited crop of new potatoes, succulent strawberry shortcakes or newly-ripened apples, the progress of the growing season is marked by one culinary feast after another. A guide has been prepared to help Islanders and visitors find those high-quality, fresh and nutritious products (www.peifarmfre sh.ca). The guide contains a listing of approximate harvest dates. You can plan to go out to the field to pick your own fresh fruits or vegetables or have them picked and packed for you.

Beginning in the fall of 2008, a Farm in the City celebration takes place, where people can wander the streets of downtown Charlottetown, sample some of the

finest food products produced on the Island and talk to the people who produce them with pride.

The provincial fisheries and aquaculture department can help you learn to prepare some of the most succulent seafood products harvested in Island waters. The Out of the Seas and Over the Coals seafood cooking demonstrations take place regularly in local provincial and national parks and other select venues. You will learn not only how to preserve the taste and freshness of seafood, but also have the chance to sample the latest treats from the grill.

Top: Freshly-dug potatoes
Above: Harvested Blue Mussels

Organizations such as the Slow Food movement are helping people rediscover the joys of eating and understand the importance of where food comes from, how it is produced and the people who produce it. On another level, buying local products links food with a sense of awareness and responsibility about the nature of the food supply in a global economy. Searching out local food is a way for people to connect with communities, strengthening a culture of place.

Prince Edward Island has been variously described as the "million-acre farm" and the "garden of the gulf." Discover for yourself the bounty of the land and sea.

Island Routes

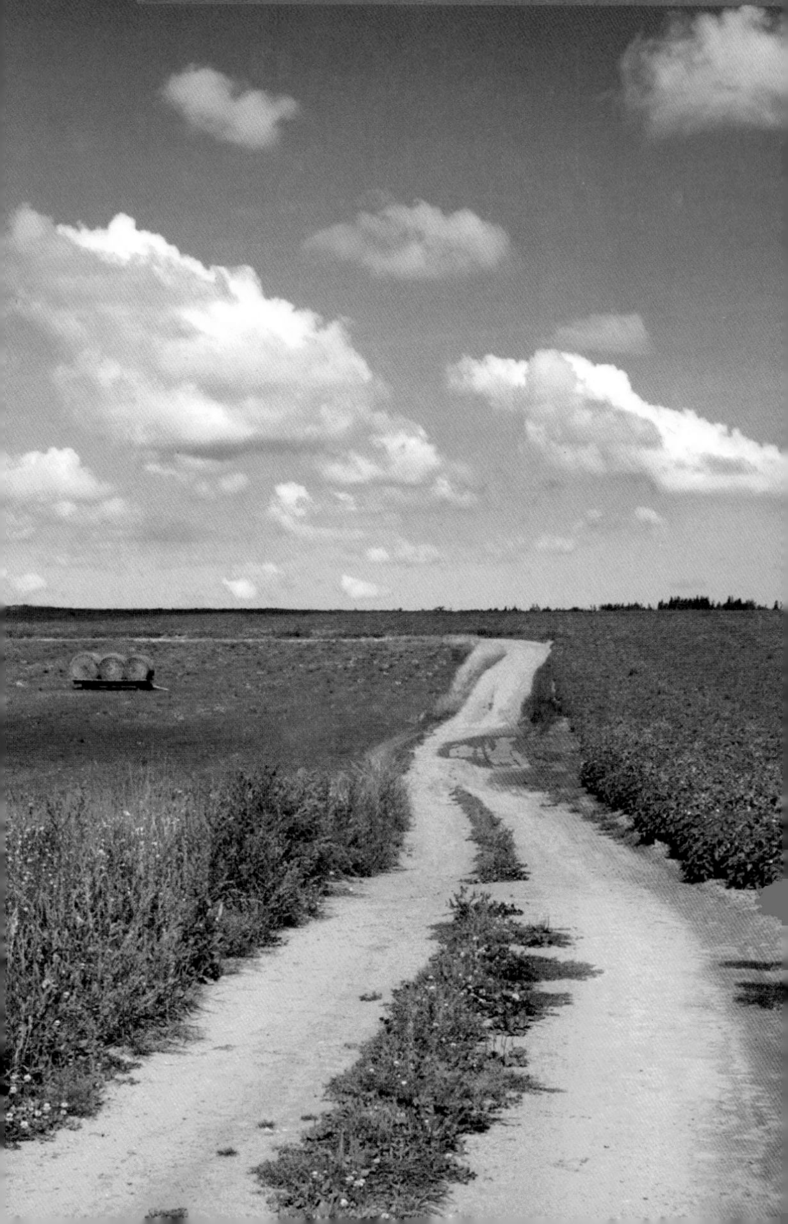

North Cape

Lobie Daughton

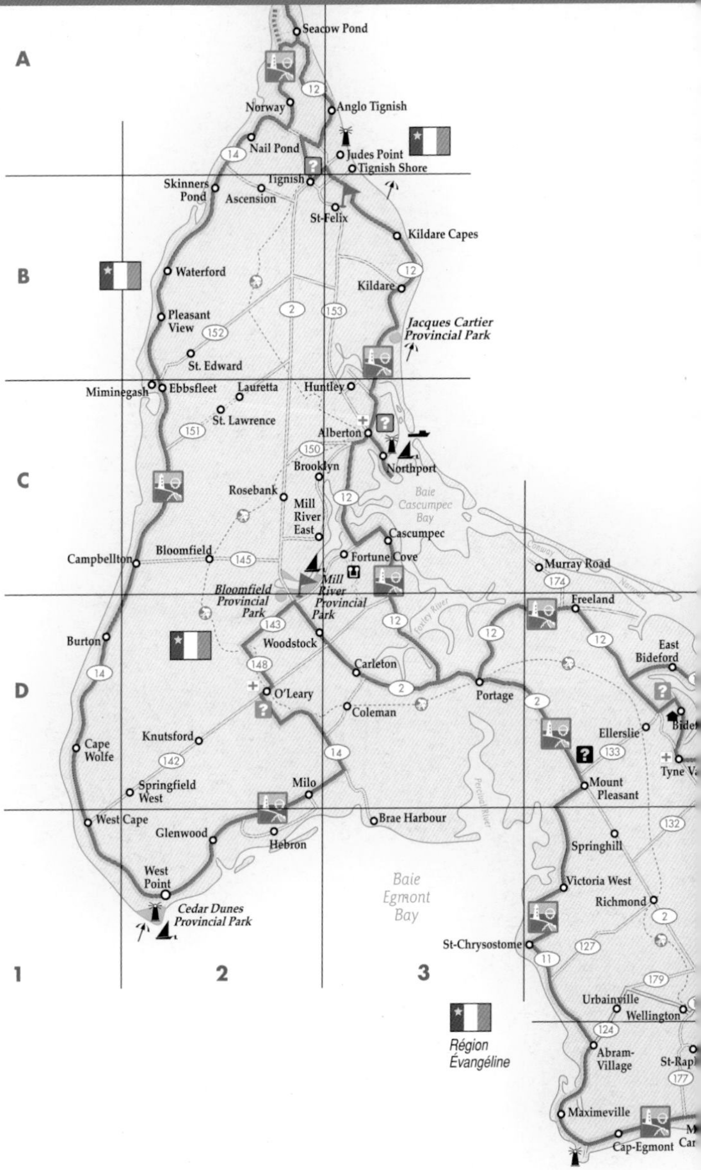

North Cape wind farm

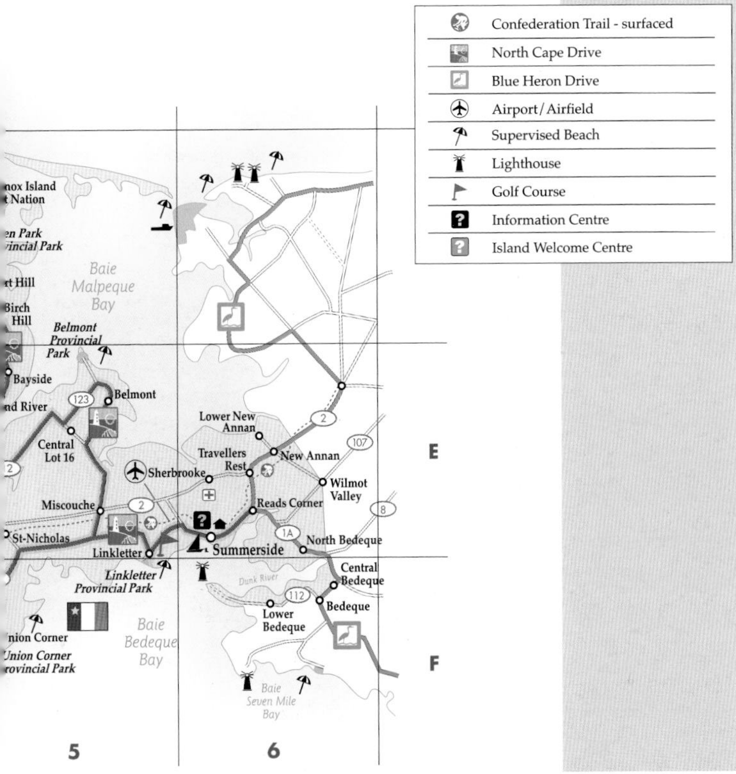

Picturesque communities, secluded beaches, historic architecture, beautiful churches and non-stop festivals and events: this is the North Cape Coastal Drive of Prince Edward Island, or what I'll call here "the Drive." This is where you can enjoy unspoiled natural wonders, succulent fresh seafood and an area rich in Acadian and Aboriginal culture.

Summerside City Hall

Just 20 minutes from Confederation Bridge, Summerside, the Island's second-largest city, has a fine harbour and a rich history as a shipbuilding centre in the Age of Sail. Between 1840 and 1890, over 3,100 wooden vessels were constructed at 176 locations. The good timber is long gone, but ships from all over the world still dock in Summerside to load Island spuds.

It's worth getting out of the car for a walk among Summerside's stately heritage homes, built over a century ago by wealthy shipbuilders and fox ranchers. A walking tour, published by the city of Summerside, is an excellent guide to the houses and their stories.

Summerside has come a long way in showcasing its historic waterfront while also maintaining a working port. Visitors can stroll the boardwalk, stop at the beach, browse the Shipyard Market, eat local seafood on the wharf or sip a refreshing brew at the Silver Fox Club by the yacht basin. The boardwalk is dotted with pictures and plaques that detail area history. Serious history buffs can find more inside the nearby Wyatt Centre, which houses the Eptek National Exhibition Centre. Eptek means "the hot place" in the language of the Mi'kmaq, who once

Lefurgey Cultural Centre, Summerside

used the area as the starting point for a portage across the Island's narrowest point (just six kilometres across).

Just beside Eptek, Spinnaker's Landing has a boat shed displaying traditional 19th-century methods of boat-building. In the downtown area, large murals grace the library and the fire hall and historical landmarks include the International Fox Museum and Hall of Fame, housed in the old Holman Homestead on Fitzroy Street. The College of Piping and Celtic Performing Arts, on Water Street East, hosts wonderful concerts throughout the summer and is home to world-champion pipers, drummers and dancers.

Spinnakers' Landing

For the more active traveller, the Confederation Trail — formerly the railway route across PEI and now a groomed walking and biking trail — passes through the centre of Summerside and on through the heart of the region.

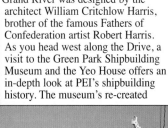

In Miscouche, about eight kilometres west of Summerside on Route 2, the Acadian Museum offers a presentation depicting the story of Island Acadians and has access to 30,000 genealogical cards. The friendly, bilingual staff can answer questions on the history and attractions of the area. Turning right onto Route 12 at Miscouche leads to beautiful countryside dotted with heritage buildings. St. Patrick's Church in Grand River was designed by the architect William Critchlow Harris, brother of the famous Fathers of Confederation artist Robert Harris. As you head west along the Drive, a visit to the Green Park Shipbuilding Museum and the Yeo House offers an in-depth look at PEI's shipbuilding history. The museum's re-created

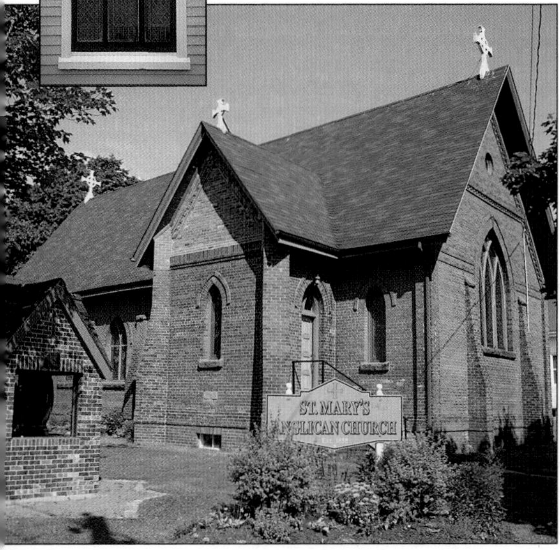

Inset: St. Patrick's Church
Bottom: St. Mary's Church, Summerside

Doctor's Inn garden

shipyard traces the rise and fall of the industry. A tour through Yeo House reveals something of the lifestyle of "ship barons" of the 1800s. The impeccably restored residence has great views of Malpeque Bay from the cupola atop the roof. Green Park is a favourite camping spot with locals and visitors alike, with some cabins for rent.

Further along Route 12 is the pretty village of Tyne Valley, where you'll find the Doctor's Inn B&B. Owners Paul and Jean Offer also serve dinners (by appointment only) featuring poultry and produce from their large organic garden. Tyne Valley plays host to the annual Oyster Festival in August, as well as to the Larry Gorman Folk Festival (Larry worked in the Maine woods and his songs and verses have become folk favourites). The Landing Pub features local beer while the Tyne Valley Studio showcases local art and knitwear.

A scant five-minute drive away in Bideford, the lovingly restored Victorian parsonage on Route 166 serves as a memento of L. M. Montgomery's first teaching post in 1894–1895. The nearby site of Montgomery's first one-room schoolhouse is marked with a cairn of stones and a small plaque. Back on Route 12, another William Harris-designed church, the small but lovely St. John's, in Ellerslie, is open for visits.

The Drive is home to the largest First Nations population on PEI. Turning right off Route 12 onto Route 163 and driving over the causeway, you will come to the Lennox Island Reserve. Mi'kmaq crafts, food and culture are demonstrated at the cultural centre and the reserve's fishing boats provide seafood for the café. An interpretive trail provides a great walking circuit and also a wheelchair-accessible route.

Lennox Island

After the reserve, a right turn back onto Route 12 will take you towards Route 2, "the Western Road," at Portage (pronounced "Portidge").

Pretty well any side road that branches off Route 12 to the right will lead down to the shore. Windsurfers, boaters and kayakers can easily find places to launch and explore bays, inlets, beaches and barachois (the French name for the shallow saltwater lagoons that run between the offshore dunes and the mainland).

Beyond Portage, West Prince is certainly less developed than the centre of PEI. This can be a source of pleasure to the visitor looking for something different: quieter, slower-paced, less "touristy." The area's farms and fishing villages are still mostly peopled by descendants of the first European settlers.

The land is flat or gently rolling, but the real glory of West Prince is its seacoast: red sandstone cliffs, often carved into striking shapes and caves by waves and wind, with miles of red or white sand beaches. It's a beachcombers' and birdwatchers' heaven.

Horace McNevin at Milo

The best way to explore the coastline is to follow the Drive across the bridge over Foxley River and then across the Mill River towards Alberton. It was here that the silver fox industry began. On an island in Alberton Harbour, Robert Oulton and Charles Dalton succeeded in raising the black foxes with white-tipped tails whose pelts created the

Red sandstone cliffs at Cap-Egmont

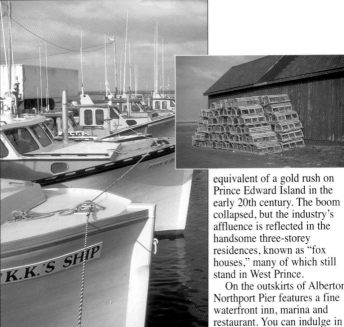

Tignish Harbour

equivalent of a gold rush on Prince Edward Island in the early 20th century. The boom collapsed, but the industry's affluence is reflected in the handsome three-storey residences, known as "fox houses," many of which still stand in West Prince.

On the outskirts of Alberton, Northport Pier features a fine waterfront inn, marina and restaurant. You can indulge in delicious food and a glass of wine while enjoying a view over the bay. Birdwatchers will appreciate a tour on a pontoon boat or a kayak on the shallow strip of water along the region's north shore, protected by ramparts of deserted sand dunes.

A few kilometres past Alberton, the Drive begins to hug the coastline. Jacques Cartier Provincial Park is named for the great French explorer, who may have first come ashore here in 1534. The beach runs virtually unbroken, at low tide, all the way to North Cape.

Opportunities for side trips to the shore abound. A short walk through the churchyard of the little white Anglican church at Kildare Capes brings you to sandstone cliffs overlooking the Gulf. The beach runs north as far as the eye can see and is often entirely empty. At low tide, you can wade to tiny, secluded beaches sheltered on either side by the cliffs.

A few miles up the coast and a little inland, Tignish is a predominantly Roman Catholic community with strong co-operative traditions. The church dominates the landscape in the form of the soaring spire of St. Simon and St. Jude, a brick building unusual in this province of wooden churches. The magnificent pipe organ, built in Quebec, is almost as old as the 1860 church. Several years ago, the neighbouring convent was converted into the Tignish Heritage Inn.

At the Tignish Cultural Centre, visitors can learn about the early days of the Irish and Acadian settlers. The Green, an eco-tourism site, depicts the landing of the eight founding families in 1799. Certain surnames, such as Gaudet, Perry/Poirier, Gallant and Arsenault, still predominate to this day.

Approaching the tip of the Island, you come to Seacow Pond, a tiny harbour named for the walrus once slaughtered for their hides, tusks and oil. Walrus herds no longer visit, but seals are a common sight off western beaches. Keep your eyes peeled for the spout of a passing whale.

At North Cape, the lighthouse has been joined by the Atlantic Wind Test Site with its array of towering windmills and by an interpretive centre where visitors can learn all about this elegant, sustainable power source. A meal at the site's Wind and Reef restaurant offers spectacular views across the water. Running out from the Cape is what may be the longest natural rock reef in the world.

You'll see many splendid draft horses in the fields of West Prince. Horses haul the scoops which rake up the Irish moss washed ashore after a storm. The moss is processed for carrageenan, a gelling agent used in a wide range of products, including ice cream. Carrageenan was a favourite dietary supplement for reggae legend Bob Marley, and you can try it for yourself at the Seaweed Pie café in Miminegash. Miminegash also boasts the childhood home of a Canadian cultural icon, singer/songwriter Stompin' Tom Connors.

For swimmers, there are beaches all along the coastal route, or you can watch the fishing boats tie up along the wharves at communities such as Howards Cove and Cape Wolfe. At Cedar Dunes Provincial Park, there's prime white sand beach as well as camping facilities. The nearby West Point Lighthouse, built in 1874,

Atlantic Wind Test Site

Harvesting Irish moss

Cedar Dunes Provincial Park

was converted into a community-owned restaurant, inn and craft shop. It is also the provincial lighthouse museum. Cedar Dunes makes a great stop for a refreshing snack, swim and stroll along the beach, or you can settle in for a long stay…West Prince is no place to rush.

From West Point, the Drive turns inland again through farms and woodland and back to Route 2, but there are options. With a left onto Route 2, then left on Route 142, you'll reach O'Leary, the home of the Prince Edward Island Potato Museum. The idea of a whole museum devoted to a vegetable may be amusing, but potatoes are to the Island what wheat is to the Prairies. Displays of machinery help to explain the central role that the potato has played in the province's agriculture. A 4.5-metre potato marks the entrance!

Potato blossoms

Just a few miles farther west along Route 2 is the principal tourist complex in West Prince: the Mill River Provincial Park and Resort. The 18-hole championship course is one of the best in Canada and the Rodd Resort is a family favourite, with everything from golf and nature walks to an indoor pool with waterslide. Less than a kilometre along the road is the Mill River Fun Park, with even bigger waterslides and many other attractions.

Across the highway, MacAusland's Woollen Mill welcomes visitors to watch as wool is carded, spun and woven into the warm blankets for which MacAusland's is known. Knitters prize the wool, and both yarn and

MacAusland's Woollen Mill

blankets are for sale.

Finally, visitors should not be reluctant to explore off the beaten track. Route 145, for example, passes through some of the prettiest pastoral scenery in the province. Many roads lead to the coast. Even if you get lost, you're never far from somewhere, and even the smallest roads are shown on the maps that are available from any tourism office or visitor information centre. Locals are glad to give visitors directions; people up west are helpful types and generous with their advice.

Bottom: Island farmland

A right turn from the Drive onto Route 2 brings you back towards Portage. After coming to Mount Pleasant — where a bustling Second World War air force training base once stood — you regain the Drive as you take a right turn and follow Route 11 through Enmore and Victoria West, into the main francophone area of the Island.

The next several kilometres follow the coastline along Egmont Bay into the heart of "La Région Évangéline" (named after Longfellow's famous poem about the Acadian deportation). Acadians are a lively bunch; local musicians and dancers know how to throw a party! Acadians love to eat as well, whether it's râpé pie, tourtière or a lobster dinner. The Acadians are famous for their friendliness and hospitality, so you might

Church of our Lady of Mont-Carmel

find yourself planning to stay a while longer.

A tour around this French-speaking area will give a taste of Acadian pride as well as Acadian food. The Acadian flag (a tricoleur with a single star) adorns many houses and local people are proud of their resilience in hard times. The region is known for beautiful churches, such as the Church of St. Phillip and St. Jacques in Egmont Bay and the Church of Our Lady of Mont-Carmel. The people of the area are also renowned for their annual Agricultural Exhibition and Acadian Festival, held on Labour Day weekend in Abram-Village.

The Bottle Houses (Les maisons de bouteilles) in Cape Egmont feature over 30,000 bottles built into colourful buildings. A little further east in Mont-Carmel you'll find

Bottle house, Cap-Egmont

Union Corner Schoolhouse Museum

Le Village de l'Acadie, which includes the Acadian Pioneer Village, L'Auberge du Village (a comfortable inn), "La Cuisine à Mémé" dinner theatre (in both English and French) and the restaurant L'Étoile de Mer.

From Union Corner, the Drive passes through St. Raphael and St. Nicholas, back into Miscouche, or a side trip on Route 177 will take you into the little village of Wellington. By following Route 124 from Wellington to Route 2, you'll come across the Promenade Acadienne Boardwalk, which replicates the commercial architecture of the late 1880s with attractions such as the Évangéline Tourist Information Centre, and the Quilt Eco-museum. Another three kilometres west on Route 2, towards Richmond, finds the Basket Weavers Co-op on the right-hand side. The Co-op's artisans preserve and showcase age-old basket-making artistry. Their beautiful split-ash baskets last for decades and are useful as well as decorative.

Whether you want to head back towards the bridge to New Brunswick, take the ferry to Nova Scotia or go to central PEI, all roads will take you through Summerside. But you mustn't be in a hurry — if you're interested in shipbuilding, in natural history, or in Mi'kmaq, French, British, Irish, Scottish, Welsh and Loyalist history, or if you just like lush countryside and curving coastline, it's worth the wander through the western part of Prince Edward Island known as the Drive.

Acadian Craft Co-op

Anne's Land

Shirley Horne

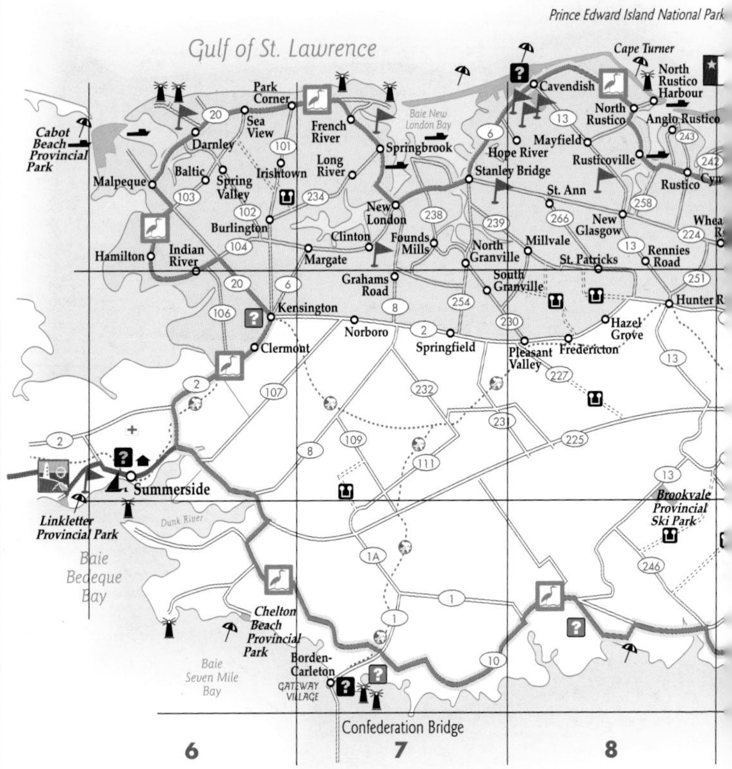

Of all the scenic beauty of Prince Edward Island, some of the most striking is found along the north shore and in the Prince Edward Island National Park. There you'll see views of the sparkling Gulf of St. Lawrence from the road that runs through the Park and parallel to the Gulf. Often there's a "sea on" and waves foam and splash up over the creamy pastel beaches. The sand dunes between the Gulf and the road are the same pastel colour, but their cover of spiky green marram grasses makes a brilliant contrast.

Along the roadside the grasses are interspersed with fragrant bay leaves and clumps of rugged spruce. The effect is as exhilarating as a breath of salt air. Marshlands and spruce groves line the opposite side of the road, and great blue herons, which feed in the ponds and harbours, can often be seen standing motionless, with one long, slim

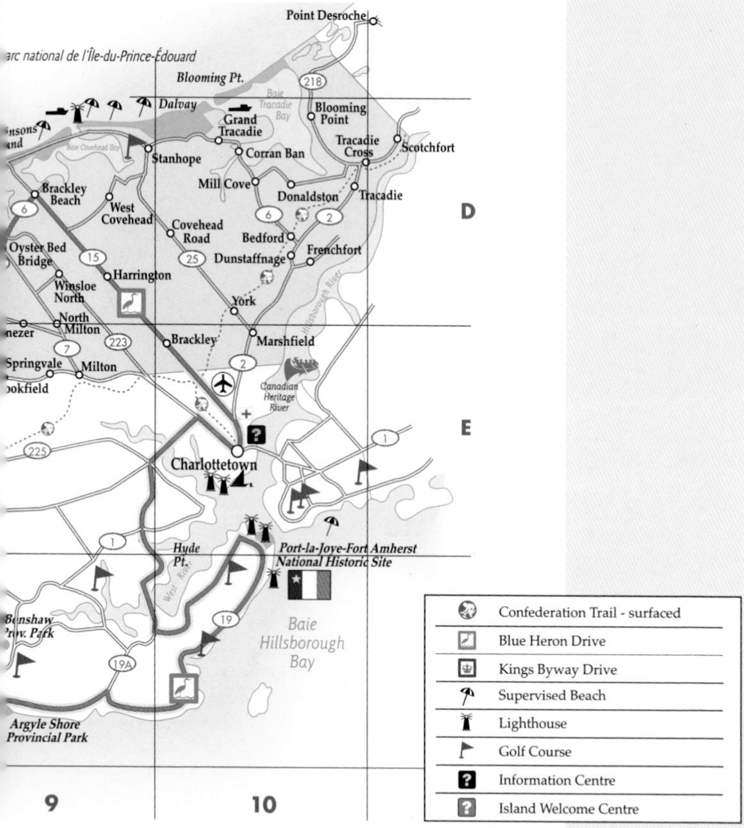

leg raised and gracefully crooked.

While admiring the grandeur of the shore, one cannot neglect the simple wonders inland. The Park is also home to several woodland hiking trails. The Bubbling Springs Trail is a relaxing two-kilometre hike with a real bubbling spring and a bench from which to admire it. Along the Trail you'll notice an old cemetery with small stubby headstones made of brown sandstone, although the names of sailors lost in the Yankee Gale of 1851 have long since worn away.

If, while at the entrance to Prince Edward Island National Park at Dalvay, the Island's most luxurious summer cottage seems vaguely familiar to you, you've probably seen it before. On the made-for-TV movie "Anne of Green Gables" and the "Road to Avonlea" TV series,

Stanhope Beach, Prince Edward Island National Park

Dalvay appears as the White Sands Hotel.

Dalvay was built as a summer home by Alexander MacDonald in 1896. At the time he was president of Standard Oil and a cohort of Rockefeller; he didn't have to pinch pennies. He built it for his family from the finest Island materials: hand-picked pine paneling — without a knot — and floor-to-ceiling fireplaces made from rough, red sandstone boulders. He furnished his summer place with beautiful items brought back from his many travels. MacDonald called his summer home Dalvay, after his ancestral home in Scotland. He employed numerous servants and the operating cost was said to be $10,000 a year — a hefty sum in those days. MacDonald, his wife and their two granddaughters spent many happy summers at Dalvay.

Dalvay passed through several owners until it was finally purchased by Parks Canada. It is currently operated as a summer hotel that features fine dining in a relaxed yet elegant ambience.

Prince Edward Island National Park is one of Canada's smallest — only 31 square kilometres — but it is one of the most popular. The Park consists mainly of marshland and spruce woodlands, which include hiking trails and campgrounds. But its fine sandy beaches — among the best in the world — are its main attraction. Wading in the clear salt waters of the Gulf of St. Lawrence, you can see your toes on the sandy bottom; you will be hard-pressed to find a stone on which to stub your toe.

This coastline was once the setting for the infamous but profitable rum-running trade. During prohibition, when the Island was dry, ships sailed in from the French islands of St. Pierre and Miquelon, located off the south coast of Newfoundland. Laden with rum, they dropped anchor offshore and blinked their lights to signal fishermen standing by, their small boats at the ready. As soon as the coast was clear they rowed out, usually after dark, to claim their liquid gold. Fishermen carried on a brisk rum-running trade and many homes had clever hiding places such as false cupboards and floorboards.

The Dunes

It was along this coastline, too, that wooden sailing ships were built and launched. Shipbuilding brought much prosperity to the Island during the mid-1800s, "The Golden Age of Sail." In this area alone, 43 ships were built and launched from 1786 to 1890.

After leaving Dalvay, it's worth the few minutes' drive towards Covehead Bay to see the newly restored palatial Stanhope Bay and Beach Resort. It is large and yellow with a wrap-around veranda. The hotel stands out amid its wide lawns and gardens. It has been operated as a hotel since 1860 but, in fact, the building is even older. During the restoration in 2005, workmen discovered walls of the original log cabin (circa 1760) around which the hotel was built.

In the 1860s the proprietor said of his hotel: "For bathing, fishing, shooting, pleasure seekers will find it unequaled in the Dominion."

The 2005 restoration blends an atmosphere of a heritage property with all modern conveniences like air conditioning and high-speed Internet. The hotel is furnished with handsome antiques and a number of rooms have Jacuzzis and fireplaces and semi-private balconies with views of the gardens and the bay. With its wide lawns and plenty of parking, the hotel has a country mansion feel and is particularly suitable for convention groups. It also has the advantage of being close to such activities as golf, kayaking, biking and hiking.

Shaw's Hotel

As you continue along the coastline of the Gulf of St. Lawrence, you will come to Brackley Beach, where there are excellent beach houses with change and shower facilities. Located on Brackley Bay is Shaw's Hotel, a relaxing country lodge. This traditional inn, with its first-class

North Rustico

dining room and several cottages, is a favourite place for families. The inn was opened by the Shaws in 1860 and is still run by the family.

Outside Prince Edward Island National Park, The Dunes Studio Gallery and Café is worth a stop just to see the interesting architecture, right from the outdoor gardens to the tiny water garden on the roof and down the spiral stair to the third floor observatory tower or the "The Muise" for a view of the reflecting pools and the bay. The Dunes, the Island's most elegant craft shop, displays beautiful crafts by Canada's finest artists and artisans. Peter Jansons and Joel Mills can often be seen at work in the studio where they produce award-winning pottery. Also on display is one of the finest exhibitions of Prince Edward Island art. A wing with marble floors and a European-style fountain is a showroom for furniture, housewares, paintings, jewelry and fashions. In the gardens there are beautiful fountains and sculptures available for purchase. At The Dunes Café, Emily Wells has been building a reputation for delicious and unique cuisine over the past ten years.

Gift Shop, North Rustico

Back on the main road you will see the signs designating Blue Heron Drive. Along the way there are signs to Rustico, Anglo Rustico, South Rustico, Rusticoville and North Rustico. Rustico used to be mainly a fishing area with a few craft shops and some tourist accommodations, but new attractions have recently been added.

Kayaking

Miniature fishing boat, Aiden's Deep Sea fishing, Rustico

The scenery is green and pastoral, with glimpses of Rustico Bay. Most fishermen here work in the lucrative lobster fishery during its season — the months of May and June — and then paint and "gussy up" their boats to take tourists out deep-sea fishing for the summer and fall. By asking around the area you can usually arrange an excursion in a genuine fishing boat. Upon your return, you'll have a healthy appetite and a fresh catch for your supper. If you didn't catch anything (or even if you did), Dayboat restaurant serves the best Island seafood you're apt to find anywhere.

The Rustico region was the first Acadian community settled in PEI after the expulsion in the late 18th century, and is still thought of as Acadian. Though French inflections are still heard, very few of its residents speak French as a first language. For a flavour of Acadian history, one can turn right near Gallant's grocery store (Route 243) at South Rustico and visit Belcourt Centre. The Centre is

Farmer's Bank

named after Father Georges-Antoine Belcourt, who served in South Rustico in the mid-1800s. Father Belcourt was committed to helping the Acadians make a better life for themselves. One of his first projects was to establish the Farmers' Bank so that residents could borrow money at a

Dayboat

preferred interest rate to buy seed. The bank was operated as a co-operative, or credit union — one of the first in the country. The slate-roofed Island stone Farmers' Bank is now a museum. On display are numerous artifacts, including Father Belcourt's robes; one of the most recently

Fisheries Museum

acquired treasures is a handsome bronze bust of Napoleon III that was brought from France with great ceremony in 2004. A forward-thinking man for his time, Father Belcourt is remembered as the first Islander to own a car. He is revered for his efforts on behalf of the Acadian people.

In Belcourt Centre stands St. Augustine's Church, the Island's oldest Roman Catholic church, with its lovely paired Gothic windows. Bed-and-breakfast accommodation is available at the 15-room Barachois (Bar-a-shwa) Inn, originally a Victorian country house built in 1880 for a local merchant, Joseph Gallant. It is one of the Island's few rural five-star bed-and-breakfast establishments. MacDonald House, located next to the main building, offers guests of the Inn an exercise room, a sauna and meeting rooms, making the Barachois Inn a favourite choice for executive retreats, intimate gatherings and small weddings. The inn is open year-round.

Next door is the Belcourt Centre, once a convent used for teaching French but now used for retreats. One of the most exciting and most recent additions to the Centre is Doucet House. Built in 1772, it was constructed of logs in the Acadian style by Jean Doucet in the nearby community of Cymbria. Slated to be torn down, the building was rescued by the Friends of the Farmers' Bank, who had it moved to Belcourt Centre. Restored, furnished and staffed, it is an authentic example of early Acadian life. Connecting Doucet House and the Farmers' Bank is a landscaped boardwalk with benches, offering a fine place for a picnic.

Below: Doucet House
Bottom: North Rustico

Continuing on Blue Heron Drive (Route 6) to North Rustico, you will pass the road down to the wharf to the Fisheries Museum and the nearby Blue Mussel Café. After some fresh mussels and a pleasant walk along the seaside boardwalk, you might even work up an appetite for a lobster dinner at the Fisherman's Wharf Restaurant nearby.

A return to Route 6 to Cavendish and a right turn at the intersection with traffic

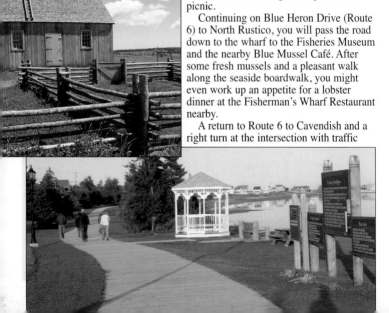

Green Gables

lights will bring you to the Cavendish Information Centre. A short distance down the side road you will find the creamy sands of Cavendish Beach. A majority of the Island's first-time visitors feel they can't miss Cavendish, and for those traveling with young children it is a must.

A new attraction at Cavendish is the Shining Waters Family Fun Park, a 36-acre complex of activities and attractions for the whole family, including the adventure woods, the storybook forest and a boating lake. Big kids may enjoy the large water slide complex while little ones can splash around in Turtle Cove. Chester's Farmyard features many small farm animals. There is live entertainment in the outdoor theatre. Picnic tables, food and gifts are available on-site.

Rollercoaster at Sandspit

Another well-run attraction is Sandspit, which includes a rollercoaster, racing cars, bumper boats, mini-rides, mini-golf and a canteen. In Cavendish you can find every kind of fast food imaginable. Most kids — big and little — think they have to "do" the Cavendish scene at least once. On a summer's day you might find a few thousand people enjoying the attractions and the spacious green areas and beaches.

Many visitors will not want to leave Prince Edward Island without having their photo taken with Green Gables in the background. If you know the story, it is captivating to walk through the home, which is believed to be the setting for the novel *Anne of Green Gables*. It's easy to imagine yourself in the milieu where the spunky, much-loved, red-haired Anne used to roam, and to walk into the kitchen and imagine Marilla at work. You'll even find Matthew's bedroom, with his big work boots under his patchwork quilt-covered bed. (Matthew had to sleep downstairs because of his bad heart.) Anne's little room upstairs is precious. There you see her tiny boots, the plain dresses she hated and, on the floor, the slate she cracked over Gilbert Blythe's head.

It is not uncommon to see smiling young Japanese couples posing for photos at Green Gables. A number of Japanese visitors come to the Island to be married. In Japan, the love for their heroine Anne and her creator, Lucy Maud

Frog Bog at Sandspit

Japanese Wedding

Montgomery, has inspired several fan clubs. The Japanese have even established a replica of Green Gables at Canada World in Japan.

Chief among the attractions and the place where many young Japanese choose to be married is the home of Montgomery's aunt and uncle at Park Corner, referred to as "Silver Bush" in her novels — now the Anne of Green Gables Museum. It is where Montgomery herself was married and where young Maud spent happy times with her cousins, the Campbells. One of their descendants, George Campbell, has turned Silver Bush into a museum and he delights in showing visitors around. On the grounds, nestled in a grove of trees, the family has built the charming Shining Waters Tea Room.

Montgomery's ivory-coloured wedding gown is kept at her birthplace at New London. This charming little home is probably where the ghost of Montgomery is most strongly sensed. Her wedding dress, her old scrapbooks and samples of her writing are all on display. In the kitchen of the tiny home it's easy to imagine the young parents, Hugh Montgomery and Clara Macneill, living as a happy family with Maud, their vivacious, chattering toddler. But it's upstairs in Maud's room, with her baby furniture and pinafores, that the tragedy of this little family hits you. When baby Maud was just two years old her young mother was struck down with tuberculosis. The author later wrote in her journal: "My earliest memory is of being held in my father's arms and reaching down to touch my mother's cool cheek with my baby hand."

Another of the area's Anne-related attractions is Avonlea Village. Here the church Maud attended, and the schoolhouse where she taught, have been brought together in a village constructed to represent the period in which the Anne books were set. To mark the 100th anniversary of the publishing of *Anne of Green Gables* in 2008, the church has been named The Montgomery Theatre. There you may enjoy live theatrical productions by such authors as George Bernard Shaw and Oscar Wilde. Find out more from their website: www.themontgomerytheatre.com. There is an

Malpeque Harbour

Roadside, near Malpeque

admission charge to the entire Village, but a horse-and-wagon ride around the square and entrance to each of the buildings is free.

For a change of pace — especially for those travelling with children, or who have children on their gift lists — it's worthwhile to find Route 13 and tour the rolling hills to New Glasgow for a visit to the Toy Factory. In this charming little factory, toys are made from Island wood and guaranteed to last a lifetime, according to the proprietor. Children are welcome in the factory and they can have their names stamped on their new toys. The famous New Glasgow lobster suppers are also in the vicinity.

The big yellow PEI Preserve Company building is located nearby, in a renovated 1913 butter factory on the little Clyde River. The small preserve factory has installed an observation window through which visitors can watch preserves being made. Then, they are welcomed at the tasting table.

Also located within the building is the Café on the Clyde for a tasty meal overlooking the Clyde and gardens. Afterwards a stroll through the 12 acres of gardens and a walk along the two kilometres of walking trails would be enjoyable.

St. Mary's Church

An early evening tour on Blue Heron Drive through French River to Malpeque is a pleasant way to finish the day. Glimpses of water are seen around each curve in the road. Indeed, no Prince Edward Island community is more than 20 km from the sea. This is one of the Island's most beautiful areas — just as Montgomery described it in her novels. Its beauty has inspired an L. M. Montgomery Land Trust to begin preservation of this scenic, coastal region. Thus far, it has preserved 130 acres and the ultimate goal is 622 acres. The aim is to keep it in production but not to be subdivided.

Further south on Blue Heron Drive is Indian River, home to a world-class classical summer music festival. The French Gothic-style St. Mary's Church is the largest wooden church remaining on the Island. Built in 1902, it is an acoustical wonder — the perfect setting for musical performance. The festival attracts internationally known vocalists and instrumentalists throughout the summer. The seats are hard but the music is heavenly. A concert at St. Mary's Church is a fitting finale to a visit in this particularly lovely section of Prince Edward Island.

New Glasgow's Toy Factory

Charlotte's Shore

Anne McCallum

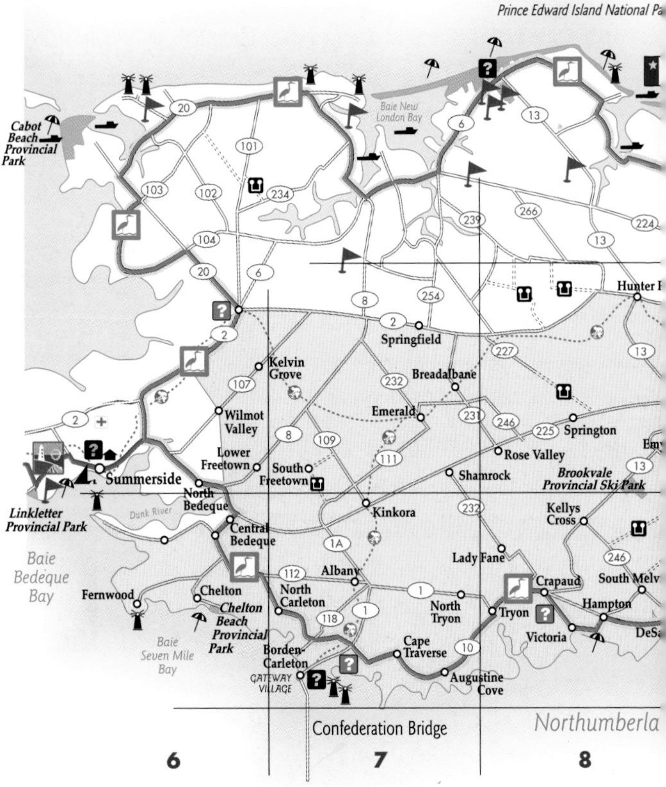

Charlotte's Shore is a patchwork of small farming communities interspersed with natural woodlands and bordered by a series of picturesque fishing villages along the Northumberland Strait. What strikes you most when you catch the first shimmering glimpse of Prince Edward Island from the high centre point on Confederation Bridge is the rich, red hue of the sandstone shoreline, especially if the sun is setting. Much of the Island's natural beauty comes from its strong colour contrasts — the burnished red of the earth, the innumerable green shades of fields and forests and the brilliant blues of sky and ocean. These colours dominate your first images of Charlotte's Shore and stay with you long after the smaller details of your trip have faded.

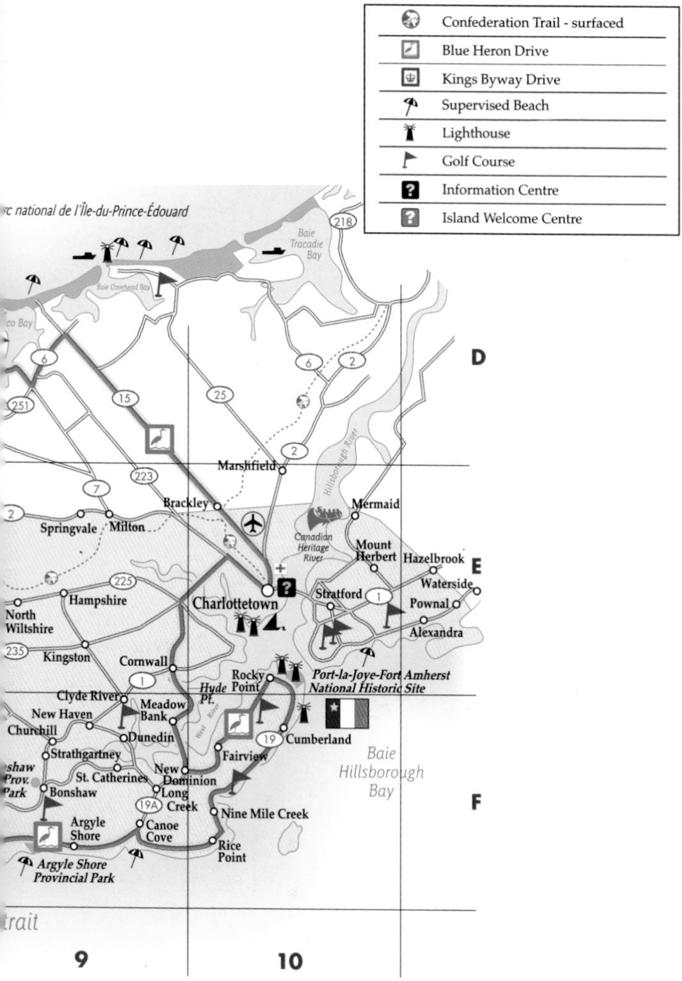

After you drive off the bridge near the village of Borden-Carleton, it is well worth spending an hour or so at Gateway Village, opened as part of the Confederation Bridge development to welcome visitors to the Island. You will notice it immediately to your right as you arrive. It is a first-rate interpretive centre where you will learn about the history, geography and economy of Prince Edward Island through a series of interactive multimedia exhibits. You will be introduced to the work of some of the province's most creative craftspeople and also find out how much effort and expertise it took to construct the world's longest continuous marine span bridge over waters that are often covered with ice.

Just west of Confederation Bridge is Chelton Beach

Sandstone cliffs

Provincial Park, the region's only dune beach. The water is warm and the Park has supervised swimming and picnic tables.

Another point of interest in the area is Seacow Head lighthouse. It is an eight-sided wooden structure over 18 metres above water level, built in 1863 and moved back from the eroding cliff edge to its present location in 1979. Black guillemots lay their eggs on the cliff's ledges. Watch for eiders, scoters and oldsquaws in the water.

Nearby Bedeque is a sleepy country village, but over a century ago it was a bustling shipbuilding centre. One of the most influential shipbuilders and merchants from the area was James Pope, the first Island premier after Confederation. You'll find the J. C. Pope historic site near Bedeque.

Farm on Route 1

From Central Bedeque and Middleton, Route 225 will take you through the Island's potato-growing heartland. The area was initially settled by Loyalists, but, as the nearby place names of Shamrock and Emerald indicate, it became home in the first half of the 19th century to Irish immigrants. Every July residents celebrate their Irish heritage with a three-day festival in Emerald Junction.

The focal point of Kinkora is the "new" St. Malachy's Catholic Church, opened in 1901. Its Gothic Revival design and beautifully carved interior make it one of the region's most impressive churches.

Farming communities around Kinkora have flourished, thanks to the potato. The Island's most prized export, the white seed potato, was developed in this area. The immaculately cultivated fields of green foliage topped with white blossoms present a healthy, fertile image, but from an environmental perspective, some of today's potato production methods have proved less than benign. Soil erosion and river siltation are serious problems in many areas where potato monoculture is common. Fortunately, the more progressive farmers now practise across-the-slope plowing and plant strip crops to conserve the Island's fragile topsoil from the ravaging effects of wind and water.

Potato fields in bloom, Meadowbank

When you reach the Route 231 intersection at Rose Valley, travel north to Breadalbane. Ask at the library/community centre about the hiking trail that village residents

have developed. Include a visit as well to Malcolm Stanley's pottery studio on Route 246, known locally as the Dixon Road. This little red road is home to numerous artists and musicians who settled on the Island in the 1970s as part of the "back-to-the-land movement." Rural life and nature provide the inspiration for the hand-painted trees, flowers and Island scenes on the Stanley family's hand-thrown pottery.

From Breadalbane, you can head north to join Route 2, one of two main roads running east-west from Summerside to Charlottetown. It passes through the picturesque village of Hunter River, where you might catch sight of a flock of Canada Geese on the river below the Presbyterian Church. A less travelled route would be to backtrack from Breadalbane to Rose Valley and follow Route 225 through the rolling hills to North River. This is dairy farming country.

Throughout the summer, the hayfields and roadsides are ablaze with wildflower colour — dog daisies and dandelions, purple vetch and white clover, black-eyed Susans and Queen Anne's lace. If you have young children along, you'll want to stop at the Toy Factory in New Glasgow, which offers an assortment of unique wooden toys that are handcrafted while you watch.

At North River, if you turn left onto the Trans-Canada Highway and drive across the causeway — watching out for great blue herons, Bonaparte's gulls and factory outlets as you do so — you will find yourself at the western entrance to Charlottetown.

Farm near Victoria

Charlottetown offers everything you would expect of a provincial capital: elegant hotels and historic inns, fine dining, professional theatre, night life, art galleries, museums and shopping. All these and more are encapsulated in a small city of historic charm and natural beauty. All summer long there are historic walking tours, festivals and celebrations. On the edges of town you will find harness racing and first-rate golf courses.

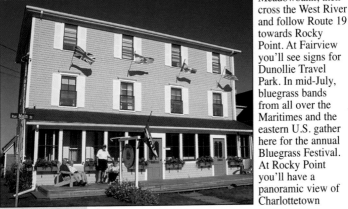

If you turn right at North River and travel west to Cornwall, you will be at a perfect starting point to explore the bays and beaches of the south shore. South shore beaches are unsupervised and much coarser than those on the north shore. But the water is considerably warmer and, at low tide, they're great for digging clams or searching for sea treasures in nooks and crannies of rock pools. Turn left onto Route 19 and follow the Blue Heron Drive through Meadowbank, then cross the West River and follow Route 19 towards Rocky Point. At Fairview you'll see signs for Dunollie Travel Park. In mid-July, bluegrass bands from all over the Maritimes and the eastern U.S. gather here for the annual Bluegrass Festival. At Rocky Point you'll have a panoramic view of Charlottetown Harbour.

Orient Hotel, Victoria

Continue west about two kilometres on Route 19 to Port-la-Joye-Fort Amherst, a national historic site. In the early 1700s the French established a settlement here. When the British took possession of the Island in 1758 they built Fort Amherst. At its peak the Fort served an important military function. At the interpretive centre you can learn about early Island settlement. The grounds and shoreline are pleasant places to walk, picnic or fly kites.

If you follow Route 19 around Rice Point you will reach Canoe Cove. When the Island was in French possession, the Mi'kmaq took the British ashore in their canoes and it is said that those soldiers gave the name to the district.

Cornwall United Church

Victoria-By-The-Sea

Some cove people of the past claim to have sighted a flaming sailboat or steamer off this shore. It is known in local folklore as "The Phantom Ship," and sightings have been reported from both sides of the strait. Swimming is good in this large sheltered cove, and Argyle Shore Provincial Park, a few kilometres west, is another great swimming and picnicking spot.

At Desable, Route 19 joins the Trans-Canada again. The Free Church of Scotland here reflects distinctive Scottish tradition in its architecture, and its steeple is topped with a thistle. The church holds 500 people, but is known to have held twice that number when the Reverend Donald McDonald preached in the mid-1800s. He established a local sect called the "McDonaldites." His powerful sermons in Gaelic and English attracted close to 5,000 followers.

By following the coastline you will have missed Strathgartney Provincial Park in the Bonshaw Hills. It is well worth backtracking a few kilometres along Route 1 to Strathgartney to experience the excellent hiking trails that have been developed. The nearby Strathgartney Inn was built by landowner and land agent Robert Bruce Stewart in the mid-1800s. At St. Catherines Cove off Route 9, you can rent a canoe and paddle the tidal West River.

If you are travelling in July or August, you can pick your own strawberries or raspberries at local fruit farms. The area around South Melville is also a paradise for hikers and cyclists.

From Desable it is a short drive to Victoria-by-the-Sea. Many homes in this charming village are notable examples of 19th-century architecture. Victoria did not develop at random, but rather was built by design on one family's farm, to serve as a seaport for nearby agricultural communities. In its heyday, it was the fourth-busiest port on the Island, but when transportation methods switched from water to land, it declined. In recent years it has enjoyed a resurgence because of its popularity among visitors.

Although a small village, Victoria offers quite a range of attractions. There is a warm-water beach and picnic area at Victoria Provincial Park — great for beachcombing. Look for bank swallows nesting on the cliff edge. Victoria Village Inn and the Orient Hotel offer excellent

Island Chocolates, Victoria

accommodations in heritage surroundings. There are several tea rooms, a chocolate factory and some first-rate arts and crafts outlets. Professional repertory theatre and musical concerts are presented nightly at the Victoria Playhouse. The hall's sloping floor design ensures that there isn't a bad seat in the house.

One of the Island's largest salt marshes is in this area — the Tryon Marsh. The Tryon River is of historical interest because it was the site of the Island's first woollen mill, built by Charles E. Stanfield in 1856.

From Tryon it is just a short drive back to the Confederation Bridge where, incidentally, you will be asked to pay a bridge toll if you are leaving the Island. The toll actually pays for the two-way trip, but is collected on the Island side. If you are staying, you can travel east to Route 13 from Crapaud to the north shore. This meandering route will take you past the Brookvale Demonstration Woodlot, where you can follow an interpretive walking tour. Brookvale is also the site of the Island's only downhill ski park, open from December to March. Route 13 continues through Hunter River. At this point you will be entering the popular tourist area known as Anne's Land.

Victoria Playhouse

Points East Coastal Drive

Kumari Campbell

Confederation Bridge

Unlike the busy central region of the province, life in the eastern region is unhurried. Simple treasures of nature are abundant and peace and solitude are tangible commodities. Unbelievable as it may seem, this is largely virgin territory, virtually undiscovered by the masses.

You won't find many commercial attractions or grandiose structures along the way. The only items of large proportions here are the great outdoors and the hearts of our residents. But be assured, that is all you will need for a splendid vacation.

Residents of eastern Prince Edward Island are determined that their region remain as close to nature as possible, and this end of the province has developed a reputation as a "green tourism" destination. Two green tourism products help visitors get a closer look at the natural beauty of the region. The Confederation Trail, which uses the former railbed of the Prince Edward Island Railway as a hiking and biking trail across the province, had its beginnings in this region. This Trail provides vistas of the interior that cannot be had from your car window. The Points East Coastal Drive, which almost encircles the

Orwell Corner

entire region, offers the visitor a complete eastern PEI experience, by linking its natural, cultural and historic sites.

Most visitors these days arrive in PEI via the Confederation Bridge. Highway 1, the Trans-Canada Highway, leads to

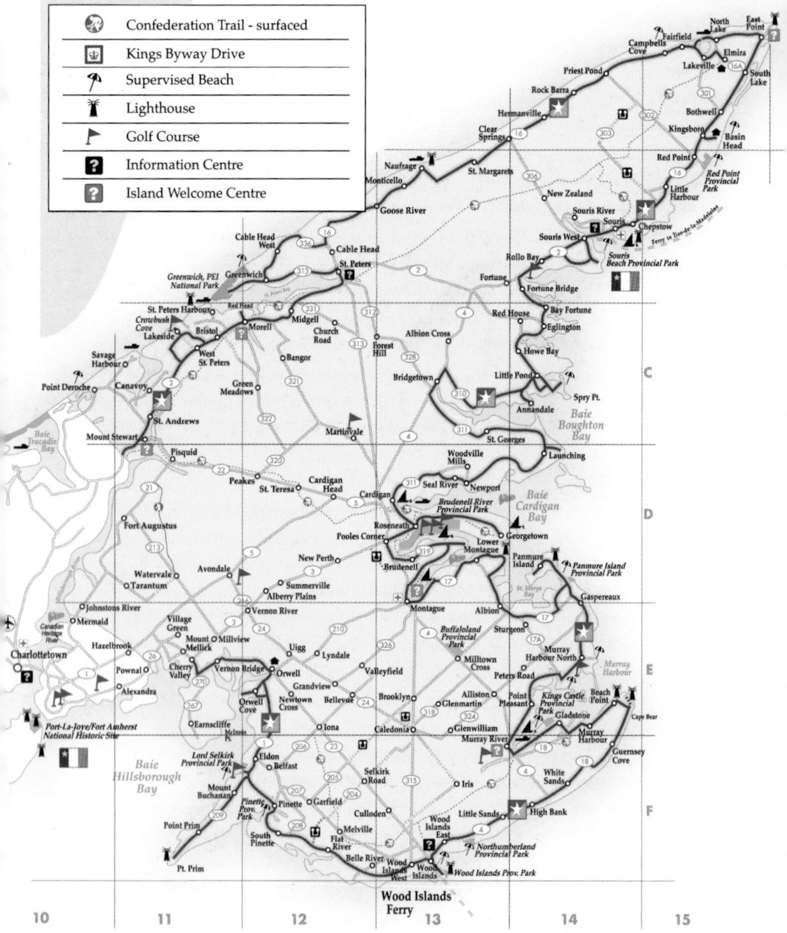

Charlottetown, the capital city, and continues on to Cherry Valley where this tour of Points East begins. You can just as easily travel the route in a counterclockwise direction. An authentic Island visit ought to involve a trip by ferry at least one way. A run across Northumberland Strait by ferry is a genuine luxury — a mini ocean cruise. Especially for anyone coming from Cape Breton or mainland Nova Scotia (anywhere from Truro north), the trip by ferry is a good alternative to the Confederation Bridge. If you have arrived on the Island by ferry, the Points East Coastal Drive may be joined by taking Route 23 to Orwell and starting the tour there.

Schoolhouse at Orwell Corner

Watch for a sign that announces the Orwell Corner Historic Village. The village transports visitors back to a less complicated age. You can visit the store or the church, or wander at will. If you're lucky, there will be a ceilidh in the hall later on. If not, there's always homemade ice cream to enjoy, an ancient piece of farm machinery to climb on or some warm sun to sit in and dream.

Sir Andrew Macphail Homestead

A minute or two down the road is the stone gate that marks the entrance to the Sir Andrew Macphail Homestead. A cup of tea awaits in the restored house. A series of walking trails take you under big pines and huge hemlocks and yellow birches, especially the trail that goes down by the brook. Here you can catch a glimpse of how the original forest cover of Kings County once looked. Some of the trees are over 150 years old. In the spring, the big linden in front of the house bursts into bloom and hums with thousands of bees. The property has a tree nursery that specializes in native trees and shrubs.

At Eldon, turn off Highway 1 and follow Route 209 to Point Prim, where you can climb to the top of the oldest lighthouse in PEI. This is the first in a little string of four lighthouses. The next one is just past the ferry terminal at Wood Islands.

From Wood Islands continue on Route 4. Here you will travel through some of the most beautiful acreage on earth. Pull into Northumberland Park. Take off those shoes and socks. Dip those sore toes into balmy salt water. Feel the sun-warmed sand beneath your feet. If you stay around here for a while, you can dig a few clams and bake them, or put on a snorkel and a mask and float out on the water, barely rippling the smooth surface.

When you leave the Park a right turn

MacPhail Woods

Sunset at Wood Islands

will take you, 6.5 kilometres later, to the Rossignol Estate Winery, where you can sample their award-winning fruit and table wines. It costs nothing to visit the meticulously tidy farm, winery, vineyard and art gallery. The owner, John Rossignol, is happy to chat about the beautiful sandy loam, or about how he is using former tobacco greenhouses for grape varieties previously considered too tender to grow on the Island. From this splendid farm you'll see breathtaking vistas of the Northumberland Strait.

These views of the Strait, with Pictou Island and Nova Scotia in the distance, continue as you glide through the communities of Little Sands, High Bank and White Sands. Route 4 will become Route 18, and you'll veer to the right past Guernsey Cove where Huguenots, descendants of settlers from the Isle of Guernsey, have raised their families for generations. You'll pass through historic Cape Bear, whose lighthouse picked up the first distress signal from the *Titanic*; then back to the pavement and around Beach Point. By now you will probably have noticed the lovely orderliness of local fishing villages and you'll have watched dozens of Cape Island fishing boats rumble in and out of the harbour mouth. If you follow Route 18 to its end you'll visit two more working fishing villages, Murray Harbour and Murray River. The entire area is a delight for the nature-lover, with its magnificent variety of birds and animals. You may decide to join a charter or a seal-watching expedition, or perhaps just explore the exquisite river systems or the Murray Islands.

Murray House

A visit to the Old General Store in Murray River, famous for its mural, quilts, linens and handicrafts, will take you back in time to a general store from the 1860s. Golfers may want to stop for a quick round at Eagle's View, Eastern PEI's newest course.

Rossignol Estate Winery

A turn onto Route 17 will take you along the coast, past numerous fishing harbours. Local waterways are popular with yachting enthusiasts from all over the Island, partly because of their many beautiful, secluded inlets and coves. The Panmure Island Cultural Grounds are open for walking and admiring their natural beauty anytime, but in the third week of August you can join 4,000 people in a celebration of Mi'kmaq culture, which even includes tasting some moose, deer or frybread. You can visit Panmure Island lighthouse and the wonderful beach. There is a campground located here and a very good B&B. Route 17 continues through scenic countryside and finally follows the Montague River up to Montague. The signs outside Montague welcome visitors to "Montague the Beautiful." There's lots of fast food, but the kids will particularly love the Gillis' Drive-In Restaurant. It's a local institution, a real drive-in restaurant.

Montague boasts the Garden of the Gulf Museum, as well as good shopping, an excellent health food store, an indoor pool and fitness centre and a small marina. The Montague River flows from its source several miles above town, down toward Georgetown and into Cardigan Bay. Seal-watching boat tours leave from Montague Bridge or you can take a cruise and munch on locally grown blue mussels.

Panmure Island

Garden of the Gulf Museum, Montague

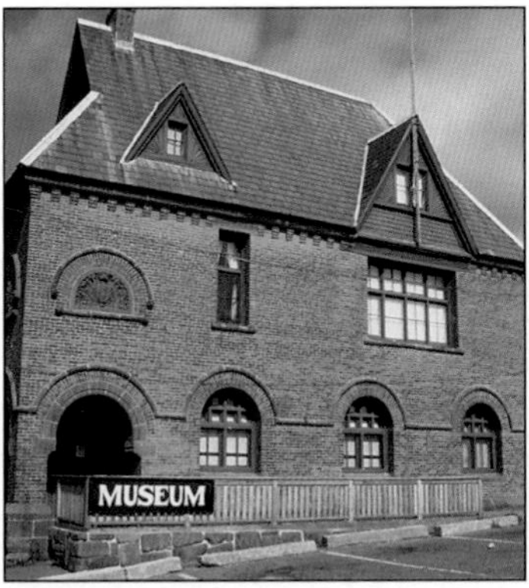

There's enough to do in the area to warrant a few days' stay. A new park, Roma at Three Rivers, is an historic site commemorating a 1700s French settlement, Victorian shipbuilding and the birthplace of Father of Confederation A. A. Macdonald. There are archaeological displays, nature trails, picnic facilities, beach and river access, and occasional re-enactments.

It's not a long drive to the Brudenell Provincial Park, where Brudenell and Dundarave golf courses are world-class. The Rodd Brudenell River Resort has excellent accommodations, several good restaurants and even a spa. Or, you may opt for one of the many bed-and-breakfasts in the area. They are run by friendly people who know the area intimately. Brenda and Edgar Dewar's comfortable 1868 farmhouse, Roseneath, just off Route 4 (take Dewar's Road on the right just before Pooles Corner), is one of the most interesting and relaxing bits of real estate around. Edgar's family operated a mill there for generations and the house is chock full of art and artifacts from his and Brenda's years in the Near and Far East. Outside, it's paradise for birders or trout fishers who follow the walking trail along the Brudenell River to where it joins the Confederation Trail. Bordering the trail and the golf course there's high-end cottage accommodation at Brudenell Fairway Chalets. Or, for camping enthusiasts, the Brudenell River Campground is right beside the golf course; it features a marina, canoeing,

Historic Roma site at Three Rivers

horseback riding, campfires and not too many bugs.

Continuing on Route 3 past the resort, you arrive in Georgetown, the capital of Kings County. Lately it's been prospering. The Irvings recently began operating the shipbuilding plant, rejuvenating something that's been a part of this town since its inception. Shipbuilding used to be what people here did for a living. At one time, it's been said, one could walk across the Georgetown harbour on the decks of wooden ships. Now it's a quiet little place, filled with friendly people, and it's an easy place to walk around.

Dundarave Golf Course

Rosenheath Bed and Breakfast

Cardigan River Heritage Centre

A block away from the harbour is Georgetown Inn, a refurbished 1840s heritage home, now a comfortable B&B. You can learn all about the history of the town and enjoy a tasty bit of Island seafood at Engine Number 6 Café and Interpretive Centre. Just down the street is the King's Playhouse, where you might catch a good concert. Behind the theatre is the A. A. Macdonald Memorial Gardens, honouring the Father of Confederation who was a long-time resident of the town.

Lobster lovers can go down to Georgetown Packers lobster pound on Water Street; it's the big red brick building on the large government wharf at the end. If asked, they'll show you some big lobsters or, even better, some weirdly coloured lobsters. If you ask me, lobster from southern Kings is the best in the Maritimes. It's easy to cook the lobsters yourself. You'll need a pot, a fire and some sea water or clean tap water laced with a fistful of pickling salt. Place the lobster in boiling water head first. When the water begins to boil again, cook for 12 minutes, then serve. The shells are packed tightly with tender, sweet meat. Enjoy the pleasure of digging it out with your fingers and getting messy.

The Wharf at Cardigan

The next stop on the drive will be Cardigan. One of many picturesque little villages that dot the shoreline of Prince Edward Island, this is a cohesive community where group spirit runs high. A new marina and interpretive centre, a five-kilometre section of the Confederation Trail through the village, a community centre, and a craft shop and tea room in the former Cardigan railway station are accomplishments of which residents are rightfully proud. You'll also find a lobster supper and a magnificent Tudor mansion, now the five-star Cardigan River Inn, on the Cardigan River.

Route 311 takes you around the Launching Peninsula. While Island woodlands are experiencing a period of intensive harvesting, this area has retained more of its woodlands than have other parts of the province. As you enter Launching, you can catch a glimpse of heavily wooded Boughton Island to your right. This is one of many islands off the coast of Prince Edward Island that provide nesting places for colonies of terns, cormorants and blue herons. A new way to explore the natural environment is by boat on the 16-kilometre Boughton River Water Trail from Bridgetown to the Annandale wharf.

Driving down into Bridgetown, you will notice that the forests have given way to farm fields. In the adjoining community of Dundas, the annual Dundas Plowing Match has been celebrated for over 100 years.

The Fortune Peninsula has several secluded beaches that can be reached from side roads leading off Route 311. Local residents would be happy to provide directions. The

area also has many interesting craft shops and accommodations. Of particular interest is The Inn at Spry Point, which also houses a distinctive restaurant. Nature trails and the local beach add to the allure of this charming hideaway.

A stroll through the Sailor's Hope Bog in Howe Bay will take you through an area rich in flora such as the insect-eating sundew, pitcher plants and calapogan orchids. This area is also rich in human history, from the early 18th century when Acadians built dykes around the salt marshes to harvest the rich marsh hay, to the desperate young tenant farmer who killed a land agent in 1819, to the Cooper Rebellion of the early 1830s, in which William Cooper of Sailor's Hope organized tenant farmers to rise up against their absentee landlords.

Dundas Plowing Match and Fair

During the 1920s, a thespian colony flourished in Bay Fortune, and renowned American playwright Elmer Harris's dramatic work *Johnny Belinda* had its roots in this community. Harris's original home later became the home of Colleen Dewhurst (the well-known actress who played Marilla in the motion picture *Anne of Green Gables*). Today, the home has been restored and houses an elegant inn and restaurant. The Inn at Bay Fortune certainly offers one of the Island's premier culinary experiences.

Stop for a few moments at the Rollo Bay scenic lookout and enjoy a long view of the bay with its salt marshes and the potato fields in the foreground. A short distance down the road is the home of the Rollo Bay Fiddle Festival, an important event for ardent fiddlers across the Maritimes.

Souris is the economic hub of the easterly point of the province, with retail stores, restaurants and public services. Here a Victorian heritage home, the four-star Matthew House Inn, offers charming accommodations. Souris is also the terminus of the passenger ferry to the Îles-de-la-Madeleine or Magdalen Islands. The town's rather unusual name originated with several plagues of mice that beset the early 18th-century settlers of the area. Sailing into the harbour filled with floating dead mice, a group of French fishers dubbed it Havre à la Souris, or Mouse Harbour, which was eventually shortened to Souris.

For a change of pace, a drive down the Scenic Heritage Road on Route 303 can take you back a century. Originally used by farmers heading out to their fields, Scenic Heritage Roads are specially designated provincial clay roads, bordered by lush vegetation that often forms a leafy canopy overhead. If you follow this with a walk along the trails of the adjacent Townshend Woodlot, you will slip into a peaceful world of unspoiled natural beauty.

Some of the most spectacular beaches in the Maritimes are to be found east of Souris. Magnificent pearly white beaches stretch endlessly, bordered by delicate marram grass dunes. It is truly memorable to watch the sun rise as you walk along the sand and listen to the music of the waves, or spend a romantic evening admiring the sunset to the cacophony of shore birds. Nature just does not get more exotic than this. Basin Head and Red Point, both situated within provincial parks, are the most popular beaches, while Little Harbour, Bothwell and South Lake are more secluded.

The South Side, as this area is called by residents, is simply awash with wildflowers between early spring and late autumn. Dandelions, marsh marigolds, ox-eye daisies, devil's paintbrushes, Queen Anne's lace, clover, purple loosestrife, fireweed and tansy ragwort are some of the most common. But none is more beautiful and plentiful than the common lupine.

The Inn at Bay Fortune

The Fisheries Museum at Basin Head will guide you through all the arcane aspects of the fishery as it is practised on PEI. The boardwalk boasts some charming craft and gift shops. While at Basin Head, be sure to walk on the beach and listen to the "singing sands" — a phenomenon caused by high silica content in the sand and ages of polishing by heavy surf.

The little white church in South Lake, on the hill to your left, has long been called "The Fisherman's Church" because of the beacon it provides for home-bound fishermen. The nearby Elmira Railway Museum chronicles the history of railroading on the Island. One of the largest model railway collections in Canada, along with a miniature railway that offers rides around a beautiful woodland track, are sure to excite model railway buffs and youngsters alike. Elmira is also the easternmost entry point

Basin Head Fisheries Museum

of the Confederation Trail. The rolling landscape of this area, with its prevalent ocean vistas and patchwork fields, makes this a singularly attractive drive. On a clear day, if you look to the horizon on your right, you can easily see Cape Breton.

East Point is land's end. You can climb to the top of the lighthouse and witness the meeting of the waters as the Gulf of St. Lawrence tides collide with those of the Northumberland Strait. If heights don't appeal to you the craft shop might, and if you're lucky one of the guides may tell you a salty yarn or two.

East Point Lighthouse

Once you have rounded the Point you are on the North Side. Campbell's Cove, a few kilometres down the road, is believed to be the jut of land that Jacques Cartier first spied when he spoke those memorable words, "the fairest land 'tis possible to see."

The landscape on the North Side is vastly different from that of the South Side. Here you see more woodland and a rugged coast. The white marram grass-covered dunes are interspersed with red sandstone cliffs. The trees speak of cruel north winds — a very different kind of beauty.

In the Rock Barra-Hermanville area you will notice several hundred acres of blueberry barrens. Sometimes in August the fields are literally tinged with blue. Later, in the fall, the plants turn bright red, presenting a feast for the eye. In recent years, blueberries have consistently increased in value as an agricultural crop on PEI. The four-star Johnson Shore Inn, which offers magnificent ocean vistas from every one of its rooms, is located in this community.

The North Side beaches are smaller than their South Side counterparts. But, for this very reason, they are less known and therefore offer greater privacy. They also have white-sand beaches, although many have captivating red sandstone cliffs rising behind them. North Lake, Campbell's Cove, Johnston's, Bear River, Naufrage, Cow River and Cable Head are the most accessible of these beaches.

A typical rural lobster supper is served in the St. Margaret's Church hall. And a few kilometres to the west, there is not a more picture-perfect fishing harbour than Naufrage, with its unique hump bridge.

Just down the road at Monticello is a re-created, authentic one-room schoolhouse, which offers up a Scottish ceilidh every summer Sunday night.

A right turn at the large white church on the hill in the village of St. Peters will take you to the Greenwich dunes, an adjunct to the Prince Edward Island National Park. This spectacular dune system is the jewel of the region. Although they have existed for thousands of years, the

East Point

Naufrage Harbour

dunes are nevertheless extremely fragile, being susceptible to the prevailing ocean winds that cause them to change shape and migrate. The immense parabolic crater-like dunes, anchored by coarse marram grass, along with adjacent ponds, wetlands, forests and attendant rare plant species, form this unique ecosystem now under the protection of Parks Canada.

Greenwich is also the guardian of an ancient cultural history legacy, as the site of confirmed human habitation dating back 10,000 years. Since receiving National Park status in 1998, the site has been developed to include a state-of-the-art interpretation centre, with many static exhibits and a delightful multimedia presentation entitled "Wind,

Church Near St. Peters

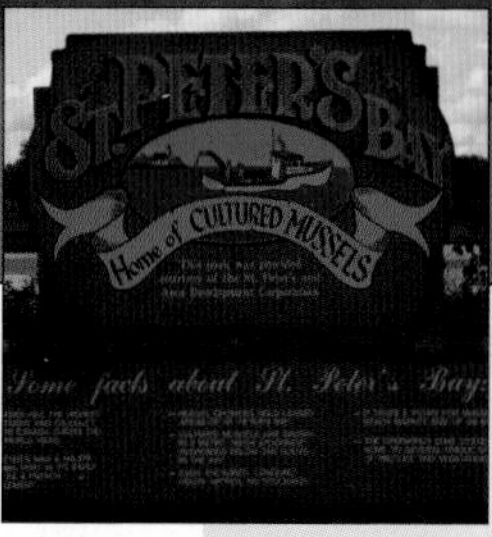

St. Peters

Sea and Sand — the Story of Greenwich." Trails, including a floating boardwalk over a pond teeming with plant and animal life, lead through the various features of the site. A commitment to maintaining the integrity of the dunes has necessitated certain ultra-sensitive areas being closed to public access, while sustainable energy and waste systems have been installed to service the site. There are only a handful of dune systems like Greenwich on the planet and given its accessibility, this one is well worth a visit.

En route to Greenwich you will encounter the Inn at St. Peters, offering lovely four-star accommodations and fine dining. You may wish to stop for a few minutes at the beautiful wayside park in the little village of St. Peters and visit the Estuary Interpretive Centre and Shops. Or take in a demonstration of pewter casting at the St. Peters Bay Craft and Giftware centre and stop for a bite at the popular Rick's Fish & Chips, which serves fresh catch from local waters and hand-cut PEI fries. If you happen by in the evening, enjoy some community theatre in the 160-year-old Courthouse Theatre, which served as a courthouse until the 1960s. In August, this community celebrates its ever-popular Blueberry Festival.

The next sizeable community is Morell. The short jaunt to Red Head Harbour is recommended if you are in the market for fresh fish, lobster or the Island's most luscious

Hillsborough River Eco-Centre

Island blue mussels. Not far from Morell is the challenging Links at Crowbush Cove, the Island's premier 4 1/2-star golf course, and the adjacent Rodd Crowbush Resort, the Island's only five-star resort.

At St. Andrews is the historic St. Andrews Chapel. Built in 1803, it was moved to Charlottetown in 1864, where it was used for over a century. Virtually destroyed by fire in 1987, the gutted structure was moved back to its original site in the late 1980s to be reconstructed and put back in use.

In the village of Mount Stewart, the Hillsborough River Eco-Centre interprets the history of PEI's only National Heritage River. This rich and diverse river system provides habitat for salmon, trout, striped bass and 1/3 of the Island's oyster harvest. Mink, red foxes, bald eagles and ospreys live in the system's salt marshes. Across the road, at the rustic Trailside Inn, Café and Adventures, you can rent bikes for riding the adjacent Confederation Trail and canoes for paddling the river. When you return your rentals at day's end, stay for dinner and enjoy some of the Maritimes' most popular entertainers.

Mount Stewart is the end (or the beginning) of Points East Coastal Drive. Hwy 2 continues on to Charlottetown where you might stop for a bit or carry on westward to continue your exploration of Prince Edward Island.

Canoeing at Brudenell River

Listings: Contents

★ denotes a location recognized by the publisher for its high quality.

Getting There

By Bridge

There used to be only one way of bringing a car to Prince Edward Island, and that was by ferry. The Confederation Bridge, which opened on June 1, 1997, changed all that. Now it's an easy 10-minute drive across a 13-kilometre bridge that, unless you're in a truck or a van, seems for all intents and purposes a highway with high concrete sides. For foot passengers and cyclists, Strait Crossing offers a complimentary shuttle service from either side (accessed from the Cape Jouriman Nature Centre in New Brunswick or at Gateway Village in Borden-Carleton, Prince Edward Island). Maximum wait time is two hours.

A return trip on the Confederation Bridge (payable when you leave the Island) costs $17 for a motorcycle, $42.50 for a car with two axles and $7.25 for each additional axle, payable by cash, credit card or debit card. Foot passengers pay $4 and cyclists $8. The toll booth is on the Prince Edward Island side of the Strait.

The bridge is sometimes closed to tall vehicles during high winds. For bridge conditions, call 888-437-6565, visit www.confederationbridge.com, or tune into the bridge's radio station at 93.9 FM.

By Sea

Between May and December, Northumberland Ferries sail several times a day between Caribou, Nova Scotia, and Wood Islands, Prince Edward Island. Reservations are not required. Larger ferries have reduced wait times at the terminals in recent years. The trip takes an hour and 15 minutes, during which time you can stroll the decks, have a meal or light refreshments or relax with a book in the lounge. The cost is $61 per car with any number of passengers, payable when you leave the Island. Campers 30–40 ft long must pay $82, and it's $98 for campers longer than 40 ft. Motorcycle fare is $38 and foot passengers pay $15 for adults, $13 for seniors; children 12 and under are free. For a detailed schedule, call 888-249-7245, or check www.nfl-bay.com.

By Bus

SMT (Eastern) Ltd. buses leave Charlottetown and other Island locations for the mainland twice daily, connecting in Moncton with coaches bound for major Canadian destinations. For information and schedules, call 800-567-5151. The SMT bus station in Charlottetown is located at 156 Belvedere Ave.; telephone 902-628-6432. SMT buses also connect with VIA Rail trains and the airport in Moncton; for information and reservations call 888-VIA RAIL (842-7245). Several shuttle services offer van transportation between PEI and Halifax/Dartmouth, NS: Express Shuttle (877-877-1771, www.peishuttle.com); Advanced Shuttle Service (877-886-3322); NS-PEI Go Shuttle (877-886-3322). Square One Shuttle services PEI, New Brunswick and Nova Scotia (877-675-3830).

By Air

Charlottetown is a 25-minute flight from Halifax, with connections to major cities in Canada and the U.S. Air Canada and Air Canada Jazz (888-247-2262; www.aircanada.com) offer direct flights from Toronto, Ottawa and Montreal. Northwest Airlines now offers direct daily service from Detroit to Charlottetown with connections from U.S. cities as well as Asia. For flight information, check their website, www.nwa.com. WestJet, Delta and Sunwing also offer flights to Charlottetown.

The airport is located about a ten-minute drive from downtown Charlottetown. Taxi service is available, with fares around $11 per single passenger. Several car rental agencies have stands at the airport. For information on flights and services available at the Charlottetown Airport, check their website, www.flypei.com.

Travel Essentials

Money

American currency can be exchanged at any Prince Edward Island bank or credit union at the going rate. Units of currency are similar to those of the United States, except for the Canadian two-dollar ("Toonie") and one-dollar ("Loonie") coins.

Travellers' cheques and major credit cards are accepted throughout Prince Edward Island, although you may require cash in some rural areas. Cheques issued by Visa, American Express and Thomas Cook are widely recognized.

American visitors may also use bank or credit cards to make cash withdrawals from automated teller machines that are tied into international networks such as Cirrus, Interac and Plus. These can be found in the larger communities on the Island.

Passports

American citizens are required to carry proof of citizenship, such as a U.S. passport or a birth certificate, plus photo identification. Naturalized U.S. citizens should carry a naturalization certificate, plus photo identification. Permanent U.S. residents who are not citizens are advised to bring their Alien Registration Card (Green Card) or a valid 1551 stamp in their passport. Note that other documents such as a driver's licence or voter registration card will not be accepted as proof of U.S. citizenship. Visas are not required for U.S. tourists entering Canada from the U.S. for stays up to 6 months.

Citizens of most other countries must bring a valid passport. Some may be required to obtain a visitor's visa. For details, please consult the Canadian embassy or consulate serving your home country. Visit www.cic.gc.ca for more information.

Customs

Arriving

Visitors to Canada may bring certain duty-free items into the country as part of their personal baggage. These must be declared to Customs upon arrival in Nova Scotia or New Brunswick, and may include up to 200 cigarettes, 50 cigars, and 200 grams of tobacco. Visitors are also permitted 1.14 litres of liquor, 1.5 litres of wine or 8.5 litres (24 x 341-ml cans or bottles) of beer.

Gift items — excluding tobacco and alcohol products — for Canadian residents that do not exceed $60 are also duty-free. Packages should be marked "gift" and the value indicated.

Boats, trailers, sporting equipment, cameras, and similar big-ticket items may enter Canada free of duty. However, Canada Customs may require a refundable deposit to ensure that these goods are not sold for profit. It might be better to register such items with customs officials in your own country, so that when you re-enter you have evidence that they were not bought in Canada.

Some items are strictly controlled in Canada. Firearms are prohibited, with the exception of rifles and shotguns for hunting purposes. Plant material will be examined at the border. Veterinary certificates are required for all pets.

For further information on Canadian Customs regulations call 800-668-4748 (inside Canada), 902-432-5608 (outside Canada) or visit the website at www.cbsa-asfc.gc.ca/travel/visitors-e.

Departing

Visitors from the U.S. who have been out of the country for a minimum of 48 hours may take back goods to the value of U.S. $400 without paying duty (provided no part of the exemption has been used within the previous 30 days). Family members may pool their exemptions.

There are restrictions on alcohol and tobacco products, among others. Visitors may bring back one litre of alcohol free of duty and up to 200 cigarettes and 100 non-Cuban cigars.

To find out more about U.S. customs regulations and what other restrictions and exemptions apply, contact your local Customs office or the U.S. Customs Service, PO Box 7407, Washington, D.C., 20044; 202-927-2095. Ask for a copy of *Know Before You Go*.

Travellers from countries other than the U.S. should check on customs regulations before leaving home.

Taxes

There is a 5% federal tax (GST) on almost all goods and services sold in Canada (basic grocery goods are excepted). Prince Edward Island has an additional 10% provincial sales tax on purchased goods and some services. Short-term accommodations and restaurant meals are subject to this tax. Accommodations may also be subject to a 2% marketing levy. Articles of clothing and shoes are exempt, as are most basic grocery items. The PST is applied on top of the GST.

Guides

The *Prince Edward Island Visitors Guide* contains excellent accommodation, restaurant and attractions listings. To obtain a copy, write to Visitor Services, PO Box 940, Charlottetown, PE, Canada, C1A 7M5, or, in North America, call toll-free 888-734-7529; outside North America, call 902-368-4444 or fax 902-368-4438. The *Guide* is also accessible on the Internet at www.peiplay.com and available at visitor information centres throughout Prince Edward Island.

For booking accommodations, an online reservation system offers real-time vacancy information. The website is www.peiplay.com/bookonline.

For further information, e-mail Tourism PEI at peiplay@gov.pe.ca.

Getting Acquainted

Time Zone

Prince Edward Island falls within the Atlantic Time Zone, which is one hour later than the Eastern Time Zone. Daylight Saving Time, when the clocks are advanced one hour, is in effect from early April until early November.

Climate

Summers on Prince Edward Island are hot, but rarely humid. The average daytime temperature is 22°C (72°F). A T-shirt should be comfortable during the day, with a light sweater or jacket for evening. Bring your bathing suit: the water here is as warm as any north of the Carolinas, thanks to our sheltered location in the Gulf of St. Lawrence. The fall is an especially beautiful time on Prince Edward Island, with warm clear days and gorgeous fall colours. There is lots of snow in the wintertime, which makes for great downhill and cross-country skiing, snowmobiling and snowshoeing. Daytime high temperatures in winter are usually in the range of -8° to 2°C (18–36°F).

Average daily maximum temperatures for Charlottetown are:

Jan.	-3.4°C	25.9°F
Feb.	-3.6°C	25.5°F
Mar.	0.6°C	33.1°F
Apr.	6.3°C	43.3°F
May	13.8°C	56.8°F
June	19.6°C	66.9°F
July	23.1°C	73.6°F
Aug.	22.5°C	72.5°F
Sept.	17.8°C	64.0°F
Oct.	12.1°C	53.8°F
Nov.	5.9°C	42.6°F
Dec.	-0.3°C	31.5°F

Metric System

Prince Edward Island, like the rest of Canada, uses the metric system of weights and measures. Some useful conversions are:

1 kilometre = 0.62 miles
100 kph = 62 mph
4 litres = 1 U.S. gallon
1 metre = 3.28 feet
1 centimetre = 0.39 inches
1 kilogram = 2.2 pounds
20° Celsius = 68° Fahrenheit

To convert degrees Celsius to Fahrenheit, multiply by 2 and add 30 (accurate within 2 degrees).

Staying Healthy

If you are not a Canadian citizen, you should obtain or extend health insurance coverage before leaving home. Only prescriptions written by Prince Edward Island doctors can be filled here, so bring an adequate supply of medication. Hospitals are located in Alberton, O'Leary, Summerside, Charlottetown, Montague and Souris. Clinics can be found in Tignish, O'Leary, Parkdale, Tyne Valley, Summerside, Bedeque, Kensington, Cornwall, Crapaud, Hunter River, Lennox Island, Charlottetown, Montague, Sherwood, Souris and Wellington.

For all emergency services, dial 911.

Getting Around

By Bus

Scheduled public transportation on PEI is limited: visitors headed off the beaten path must make their own arrangements. SMT offers daily service connecting Charlottetown and Borden-Carleton via Kensington and Summerside. From Charlottetown to Summerside costs about $13. The bus leaves Charlottetown daily at 7:45 a.m. and 2 pm and Borden-Carleton at 11:15 a.m. and 3:10 pm. On Friday and Sunday, a second bus leaves Charlottetown at 5:15 pm, arriving at Borden-Carleton at 6:35 pm. In the peak season, another run later in the day is usually added. Schedules are subject to change, so call 800-567-5151 for current information, or check their website, www.smtbus.com.

A transit bus operates in Charlottetown. For information, call 902-566-9962 or visit www.peisland.com/triustours.

Shuttle Service

East Connection offers year-round passenger shuttle service from Charlottetown to Morell, St. Peters, Souris, Montague and Wood Islands. Island-wide tours are also available through this service. For information, call 902-892-6760.

A beach shuttle service (902-566-3243) runs between Charlottetown and Cavendish Beach in the summer. Several companies offer guided sightseeing tours by bus. Abegweit Tours (902-894-9966; www.abegweittours.ca) offers seven daily one-hour tours of Charlottetown, as well as tours of the north and south shores in a double-decker bus. Trius Tours (902-566-5664; www.peisland.com/triustours) Prince Edward Tours (877-286-6532; www.princeedwardtours.com), and Capture the Spirit of Prince Edward Island (866-836-4200; www.capturepei.com) are among the companies that provide guided tours and will arrange custom tours for groups and individuals.

By Car

The Prince Edward Island Visitors' Map is available at visitor information centres throughout the province. Highways are generally well maintained. Speed limits are as follows: 90 kilometres per hour along the main highways, 80 kph along secondary roads and 50 kph in cities and towns. On Prince Edward Island, seat belt use is compulsory for driver and passengers.

A valid U.S. driver's license is also valid in Prince Edward Island. Evidence of the car's registration is required (a car rental contract will serve). U.S. motorists may obtain a Non-Resident Inter-Province Motor Vehicle Liability Insurance Card through their own insurance companies as evidence of financial responsibility within Canada.

Car Rentals

All major car rental agencies are represented in Prince Edward Island.
Avis: 800-437-0358; www.avis.com
Budget: 800-314-5885; www.budget.com
Discount: 888-820-7378; www.discountcar.com
Enterprise: 888-261-7331; www.entertprise.com
Hertz: 800-263-0600; www.hertz.ca
National Car Rental: 800-227-7368; www.nationalcar.ca
Rent A Wreck: 566-9955; www.rentawreck.ca
Thrifty: 800-892-3600; www.thrifty.com
Consult the Yellow Pages of the Prince Edward Island telephone directory under Automobile Renting for local numbers and agencies.

Lodging

For a complete list of accommodations in the province, consult the *Prince Edward Island Visitors Guide*. For visitors who are interested in B&B-style accommodation, a pamphlet called "PEI Bed and Breakfasts and Country Inns" is a good source of information. Write to PO Box 2551, Charlottetown, PE, C1A 8C2.

There are several hostels in Prince Edward Island offering good economical accommodation for backpackers, cyclists and budget-conscious travellers. Check www.hostels.com/en/ca.pe.html for rates, locations and availability.

The following list of accommodations includes those already mentioned in this book and other selected locations. Immediately following the name of each establishment is an abbreviation indicating whether it is an inn (I), bed and breakfast (B&B), hotel/motel (H/M), resort (R), cottage (C) or hospitality home (HH). For detailed information on these categories, see the Visitors Guide.

Approximate prices are indicated, based on the average cost at time of publication, for two persons staying in a double room (excluding taxes): $ = under $100; $$ = $100–150; $$$ =

more than $150.

The area code for all local phone numbers is 902.

North Cape

- Art Gallery Bed & Breakfast (B&B), 470 MacMurdo Rd., North Bedeque; 902-887-2683; www.bbcanada.com/art gallery. Century home with modern amenities, wireless Internet and ensuite baths. Breakfast included. Open year-round. $/$$
- Blue Shank Inn (B&B), Rte. 107/Blue Shank Road, Wilmot; 866-436-1171; www.blueshankinn.com. Right outside Summerside past the Red Bridge with view of Wilmot River. Breakfast included. Open May–Oct. $$
- Causeway Bay Linkletter Inn and Convention Centre (H/M), 311 Market St., Summerside; 800-565-7829; www.causewaybayhotels.ca. Convention facilities, family restaurant, licensed lounge. Indoor pool, outdoor patio. Small pets allowed. Inn has elevator, amenities for physically challenged. Open year-round. $/$$
- The Doctor's Inn (B&B), Rte. 167, Tyne Valley; 902-831-3057; www.peisland.com/doctorsinn. Thirty km west of Summerside. Beautiful gardens, organic vegetables. Breakfast included; dinner by reservation. Open year-round. $
- Historic Maplethorpe Bed & Breakfast (B&B); 902-887-2909; 866-770-2909; historicmaplethorpe.com. Central location, single rooms and weekly vacation apartment. Children welcome. Breakfast included. Open year-round. $$
- Loyalist Lakeview Resort (H/M), 195 Harbour Dr., Summerside; 877-355-3500; www.lakeviewhotels.com. Traditional inn offering all the amenities of an urban hotel, overlooking the waterfront. Licensed dining room and lounge, conference facilities. Two rooms for physically challenged, craft shop, indoor pool, sauna, bike rental, outside patio. Open year-round. $$/$$$
- Northport Pier Inn (I), Alberton; 866-887-4520; www.northportpier.ca. Luxury oceanfront inn located directly on the beach. Two rooms available with wheelchair-accessible showers. On-premise restaurant, shops, marina, day adventure centre and Sea Rescue Interpretive Centre. Open May–Oct. $$$
- Quality Inn — Garden of the Gulf (H/M), 618 Water St. East (Rte. 11), Summerside; 800-265-5551; www.qualityinnpei.com. Off Rte. 1A. Waterfront property, close to downtown. Indoor and outdoor pools, free 9-hole golf, shuffleboard, bicycling, gift shop, coffee shop, Brothers Two Restaurant and Dinner Theatre. Open year-round. $$/$$$
- Rodd Mill River Resort (R), Woodstock, O'Leary; 800-565-7633; www.roddvacations.com. Rte. 2, 57 km west of Summerside. Three-floor hotel resort. Lounge, conference facilities, licensed dining room. Gift shop, indoor swimming pool, sauna, whirlpool, waterslide, two squash courts, exercise room, 18-hole championship golf course, pro shop, tennis courts, canoeing, windsurfing, bicycling. Open Jan.–Oct. $$/$$$
- Silver Fox Inn (HH), 61 Granville St., Summerside; 800-565-4033; www.silverfoxinn.net. Historic house built in 1892. Antiques, claw-foot tubs, antique shop. Tree-top balcony, water gardens, afternoon tea. Buffet breakfast included. Lunch, afternoon tea and dinner available. Open year-round. $$
- Tignish Heritage Inn and Gardens (B&B), Tignish; 877-882-2491; www.tignish.com/inn. Elegantly restored convent. Guests welcome to use kitchen, dining area, laundry room. Children under six free. Continental breakfast included. Open mid-May – mid-Oct. $/$$
- West Point Lighthouse Inn, Restaurant & Museum (I), Rte. 14; 800-764-6854; www.westpointlighthouse.com. Canada's first inn in a functioning lighthouse. Enjoy the sea at your doorstep, supervised swimming, nature trails, fishing, biking. Museum, licensed dining room, patio, two rooms with whirlpool tub. Open mid-May–mid-Oct. $$

Anne's Land

- Barachois Inn (HH), 2193 Church Rd., Rustico; 902-963-2194. www.barachoisinn.com. On Rte. 243, six km from PEI National Park; 17 km from Charlottetown. Heritage Victorian house, built 1870; works of art, whirlpools, Victorian tubs, four suites with kitchenettes and fireplaces. Meeting rooms, sauna, exercise room. View of Rustico Bay. No pets or smoking please. Bilingual. Full breakfast included. Open year-round. $$$
- ★ Dalvay-by-the-Sea Inn (I; C), Grand Tracadie; 888-366-2955; www.dalvaybythesea.com. On Rte. 6 in PEI National Park. Victorian inn (c. 1895). Magnificent endless beach. National Historic Site. Fine dining, breakfast and dinner included. Tennis court, bike rentals, croquet, lawn bowling, golf practice range, lake, canoes, 2-hole fairway, children's recreational area, nature trails. Open mid-June to Sept. $$$
- My Mother's Country Inn (B&B; C), New Glasgow; 800-278-2071; www.mymotherscountryinn.com. Restored heritage home (c. 1860) on Rte. 13. Rooms with whirlpool tubs, breakfast. Housekeeping cottages and deluxe executive cottage. Open June–Sept. $$/$$$
- ★ Shaw's Hotel and Cottages (I; C), Brackley Beach; 902-672-2022; www.shawshotel.ca. On Rte. 15. Oldest family-operated inn and resort in Canada. Located on a 75-acre peninsula overlooking Brackley Bay. Antique-furnished guest rooms, cottages, luxury chalets. Walking distance to Brackley Beach in the Prince Edward Island National Park. Many recreational activities. Meals included. Children's programs Tues, Fri and Sun. Dine alone while children supervised. Open May–Oct; chalets open year-round. $$$
- Shining Waters Country Inn and Cottages (B&B; C), Cavendish; 877-963-2251; www.shiningwatersresort.com. Historic inn overlooking ocean. Luxury suites and cottages with air conditioning, fireplaces and whirlpool tubs. Playgrounds, two heated pools and exercise room. On-site restaurant and conference centre. No pets, please. Open May–Oct. $$/$$$
- Stanhope Bay and Beach Resort, 3445 Bayshore Road, Stanhope; 866-672-2701; www.stanhopebeachresort.com. Waterfront resort within walking distance to beaches, golf. Heated pool, tennis court and acres of land. Open mid-May to Oct. $$
- Stanley Bridge Country Resort (H/M; I; C), Stanley Bridge; 800-361-2882; www.stanleybridgeresort.com. Rte. 6. Country inn, housekeeping cottages. Convention facilities, heated pool, exercise room, playground, dinner theatre, Stanley Bridge Studios on-site. No pets, please. Open May–Oct. $$/$$$

Charlotte's Shore

- The Delta Prince Edward (H/M), 18 Queen St., Charlottetown; 866-894-1203; www.deltaprinceedward.pe.ca. Located in the old city centre, close to shopping, offices, attractions and theatre. Saunas, jacuzzis, indoor pool, spa, restaurants, lounge. Food and beverages at Fox Meadow Golf and Country Club billable to your room. Ballroom plus meeting rooms. Open year-round. $$$
- Duchess of Kent Inn (B&B), 218 Kent St., Charlottetown; 800-665-5826; www.duchessofkentinn.ca. Heritage home (c. 1875) in historic downtown. No pets or smoking. Separate fully equipped kitchen, living room. "Turret" suites with antiques available. Breakfast extra. Open year-round. $$
- The Dundee Arms (I; H/M), 200 Pownal St., Charlottetown; 877-638-6333; www.dundeearms.com. Picturesque inn located in heart of Charlottetown. Furnished in period decor and antiques. Dining room and lounge. Outdoor deck. Open year-round. $$/$$$
- Elmwood Heritage Inn (B&B), 121 North River Rd., Charlottetown; 877-933-3310; www.elmwoodinn.pe.ca. W. C. Harris-designed house (c. 1889); antiques, quilts, artwork, fireplaces, whirlpool and Victorian tubs. Bicycles. Candlelit breakfasts, gourmet entrees. Open year-round. $$$
- Fairholm National Historic Inn (B&B), 230 Prince St.,

Charlottetown; 888-573-5022; www.fairholm.pe.ca. Historic splendour and modern amenities in an elegant five-star breakfast inn close to old-town attractions. Breakfast included. Open year-round. $$$

- Fitzroy Hall (HH), 45 Fitzroy St., Charlottetown; 866-627-9766; www.fitzroyhall.com. Stately Victorian mansion built in 1872. Recently restored, antique furnishings. Relax by the fireplace or in the garden. No smoking or pets. Full breakfast included. Open year-round. $$/$$$
- The Great George (I), 58 Great George St., Charlottetown; 800-361-1118; www.thegreatgeorge.com. Completely restored buildings. Suites, flats, stylishly appointed with antiques, fireplaces; jacuzzi and claw-foot tubs available. Breakfast included. Open year-round. $$$
- Hillhurst Inn (B&B), 181 Fitzroy St., Charlottetown; 877-994-8004; www.hillhurst.com. Heritage home (c. 1897) two blocks from city centre. Elegant setting, period furnishings, Island art. Two whirlpools. Wireless high-speed internet. No smoking. Breakfast included. Open May–Nov. $$/$$$
- Orient Hotel (B&B), 34 Main St., Victoria-by-the-Sea; 800-565-6743; www.theorienthotel.com. Heritage inn (c. 1900). Located in a picturesque seaside village with views of countryside and shore. Smoke-free. Dinner/theatre packages available. Breakfast included. Open May 15–Oct 15. $/$$
- Rodd Charlottetown (H/M), 75 Kent St., Charlottetown; 800-565-7633; www.roddvacations.com. Historic Canadian National Railways hotel. Indoor pool, whirlpool, sauna, licensed dining room, pub and eatery. Dinner theatre nightly in summer. Golf and theatre vacation packages available. Open year-round. $$$
- The Shipwright Inn (HH), 51 Fitzroy St., Charlottetown; 888-306-9966; www.shipwrightinn.com. Elegant 1860s heritage home, lovingly restored in nautical theme, fireplaces, antiques, books, art. Secluded garden, balconies, whirlpool. Business centre with computer, fax, wireless LAN. No smoking. Memorable breakfast and afternoon tea. Open year-round. $$$
- Victoria Village Inn & Restaurant (B&B), Victoria-by-the-Sea; 658-2483; www.victoriavillageinn.com. Victorian sea captain's home next to Victoria Playhouse. Classically trained chef/owner serves innovative cuisine. No smoking. Full breakfast included. Open year-round. $/$$

Points East Coastal Drive

- Brudenell Chalets (C), Roseneath; 866-652-2900; www.brudenellchalets.com. Fully-equipped, three-bedroom chalets with pool, outdoor fireplaces, screened verandahs; near golf courses. Open year-round. $$$
- Cardigan River Inn (B&B), 57 Owen's Wharf Road, Cardigan; 800-425-9577. Private whirlpool bath, cable tv/vcr, air conditioning, telephone, antiques and three rooms have a wood burning fireplace for that special romantic evening. Open mid-June-mid-Oct. $$/$$$
- Chateau Bayfield (B&B), Bayfield; 888-611-3908; www.chateaubayfield.com. Master Bedroom suite with double spa, full bath and private deck. Crow's Nest Sleeping Loft with a Queen futon and private deck. Open year-round; call for Oct.–May bookings.
- Georgetown Inn (B&B), 62 Richmond St., Georgetown; 877-641-2414; www.georgetownhistoricinn.com. Tastefully decorated Victorian B&B. Licensed dining room. Open year-round. $$
- The Inn at Bay Fortune (I; C), Kings Byway Dr. (Rte. 310), Bay Fortune; 888-687-3745; www.innatbayfortune.com. Overlooking Fortune Harbour. 18 rooms, 14 with fireplace. Relaxed, casual atmosphere. Full breakfast included. Restaurant features contemporary creative cuisine using seasonal produce; dinner only. Open late May to mid-Oct. $$$
- The Inn at St. Peters (I), 1668 Greenwich Rd., St. Peters Bay; 800-818-0925; www.innatstpeters.com. Luxury inn on waterfront, minutes

from golf, PEI National Park at Greenwich. Antique furnishings, fireplaces, waterfront dining, award-winning chef. Pets welcome. Full breakfast and gourmet dinner included. Open late May–early Oct. $$$

- Inn at Spry Point (I), off Spry Point Rd. (Rte. 310), Souris; 902-583-2400; www.innatsprypoint.com. Striking inn at the tip of a 110-acre peninsula. Walking trails, secluded beach, meeting facilities, dining. Near three world-class golf courses. Full breakfast included. Open mid-June to Oct. $$$
- The Johnson Shore Inn (B&B), 9984 Rte. 16, Hermanville; 877-510-9669. Country inn located on a high, rocky red cliff with spectacular ocean views from all rooms. Adult environment. Full breakfast included. Open May–Oct. $$/$$$
- Maplehurst Properties (B&B), Panmure Island; 902-838-3959; off-season 305-318-2957; www.maplehurstproperties.com. Secluded 25-acre beachfront estate. Decorated with artwork and period antiques. Beachfront cottage located on-site. Full gourmet breakfast. Open June–Oct. $$/$$$
- The Matthew House Inn (B&B), 15 Breakwater St., Souris; 902-687-3461; www.matthewhouseinn.com. Award-winning heritage inn, near Magdalen Islands ferry. Renowned for hospitality, ambience. Close to beaches, golf, fishing. No smoking. Continental or full breakfast included. Open late June–early Sept. $$
- Rodd Brudenell River Resort (R; C), Roseneath, near Montague; 800-565-7633; www.roddvacations.com. Hotel, riverside chalets, conference facilities, licensed dining room. Two 18-hole championship golf courses, golf academy, pro shop, tennis, canoeing, windsurfing, trail riding, lawn bowling, indoor and outdoor pool, sauna and fitness centre. Kids' program. Children under 16 free. Family, golf, romance packages available. Restrained pets allowed. Open mid-May–mid-Oct. $$/$$$
- Rodd Crowbush Golf & Beach Resort (R), Lakeside; 800-565-7633; www.roddvacations.com. Golf and ocean vistas, access to white sand beach. Indoor and outdoor pools, whirlpool, tennis. Restaurant, lounge and conference facilities. Internationally-acclaimed championship golf course, The Links at Crowbush Cove, on-site. Pets welcome. Children under 16 free with parents or guardians. Open mid-May–mid-Oct. $$$
- Rollo Bay Inn (H/M), Rollo Bay, Souris; 877-687-3550; www.peisland.com/rollobayinn. Elegant Georgian-style inn in peaceful country setting. Conference facilities. Walking distance to beach. No pets, please. French spoken. No charge for two children under 12 occupying same room as parents. Open year-round. $
- Roseneath Bed & Breakfast (B&B), Roseneath; 800-823-8933; www.rosebb.ca. Adjacent to Brudenell Golf Course, half-hour from Charlottetown. Peaceful country retreat, historic 1868 home with antiques, artwork, gardens, walking trails. Smoke-free, no pets. Cat in residence. Full breakfast. Open May–Oct. $$

Dining

When it comes to food, there's more to Prince Edward Island than just potatoes. Taking advantage of the freshest produce grown in this "Garden of the Gulf," as well as the bounty of the sea, restaurant owners cook up a wide variety of meals to suit the most discriminating diner. We're home to the Culinary Institute of Canada; what more could one expect?

Island cuisine benefits, too, from a variety of cultural influences, including Scottish, Dutch, Lebanese, Acadian, Indian and German. Check out our many restaurants and cafés. And drop by the Charlottetown Farmers' Market on Saturdays from 9 am to 2 pm., and taste for yourself!

North Cape

- Boat Shop Steak and Seafood Restaurant, Rte. 152, Northport Pier Inn, Northport; 902-853-4510; www.northportpier.ca. Located in an original boathouse on the waterfront. Fresh seafood and locally inspired cuisine. Outdoor patio. Licensed. Open June–Sept.
- Brothers Two, 618 Water St.,

Summerside, 902-436-9654; www.brotherstwo.ca. Seafood, steak, fresh lobster suppers, succulent mussels, chicken and skillets. Fresh desserts, handcrafted microbrew beer and kids' menu. Fully licensed. Dinner theatre in summer. Open May–Dec.
- Centre Expo/Festival Centre, Rte. 124, Abram-Village; 902-854-3300; www.regionevangeline.com. Lobster suppers Acadian-style. Open June–Sept.
- The Doctor's Inn, Tyne Valley, on Rte. 167; 902-831-3057; www.peisland.com/doctorsinn. International cuisine using fresh organic produce from their own garden. Recommended in *Where to Eat in Canada* and *Frommers*. Evening dining by reservation only. Open year-round.
- Hernewood Dining Room, Rodd Mill River Resort, Rte. 136, Woodstock; 902-859-3555. Licensed dining room. Full à la carte menu, specializing in fresh Island cuisine. Open seasonally.
- Prince William Dining Room, Lakeview Loyalist Resort, 195 Harbour Dr., Summerside; 902-436-3302; www.lakeviewhotels.com. Seafood, steaks, Island delicacies. Licensed. Open year-round.
- West Point Lighthouse Inn, Restaurant & Museum, West Point, off Rte. 14; 902-859-3605; www.westpointlighthouse.com. Serving chowders, seafood and full menu. Vegetarian, children's and senior's dishes available. Open late May–late Sept.
- Wind and Reef Restaurant, North Cape; 902-882-3535. Where the two tides meet. Serving fresh Island clams, mussels, lobsters; steaks and prime beef. Reservations recommended. Open mid-May–mid-Oct.

Anne's Land

- Blue Mussel Café, North Rustico; 902-963-2152. Located oceanside at North Rustico Harbour. Fresh mussels and seafood. Open mid-June–mid-Sept.
- Café on the Clyde Restaurant, New Glasgow, at PEI Preserve Company; 902-964-4301; www.preservecompany.com. Famous fresh salads, sandwiches, fish cakes and homemade fruit pies. Casual dining with a great water view. Open late May–early Oct.
- Chez-Yvonne, Cavendish, on Rte. 6; 902-963-2070; www.chezyvonne.com. Family dining room and take-out specializing in fresh seafood and steaks. Bakery, gift shop. Licensed. Open early June–late Sept.

★ Dalvay-by-the-Sea, Grand Tracadie, on Rte. 6; 902-672-2048; www.dalvaybythesea.com. Executive chef creates innovative cuisine with local ingredients. Extensive wine list, panoramic views. Afternoon High Tea served July and Aug. Reservations recommended. Open June–Sept.

★ Dayboat, 5033 Rustico Rd., Oyster Bed Bridge; 902-963-3833; www.dayboat.ca. Among Canada's top ten best new restaurants 2006. Robert Shapiro serves up some of the best seafood in the country. Reservations recommended. Lovely patio. Seasonal.

★ The Dunes Café and Studio Gallery, Brackley Beach, Rte. 15; 902-672-1883; www.dunesgallery.com. Inspired cuisine featuring local produce, seafood, sumptuous desserts, beautifully presented on The Dunes' handmade pottery. Vistas of flowering water gardens and ocean dunes. Open June–Sept.

- Fisherman's Wharf, North Rustico, on Rte. 6; 902-963-2669. Fresh seafood, lobster, steaks, ham, scallops and 60-ft. salad bar. Open mid-May–mid-Oct.
- Fyfe's Landing, Stanley Bridge Country Resort; 902-886-2882; www.stanleybridgeresort.com. Breathtaking views of New London Bay and Cavendish Dunes. Quality seafood, weekend buffets, lobster dinners and dinner theatre. Children's menu. Open June–Sept.
- Millstream Family Restaurant, Brackley Beach, Rte. 15; 902-672-2644. Home-cooked, large-portion meals. Seafood pizza. Open seasonally.
- New Glasgow Lobster Suppers, New Glasgow; 902-964-2870; www.peilobstersuppers.com. Lobster, fresh from the pound, chowder, mussels, salads and dessert. Children's menu. Open June to mid-Oct.

- The Pearl, 7792 Cavendish Rd., North Rustico; 902-963-2111; www.thepearlcafe.ca. Features urban food and atmosphere in a rural setting; serving breakfast, lunch, brunch and afternoon *hors d'oeuvres*. Menu is sourced locally and changes to reflect the seasonality of ingredients. Open May–Oct.
- Rachael's Restaurant, Cavendish Corner; 902-963-3227. Three separate dining areas including oceanview deck. Italian specialties and traditional favourites. Open May–Oct.
- St. Ann's Lobster Suppers, Hope River, Rte. 224; 902-621-0635; www.lobstersuppers.com. Non-profit organization offering home cooking and professional service. Luncheon specials. Licensed. Open mid-June to late Sept.
- Shaw's Hotel and Cottages, Brackley Beach; 902-672-2022; www.shawshotel.ca. Fresh local ingredients in season, including several seafood dishes. Sunday buffet evenings during July and Aug. Open June–Sept.
- Shipwright's Café, Margate, at junction of Rtes 6 and 233; 902-836-3403. Hearty meals with organic vegetables, Island seafood beef and lamb. Seasonal.

Charlotte's Shore

- Brit's Fish & Chips, 41 University Ave., Charlottetown; 902-892-3474. Pub-style food in a family-friendly environment. Takeout available. Open year-round.
- Castello's Ristorante & Pizzeria, 146 Richmond St., Charlottetown; 902-892-6464; www.castellosristorante.com. Sicillian menu specializing in thin crust pizza, fresh breads and oils, salads and homemade pasta. Seasonal.
- Cedar's Eatery, 81 University Ave., Charlottetown; 902-892-7377; www.cedarseatery.com. Canadian and Lebanese food served in a nostalgic setting. Recommended in *Where to Eat in Canada*. Open year-round.
- China Garden, 96 Queen St., Charlottetown; 902-566-3222. Canadian Chinese cuisine. Open year-round and late into the night.
- Claddagh Oyster House, 131 Sydney St., Charlottetown; 902-892-9661; www.claddaghoysterhouse.com. Newly renovated oyster bar. Menu includes beef, lamb, seafood pasta. Irish pub with entertainment upstairs. Open year-round.
- Fishbones Oyster Bar & Seafood Grill, 136 Richmond St., Charlottetown; 902-628-6569; www.fishbonesoysterbar.ca. Pub fare, specializing in seafood. Seasonal; available for private functions in the off-season.
- Flex Mussels, 2 Lower Water St., Charlottetown; 902-569-0200. Seafood menu with some land-lover fare. Seasonal.
- Formosa Tea House, 186 Prince St., Charlottetown; 902-566-4991. Vegetarian and vegan menu, iced and hot teas. Open year-round.
- Gahan House, 126 Sydney St., Charlottetown; 902-626-2337; www.gahan.ca. Pub and brewery. Brewery tours in July and Aug. Extensive pub menu. Open year-round.
- Griffon Dining Room, Dundee Arms Inn, 200 Pownal St., Charlottetown; 902-892-2496; www.dundeearms.com. Local favourite for its great food and historic atmosphere. Reservations recommended. Open year-round.
- Just Us Girls Fashion Café, 100 Queen St., Charlottetown; 902-566-1285; www.justusgirls.ca. Licensed café offering panninis, soups and espresso. Open year-round.
- Landmark Café, across from Victoria Playhouse, Victoria; 902-658-2286; www.peisland.com/landmark/index.htm. Licensed, air conditioned, full menu. Open mid-May–Sept.
- Leonhard's Café & Bakery, 42 University Avenue, Charlottetown; 902-367-3621. Breakfast and lunch, open Monday to Saturday, closed Sunday.
- Lot 30, 151 Kent St., Charlottetown; 902-629-3030; www.lot30restaurant.ca. Fresh food, menu changes daily. Open evenings Tuesday to Sunday year-round.
- Mavor's Bistro and Bar, Confederation Centre of the Arts, 145 Richmond St., Charlottetown; 902-628-6107; www.confederationcentre.com. Light modern cuisine in a chic

atmosphere. Open-air garden and pre-theatre dining. Open year-round; closed Mon.

- The Merchantman Pub, 23 Queen St., Charlottetown; 902-892-9150; www.merchantmanpub.com. Full menu served 11:30 am–10 pm Located in historic property. Thai and Cajun fare, fresh seafood, imported and local draught beer on tap. Open year-round, 11:30 am–midnight.
- Off Broadway Café, 125 Sydney St., Charlottetown; 902-566-4620; www.offbroadwayrestaurant.ca. Intimate surroundings in cozy rooms and attentive service. Specializing in crêpes, steaks and luscious desserts. Open year-round.
- The Pilot House, 70 Grafton St., Charlottetown; 902-894-4800; www.thepilothouse.ca. Fresh seafood, prime rib and steaks, and fine wines in a beautiful heritage building. Pub with local and imported draughts. Open year-round; closed Sun.
- The Selkirk, Delta Prince Edward Hotel, 18 Queen St., Charlottetown; 902-894-1208; www.deltaprinceedward.pe.ca. Fine dining room with innovative menu, elegant atmosphere and continental service. Open year-round.
- Shaddy's Mediterranean Cuisine, 44 University Ave., Charlottetown; 902-368-8886. Falafel, shawarma and shish taouk sandwiches and other Lebanese fare. Open year-round daily; dinner only on Sat and Sun.
- Sims Corner Steakhouse and Oyster Bar, 84 Queen St., Charlottetown; 902-894-7467; www.simscorner.ca. Prime Canadian AAA beef, all-Island oyster bar, selection of new and old world wines. Open daily 4 pm-11 pm year-round.
- Sirenella Ristorante, 83 Water St., Charlottetown; 902-628-2271; www.sirenella.ca. Northern Italian cuisine, grilled seafood, veal, and homemade pasta. Outdoor patio. Open year-round.
- Tai-Chi Garden, 2 Crestview Dr., Charlottetown. Asian fare, garden patio. Open year-round.
- Urban Eatery, Second Level, Shops of Confederation Court Mall, Charlottetown; 902-566-4848; www.urbaneatery.ca. Modern dining concept with fresh, quality ingredients. Open Mon–Sat, year-round.
- Victoria Village Inn, 22 Howard St., Victoria; 902-658-2483; www.victoriavillageinn.com. Classically trained chef/owner serves innovative cuisine using fresh local produce. Open year-round.
- Water Prince Corner Shop, 141 Water St., Charlottetown; 902-368-3212; www.waterprincelobster.ca. Live Atlantic lobster, cooked lobster, Northumberland scallops, Malpeque oysters, canned clams, canned chowders, crab meat, frozen lobster, hot pack lobster, Island blue mussels, steamer clams, salmon, halibut and sole. Open daily year-round.

Points East Coastal Drive

- Cardigan Lobster Suppers, Cardigan; 902-583-2020; www.cardiganlobstersuppers.com. Licensed waterfront dining at reasonable prices. Five-course lobster supper and full family menu. Open early June–Oct.
- Club 19, Rodd Brudenell River Resort, Roseneath; 902-652-2332; www.roddvacations.com. Pub-style restaurant overlooking the Brudenell River. Casual atmosphere, casual food. Open daily for breakfast, lunch, dinner and nightlife. Seasonal.
- Gillis' Drive In, 5207 AA MacDonald Highway, Brudenell; 902-838-2301. True drive-in restaurant with deep-fried fare and ice cream. Seasonal.

★ The Inn at Bay Fortune, Bay Fortune, on Rte. 310; 902-687-3745; www.innatbayfortune.com. Recommended by *Where to Eat in Canada*. Contemporary creative cuisine in a country inn setting. Dinner only. Open late May to mid-Oct.

- Inn at St. Peters, next to Greenwich, Prince Edward Island National Park, St. Peters; 902-961-2135; www.innatstpeters.com. Award-winning executive chef, produce from on-site garden. Reservations recommended for dinner. Open late May–early Oct.
- Inn at Spry Point, off Rte. 310,

Souris; 902-583-2400; www.innatsprypoint.com. The finest ingredients are harvested locally. Airy dining room and patio. Breakfast and lunch only. Open mid-June to Sept.

- La Belle Cloche, Knights Ave., Souris (behind the school La Belle Cloche and across the street from Souris Harbour). Open seasonally.
- Rick's Fish 'N' Chips and Seafood House, Rte. 2, St. Peters; 902-961-3438. Seafood specialties, pizza, freshly battered fish and fresh-cut fries. Vegetarian items. Open May–Oct.
- Sir Andrew Macphail Homestead, Orwell, off Rte. 1; 902-651-2789; www.isn.net/~dhunter/macphailfoundation.html. Tea room and restaurant featuring heritage meals from the 1900s. Lunch, dinner and afternoon tea. Open mid-June to late Sept.
- St. Margarets Lobster Suppers, Rte. 16, St. Margarets; 902-687-3105. Licensed dining room serving lobster and ham dinners. Children's menu. Open mid-June–mid-Sept.
- Trailside Inn, Café and Adventures, 109 Main St., Mount Stewart; 902-676-3130; www.trailside.ca. Delightful café on the Confederation Trail, featuring local entertainment most weekends, seafood chowders, pizza, home-baked bread, desserts. Open July–Aug., daily; reduced hours in the off-season.
- The Whim Inn, junction of Rtes 3 and 4, Pooles Corner; 902-838-3838; 800-563-9446; www.whiminn.com. Home-cooked style meals. Lounge with pub food. Open year-round.
- Windows on the Water Café, 106 Sackville St., Montague; 902-838-2080. Locally grown produce, casual country dining. Eat on the deck and enjoy a lovely view of Montague Harbour. Reservations recommended. Open mid-May to Sept.

Attractions

Admission fees are subject to change.

North Cape

- Acadian Museum/Musée Acadien, Miscouche, on Rte. 2, west of Summerside; 902-432-2880; www.peimuseum.com. History of the Island Acadians from 1720 to present, genealogy, gift shop. Open year-round. Admission charged.
- Alberton Museum & Genealogy Centre, 457 Church St., Alberton; 902-853-4048. Artifact collection depicting activities carried out by PEI's early settlers. Historical photographs and genealogical information. Open June–Sept, daily 9:30 am–5:30 pm; Sun, 1–5 pm Admission by donation.
- Bideford Parsonage Museum, on Rte. 166, Bideford; 902-831-3133; www.bidefordparsonagemuseum.com. Community museum with displays depicting the shipbuilding era, the role of the parsons in the community and the residency of L. M. Montgomery as a school teacher. Open June–Sept, daily, 9 am–5 pm Admission: $5 adults, $2.50 students, $15 family.
- The Bottle Houses/Maisons de Bouteilles, Cap-Egmont, on Rte. 11; 902-854-2987; www.bottlehouses.com. Fantasy-like buildings made out of over 30,000 coloured bottles. Open mid-May–mid-Oct. Admission: adults $5, seniors and students $4.50, children 6–16 yrs $2, preschoolers free.
- College of Piping and Celtic Performing Arts of Canada, 619 Water St. E, Summerside; 902-436-5377; 877-224-7473; www.collegeofpiping.com. Performances, instruction in bagpiping, Highland dancing, stepdancing, drumming. Concerts, tours and Celtic Gift Shop. Celtic Festival July and Aug.; interpretive and interactive exhibit open year-round.
- Eptek Art & Culture Centre, Waterfront Properties, 130 Harbour Dr., Summerside; 902-888-8373; www.peimuseum.com. Art gallery featuring Island artists and touring Canadian exhibitions; historic

exhibits of Island culture. Open year-round. Admission charged.

- ★ Green Park Shipbuilding Museum and Historic Yeo House, Port Hill, Rte. 12, west of Summerside; 902-831-7947; www.peimuseum.com. Restored house of shipbuilder James Yeo Jr., re-created shipyard. Gift shop. Open June–Sept. Admission charged.
- International Fox Museum and Hall of Fame Inc., 33 Summer St., Summerside; 902-432-1296. This museum tells the story of the fox industry on PEI. Open June–Sept. Admission by donation.
- Irish Moss Interpretive Centre, Miminegash, on Rte. 14; 902-882-4313. Learn all there is to know about Irish Moss through displays and videos. Gift shop and Seaweed Pie Café. Open early June–late Sept, daily 10 am–7 pm Admission charged.
- Lennox Island Aboriginal Ecotourism Centre; 866-831-2702; www.lennoxisland.com/liae. "Malpeque Discoveries" program, guided tours of museum, community and Lennox Island Nature Trail. Traditional Mi'kmaq food, craft demos and ecotourism information. Open late June–early Sept. Off-season by appointment.
- Mill River Fun Park, 38016 Western Rd. (Rte. 2), Woodstock; 902-859-3915. Family activities for all ages: children's pool with waterslides, swimming pool, mini-golf, bumper boats, play area, sea of balls, giant twister slide and the Aqua Rage. Open July to Labour Day, daily, 11 am–7 pm, weather permitting. Admission $9, under 5 free.
- North Cape Nature and Technology in Perfect Harmony, North Cape; 902-882-2991; 902-882-3535; www.tignish.com/northcape. The Wind Energy Institute of Canada, Irish Moss harvesting by horse, low-tide walks along rock reef. Black Marsh Nature Trail, Wind Energy Interpretive Centre & Gift Shop and the Wind & Reef Restaurant. Open mid-May–mid-Oct.
- PEI Shellfish Museum, Ellerslie; 902-853-3225; 902-853-3374. Aquariums featuring live native fish and shellfish, artifacts relating to species identification, the history of oyster cultivation and the growth and culture of shellfish. Open June–Sept. Admission $3.
- Prince Edward Island Potato Museum, 1 Dewar Lane, Centennial Park, O'Leary; 902-859-2039; www.peipotatomuseum.com. Interpretive display of the potato's history to present day. Collection of antique farm equipment. Gift shop and resource room. Open May 15–Oct. 15, Mon–Sat 9 am–5 pm, Sun 1–5 pm Admission: $4.
- Spinnakers' Landing, on the waterfront, Summerside; 902-436-6692; www.tourismsummerside.com/spinnakerslanding2.html. Boardwalk along the edge of the water, shopping, outdoor entertainment, Boat Shed display, interpretive centre, visitor information centre in a lighthouse. Open daily early June–late Sept. Free admission, free parking.
- Union Corner School House Museum, Union Corner, on Rte. 11; 902-854-2992; www.unioncornerschoolhouse.ca. Old Schoolhouse brought back to life as small museum with original furnishings; pictures of teachers and students. Open mid-June to Labour Day, daily, 9 am–5 pm Admission: adults $3, seniors $2.75, students $2.25.
- West Point Lighthouse Inn, Restaurant & Museum, West Point, on Rte. 14; 902-859-3605; www.westpointlighthouse.com. Climb to the top of the Island's tallest functioning lighthouse (20.6 meters). Museum. Open late May–late Sept.
- Wyatt Heritage Properties, downtown Summerside; 902-432-1296; www.wyattheritage.com. Features MacNaught History Centre and Archives, historical and genealogical resources at 75 Spring St.; the Wyatt Historic House, 1867 home and gardens of distinguished Islander Dr. Wanda Wyatt at 85 Spring St.; and LeFurgey Cultural Centre, 19th-century shipbuilder's mansion, now an arts and culture centre, at 205 Prince St. Open year-round.

Anne's Land

- Avonlea — Village of Anne of Green

Gables, Cavendish, Rte. 6, across from Rainbow Valley; 902-963-3050; www.avonlea.ca. The Belmont Schoolhouse where Lucy Maud Montgomery taught in 1896 and the restored 1872 Long River Church where she attended, surrounded by reproductions of buildings and gardens of the time. Barnyard animals, horse and wagon rides, games with Anne and Diana, and entertainment. Open June–Sept., daily. Admission charged.

- Anne of Green Gables Museum at Silver Bush, Park Corner, on Rte. 20; 902-886-2884 (Sat–Sun); 800-665-2663 (Mon–Fri); www.annesociety.org/anne. L. M. Montgomery often visited the home of her uncle John Campbell and aunt Annie Campbell. She was married here in 1911. Open mid-May–mid-Oct, daily. Admission: adults $4, children $1, preschoolers free.
- Belcourt Centre, South Rustico, Rte. 6; 902-963-2877. Once the Rustico Convent, a Catholic girls' boarding school, now part of the Farmers Bank Museum historical structures. Seasonal.

★ Brackley Beach Drive-In Theatre and Mini-Golf, Rte. 15, Brackley Beach; 902-672-3333; www.drivein.ca. One of the most unusual drive-in theatres in Canada. Two first-run movies nightly. Full-service canteen. Seasonal.

- The Fantazmagoric Museum of the Strange and Unusual, Cavendish, Rte. 6, beside Sandspit; 902-963-3242; www.cavendishsavings.com. Strange and unusual facts presented in thought-provoking displays and dioramas. Open mid-June to Labour Day, 10 am–10 pm Admission: adults $7; children 6–12 and seniors $6; preschoolers $3; children under 2 free.
- The Farmers' Bank of Rustico Museum, Rte. 243, Rustico; 902-963-3168; www.farmersbank.ca. A National Historic Site operated from 1864 to 1894 as the first people's bank now houses an exhibit of the Rustico Acadians. The Doucet House, adjacent to the bank, is a restored 1772 Acadian period log house. Open June–Sept., daily. Admission charged.

★ Green Gables — Prince Edward Island National Park of Canada, Cavendish, on Rte. 6; 902-963-7874; www.pc.gc.ca. Built in the mid-1800s, this house inspired the novel *Anne of Green Gables*. Nature trails, farm demonstrations and interpretive programs by bilingual staff in July and Aug. Open May–Oct., daily. Admission charged.

- The Keir Memorial Museum, Rte. 20, Malpeque; 902-836-3054. Exhibits illustrate household, religious, farming and oyster-fishing activities; focus on early Acadian and Mi'kmaq. Open July 1–Labour Day, daily. Admission: adults $2, children under 12 $1, family $5.
- Kensington Train Station, Rte. 20, Kensington; 902-836-3031; www.kata.pe.ca. Historic train station housing the library. Tourist information and local crafts available in Kensington Railyards and Welcome Centre adjacent to the Train Station. Open May–Oct., 9 am–4 pm, July and Aug 9 am–8 pm.

★ Lucy Maud Montgomery's Birthplace, New London, at Rtes 6 and 20; 902-886-2099; 902-836-5502. Interior is decorated with authentic Victorian period pieces. The writer's wedding dress and personal scrapbook are among the items on display. Open mid-May–mid-Oct, daily 9 am–5 pm Admission: adults $2.50, children 6–12 $0.50.

★ Prince Edward Island National Park of Canada, Cavendish to Dalvay, off Rte. 6; 902-672-6350; www.pc.gc.ca. The park preserves 40 km of the Island's north shore. Facilities for camping, swimming and other activities. Admission charged. Family passes and season passes available.

- Ripley's Believe It Or Not! Museum, Cavendish, Rte. 6; 902-963-2242. Exciting collection of wonders and curiosities in over 200 exhibits in 14 galleries with 10 video screens. Open May to mid-Sept., 9:30 am–5:30 pm; July and Aug., 9 am–10 pm. Ticket sales close one hour prior to closing time.
- Rustico Harbour Fisheries Museum, 318 Harbourview Dr., off Rte. 6; 963-3799. Learn about the history of the fishing industry in the area. Climb aboard the *SilverWave* and experience lobster fishing first-hand (via video). Touch tank, gift shop on premises. Open mid-June to Sept 30.

- Sandspit, Cavendish, on Rte. 6; 902-963-2626; www.sandspit.com. Enjoy 18 attractions including a huge rollercoaster, Can-Am racers, ferris wheel, carousel, bumper boats, miniature golf, etc. Canteen and picnic facilities. Open mid-June to Labour Day. No admission charge to the grounds. All-day bracelet packages or pay-as-you-go.
- Shining Waters Family Fun Park, Rte. 6, Cavendish; 902-963-3939; www.maritimefun.com. Adventure woods, storybook forest, boating lake; barnyard animals, hayrides; waterslides, canteen and picnic grounds. Open mid-June to early Sept. All-day admission charged.
- Site of Lucy Maud Montgomery's Cavendish Home, Cavendish, on Rte. 6; 902-963-2231; www.peisland.com/lmm. Homestead fields, quiet woods and gardens surround stone cellar of old farm house where Montgomery was raised by her Macneill grandparents. Interpretive panels. Bookstore and gift shop. Open mid-May–mid-Oct, 10 am–5 pm; July–Aug., 9 am–6 pm Admission: adults $4, children $2, families $10.

Charlotte's Shore

- Ardgowan National Historic Site of Canada, 2 Palmers Lane, Charlottetown; 902-566-7626; www.pc.gc.ca. Country home of William Henry Pope, a newspaper editor, politician and one of the Fathers of Confederation. The house was once the centre of high-society life and has been restored to its Victorian grandeur. Grounds open to the public.
- ★ Beaconsfield Historic House, 2 Kent St., Charlottetown; 902-368-6603; www.peimuseum.com. Designed by W. C. Harris and built in 1877, one of the Island's finest residences. Historically furnished rooms, summer teas, music and theatre. Open year-round. Admission charged.
- Capital Area Recreation Inc. (CARI), University of Prince Edward Island, 550 University Ave., Charlottetown; 902-569-4584; www.caripei.ca. Leisure pool, hot tub and toddler's pool. Scheduled family swims. Waterslide, family change room. Open year-round. Call or check the website for rates and schedules.
- Charlottetown Driving Park Entertainment Centre, 21 Exhibition Dr., Charlottetown; 902-620-4222. Live seasonal racing, a simulcast lounge, full-service tiered dining, enclosed grandstand and an entertainment centre offering an assortment of gaming products. Open year-round, Mon–Sat.
- Confederation Centre of the Arts, 145 Richmond St., Charlottetown, 902-628-1864; 800-565-0278; www.confederationcentre.com. Three theatres, Atlantic Canada's largest art gallery, library, gift shop, restaurant. Home of the Charlottetown Festival. Open year-round, 9 am–5 pm Extended hours May–Oct.
- Founders' Hall — Canada's Birthplace Pavilion, 6 Prince St., Charlottetown Waterfront; 902-368-1864; www.foundershall.ca. Live the nation's history from 1864 to present day through state-of-the-art displays, multimedia, holivisuals and new technology. Closed Dec. and Jan.
- Gateway Village, Borden-Carleton at the foot of the Confederation Bridge. Museums, exhibits, dining and shopping. Free parking. Open year-round; some shops seasonal. Free admission.
- ★ Government House, Victoria Park, Charlottetown; 902-368-5480; www.gov.pe.ca. Built in 1832, Fanningbank is the official residence of the Lieutenant-Governor of PEI. House open to the public during July and Aug. Tours Mon–Fri, 10 am–4 pm Donations accepted.
- Harbour Hippo (Land and Sea Tours), Lower Prince St. Wharf, Charlottetown; 902-628-8687; www.harbourhippo.com. Land and sea tours of historic Charlottetown and Charlottetown Harbour aboard an amphibious vehicle. Tours June–Sept., daily, 10:15 am–8 pm (running every hour and 15 minutes). Adults $23, children (5–12 yrs.) $16, 4 and under free.
- Port-La-Joye –Fort Amherst National Historic Site of Canada, Rocky Point, off Rte. 19; 902-566-7626; www.pc.gc.ca. The French established Port-La-Joye in 1720. The British captured the area in 1758 and built Fort Amherst. Today,

only the earthworks remain. Visitors' centre features audio-visual presentation, bilingual staff.

★ Province House National Historic Site of Canada, corner of Richmond and Great George streets, Charlottetown; 902-566-7626; www.pc.gc.ca. Considered the "Birthplace of Canada"; the first meeting to discuss federal union was held here in 1864. Home of the provincial legislature. Guided tours, displays and audio-visual presentation. Open year-round. Donations accepted. Group fees apply.

Points East Coastal Drive

- Basin Head Fisheries Museum, Basin Head, off Rte. 16; 902-357-7233; www.peimuseum.com. Boats, gear, displays and photographs depict the lifestyle of an inshore fisher. Saltwater aquariums, boardwalk to beach, children's play area. Open June–Sept., daily. Admission charged.
- Buffaloland Provincial Park, Milltown Cross, on Rte. 4; 902-652-8950. A boardwalk leads to a deck overlooking an enclosure where herds of buffalo and white-tailed deer graze. Open year-round. Admission free.
- Cape Bear Lighthouse & Marconi Museum, off Rte. 18 at Cape Bear; 902-962-2917; www.eaglesviewgolf.com. Four-storey lighthouse built in 1881. Replica of the Cape Bear Marconi Station, believed to be the first Canadian land station to receive distress signals from the *Titanic*. Open mid-June–mid-Sept, daily, 10 am–6 pm Admission: adults $3.50, seniors $2.50, children 6–12 yrs $1.50, preschoolers free.
- East Point Lighthouse & Welcome Centre, East Point, off Rte. 16; 902-357-2718. Guided tours available. Admission: adults $4, students and seniors $3, children $2, preschoolers free; family $11.
- Elmira Railway Museum & Miniature Railway, Elmira, Rte. 16A; 902-357-7234; www.elmirastation.com. History of railroading on PEI. Home to the PEI Miniature Railway and one of the largest railway collections in Canada. Open June–Sept. 30, daily. Admission charged.
- Garden of the Gulf Museum, 564 Main St., Montague; 902-838-2467. Exhibit and interpretive programs on the natural history of the Three Rivers area. Open early June–late Sept., Mon–Sat (Mon–Fri in Sept), 9 am–5 pm Admission: adults $3, children under 12 free.

★ Greenwich Interpretation Centre, Prince Edward Island National Park of Canada, Rte. 313, Greenwich; 902-961-2514; www.pc.gc.ca. A rare system of parabolic sand dunes and sites of Aboriginal, French and Acadian occupation. Three walking trails, beach facilities, interpretive centre with multimedia displays of the site's natural and cultural features, interactive exhibits. Open mid-May to early Oct; call for off-season information. National Park entrance fees apply.

- Hillsborough River Eco-Centre, 104 Main St., Mount Stewart; 902-676-2050. Interpretive displays portraying the natural and cultural history of PEI's first Canadian Heritage River. Guided tours, entertainment. Open year-round: July–Sept., daily, 10 am–6 pm; reduced hours off-season.
- Orwell Corner Historic Village, Orwell, off Rte. 1; 902-651-8515; www.peimuseum.com. Experience the 1800s atmosphere of PEI's agricultural heritage. Farmhouse, church, school, community hall, smithy, shingle mill and barns. Events throughout the summer. PEI Agricultural Museum depicts the heritage of Island agriculture. Open May to mid-Oct. Admission charged.
- Panmure Head Lighthouse, Rte. 17 (the King's Byway) to Rte. 347; 902-838-3568. PEI's oldest wooden lighthouse. Climb to the lantern and view the beach. Gift shop. Open July–Aug., daily. Reduced hours in June and Sept. Admission to climb tower.
- Point Prim Lighthouse, Point Prim, on Rte. 209; 902-659-2412. PEI's oldest lighthouse (c. 1845). Climb 24 metres (80 ft.) above sea-level to view the Northumberland Strait in this round brick structure. Chowder House on-site. Open July–Aug.,

guided tours. Admission by donation.

- Roma at Three Rivers, Rte. 319 north of Montague; 902-838-3413; www.romapei.com. Historic site commemorating 1700s French settlement and Victorian shipbuilding. Archeological displays. Guided tours. Open July–Aug., 10 am–6 pm Admission charged.
- Rossignol Estate Winery, Little Sands, on Rte. 4; 902-962-4193; www.rossignolwinery.com. The Rossignol family's winery, vineyard and art gallery. Wine-tasting of premium fruit wines. Open May–Oct., Mon–Sat, 10 am–5 pm, Sun 1–5 pm Admission free.
- St. Andrew's Chapel, St. Andrew's, on Rte. 2; 902-961-2096. The church began its life in 1805 and was moved down the ice on the Hillsborough River in 1864 to become a girls' school in Charlottetown. It was returned to the original site in 1990 and restored. Open June–Aug., 9:30 am to 4:30 pm Donations in lieu of admission.
- St. Peter's Landing, St. Peters Bay; www.stpeterslanding.com. Retail shops featuring fine art, Island crafts and cuisine. Island Blue Cultured Mussel Interpretive building. St. Peter's Landing Park with boardwalk. Seasonal.
- Sir Andrew Macphail Homestead National Historic Site, Orwell, off Rte. 1; 902-651-2789. Restored historic house, museum, nature trails, ecological forestry project on site. Restaurant serves lunch, afternoon tea and dinner (with reservations). Open mid-June–mid-Oct, Wed and Thurs 11 am–4:30 pm; Fri–Sun 11 am–7:30 pm Free admission.
- Wood Islands Lighthouse & Interpretive Museum; 902-962-3110; www.woodislands.ca. Photos, displays and documentation. Over 200 artifacts. Craft and gift shop. Open mid-June–mid-Sept, 9:30 am–6 pm Admission charged.

Genealogical Research

Check out the PEI website for further information on genealogy and on-line census: www.gov.pe.ca/cca/index.php3?number=1022471&lang=E

- Alberton Museum and Genealogy Centre, 457 Church St., Alberton; 902-853-4048; www.townofalberton.ca/museum.htm
- Acadian Museum of PEI/Musée Acadien de l'I-P-E, Miscouche; 902-432-2880; www.peimuseum.com
- The Farmers' Bank of Rustico Museum, Rte. 234, adjacent to St. Augustine's Church, Rustico; 902-963-3168; www.farmersbank.ca. Rustico Acadian genealogy.
- The History Room, 12 Heritage Lane, Kingsboro, off Rte. 16, east of Souris; 902-357-2116; www.islandregister.com/leard.html
- MacNaught History Centre & Archives, Wyatt Heritage Properties, 75 Spring St., Summerside; 902-432-1332; www.wyattheritage.com
- PEI Collection, UPEI Robertson Library; 902-566-0536; www.library.upei.ca.
- Public Archives and Records Office, The Hon. George Coles Building, Richmond St., Charlottetown; 902-368-4290; www.edu.pe.ca/paro.

Festivals and Events

Hardly a weekend goes by in the spring, summer, and fall when there isn't a celebration happening somewhere in the province. Included here is a selective listing of events highly recommended if you're in striking distance. Many Island communities also go all out for Canada Day on July 1. For detailed information on Festivals & Events, check out the websites www.festivalspei.com and www.peiplay.com/festivals.

Island-wide

June:

- Festival of Small Halls, Island-wide; 902-626-8084; www.smallhalls.com.

Island musicians play small venues around the province.

- Tour de PEI. Island-wide; 902-367-3679; www.tourdepei.com. International women's professional cycling event.

September/October:

- Prince Edward Island Studio Tour Weekend. Island-wide; 902-368-6300; www.peistudiotour.com. Open houses at artists' and craft producers' workshops and studios.

North Cape

June

- Summerside Highland Gathering, College of Piping, Summerside; 902-436-5377; 877-BAGPIPE; www.collegeofpiping.com. Competitions for pipe bands, drummers, stepdancers and heavy-weight athletes. First-rate Celtic entertainment.

July

- Evangeline Bluegrass and Traditional Music Festival, Centre Expo/Festival Centre, Abram-Village; 902-854-3300; www.regionevangeline.com. A weekend of bluegrass and old-time fiddle music. Local and international artists.
- Le Fricot, Centre Expo/Festival Centre, Abram-Village; 902-854-3300; www.regionevangeline.com. Acadian-style soirée featuring music, comedy and storytelling.
- PEI Potato Blossom Festival, O'Leary; 902-859-1487; 902-859-4722; www.exhibitions-festivalspeiae.com/peipotatoblossomfestival.html. Farm show, gospel concert, parade, outdoor music festival, fireworks, dances.
- St. Ann's Sunday Celebrations, Lennox Island; 902-831-5423; www.lennoxisland.com/liae/nat_02_06.htm. Mi'kmaq food and culture.
- Summerside Lobster Carnival, Summerside; 902-436-4925; www.exhibitions-festivalspeiae.com/summersidelobstercarnival.html. Lots of lobster, a parade, talent contest, midway, nightly entertainment.
- Summerside Wine & Arts Festival, Shipyard and Wyatt Heritage Properties; 888-748-1010. Wine tasting of over 100 wines from around the world, art exhibits and demonstrations, wine bards, live entertainment.
- Tignish Irish Moss Festival, Tignish; 902-882-2476. www.exhibitions-festivalspeiae.com/tignishirishmossfestival.html. Miss Irish Moss pageant, parade, dance, food, entertainment, lobster suppers.
- West Point Lighthouse Festival & Boat Race, West Point; 902-859-1274; www.exhibitions-festivalspeiae.com/westpointlighthousefestival.html. Dances, children's events, fishing boat races, antique car show, parade, competitions and food.

July/August

- Celtic Festival, College of Piping, Summerside; 902-436-5377; 877-224-7473; www.collegeofpiping.com. A nine-week concert series featuring piping, drumming, dancing, fiddling, singing and storytelling. July–Aug., Tues–Thurs.

August

- Atlantic Fiddlers Jamboree, Centre Expo/Festival Centre, Abram-Village; 902-854-3300. Fiddlers from the East Coast as well as local talent from the Évangeline Region.
- Larry Gorman Folk Festival, Britannia Hall, Tyne Valley; 902-831-2191; www.upei.ca/~iis/gorman.htm
- Prince County Exhibition, Alberton; 902-853-3013; 902-853-2455; www.exhibitions-festivalspeiae.com/princecountyexhibition.html. Various competitions, shows and displays, midway, parade.
- Tignish Irish Folk Festival, West Prince Heritage Property. 902-882-3446; www.tignishirishfolkfestival.com
- Tyne Valley Oyster Festival, Tyne Valley; 831-3294; www.exhibitions-festivalspeiae.com/tynevalleyoysterfestival.html. Fiddling and step-dancing championships, Canadian Oyster-shucking championship, adult dance, oyster and scallop dinners.

September

- L'Éxposition Agricole et le Festival Acadien, Abram-Village; 902-854-

3300; www.expositionfestival.com. Acadian entertainment, parade, demonstrations and lobster suppers.

Anne's Land

June-Sept.

- Avonlea Concert, Avonlea Village, Cavendish; 902-963-3050. Island singing, step dancing and fiddling in the restored 1872 Long River Church.

July

- British Car Days Across the Bridge; 902-367-3675; www.bmapei.com. British car and motorcycle show with vehicles from Eastern Canada and U.S.
- Festival Rendez-vous Rustico, Rte. 243, Rustico; 902-963-3011; www.rendezvousrustico.com. An Acadian festival of traditional, contemporary and classical music, dance, food and games.
- Island Motorcylce Rally, Vacationland RV Park, Brackley Beach; 902-629-1319; www.motorcyclepei.com. Hosted by the PEI Motorcycle Touring Club. Poker run, motorcycle parade of flags, field events, tenting sites, hip-of-beef buffet, corn roast, dances, breakfasts. Supervised activities for 18 and under.

July-August

- Indian River Festival, St. Mary's Church, Indian River, Rte. 104, 5 km north of Kensington; 902-836-3733; 866-856-3733; www.indianriverfestival.com. Chamber music, jazz and choral concerts by international musicians enhanced by breathtaking acoustics of the church.

August

- Fiddlers and Followers Weekend, North Rustico; 902-836-3610. Four big fiddle shows featuring Maritime fiddle champions, step dancers, barbecues, lobster parties and picnics.
- Lucy Maud Montgomery Festival, Cavendish and area; 902-963-2078; www.lmmontgomeryfestival.com. Traditional music, readings from L. M. Montgomery's work, writers' workshops, traditional and children's entertainment.

Charlotte's Shore

May-October

- Capture PEI Writers & Photographers Workshops & Tours, Charlottetown; 902-569-3913; www.seacroftpei.com. Learn writing, publishing photography with professionals.
- Ceili at the Irish Hall, Benevolent Irish Society, 582 North River Rd., Charlottetown; 902-892-2367; www.irishisland.ca. Irish, Scottish and traditional music, song and dance. PEI's best traditional performers. Every Fri, 8–10:30 pm

June/July

- Festival of Lights, Charlottetown waterfront; 800-955-1864; www.walkandseacharlottetown.com. Buskers, midway, fireworks, concerts, pub tents.

June–September

★ Charlottetown Festival, Charlottetown Confederation Centre of the Arts; 902-566-1267; 800-565-0278; www.confederationcentre.com. Mainstage, second stage and outdoor amphitheatre productions.

July

- Crapaud Exhibition, Crapaud; 902-658-2787; www.exhibitions-festivalspeiae.com. Animals, competitions, food, children's activities, entertainment.
- Emerald Junction Summerfest, Emerald Community Centre, Rte. 113; 902-886-2400. Great Irish music, food, beer garden, children's activities, rough camping.
- Gay & Lesbian Pride Festival, Charlottetown and various locations across PEI; 902-388-0969; 877-380-5776; www.pridepei.com. Parade, entertainment and dance, sporting activities.
- PEI Jazz & Blues Festival, Charlottetown; 902-628-1870; www.jazzandblues.ca.

August

★ Old Home Week/PEI Provincial Exhibition, Charlottetown Civic Centre and Driving Park; 902-629-6623; www.oldhomeweekpei.com. Horses and livestock shows, harness racing, parade, midway, exhibits and entertainment. The Gold Cup and Saucer Race is one of eastern

Canada's most prestigious harness races.

September

- PEI International Shellfish Festival, Charlottetown waterfront; 866-955-2003; www.peishellfish.com. Maritime entertainment, PEI/Eastern Canadian Oyster-shucking Championships, PEI International Chowder Championships.

October

- Prince Edward Island Marathon, Brackley Beach to Charlottetown; 902-628-1861; www.princeedwardislandmarathon.com. Distance running event for the whole family. Health and Fitness Expo.

Points East Coastal Drive

June-October

- Ceilidh at the Corner, Orwell Corner Community Hall; 902-651-8515; www.orwellcorner.isn.net. Traditional song, stories and dance. Wed, 8 pm

July

- Northumberland Provincial Fisheries Festival, Murray River, Northumberland Arena; 902-962-3327; www.exhibitions-festivalspeiae.com/northprovfisheriesfestival.html. Pageant, golf tournament, fisherman's challenge, variety show, dances, lobster suppers.
- PEI Bluegrass & Oldtime Music Festival, Rollo Bay; 902-569-3864; www.bluegrasspei.com/rollobay.htm. Bluegrass and oldtime bands from Canada and the U.S.
- PEI Street Rod Association Show 'n' Shine, Old Brudenell Park, Brudenell; 902-962-4140; www.peistreetrod.com. Antique, special interest and classic street rod display and run.
- Rollo Bay Fiddle Festival, Rollo Bay; 902-687-2584; www.rollobayfiddlefest.ca. Open-air concert featuring talent from all over North America.
- Souris Sea Fest, Marine Terminal Wharf, Souris; 902-687-2157; www.sourispei.com. Boat races, boat poker run, Queen-of-the-Sea pageant, marine trade show, midway, children's entertainment and barbecues

August

- Annual Abegweit Pow-Wow, Panmure Island; 902-892-5314; www.ncpei.com. A celebration of Mi'kmaq culture with traditional foods and entertainment.
- Caledonia Club of PEI Annual Highland Games, Eldon, Lord Selkirk Provincial Park; 902-659-7221. Piping, dancing and traditional athletic competitions. Lobster suppers.
- Provincial Plowing Match and Agricultural Fair, Dundas; 902-583-2723; www.exhibitions-festivalspeiae.com. Country fair celebrating the land, its bounty and people. Agricultural displays, livestock, food and entertainment.
- St. Peters Bay Wild Blueberry Festival, St. Peters Park; www.stpetersblueberryfestival.ca. Open-air concert, dances, entertainment, blueberry pancake brunch and parade.

★ Pick up a copy of *The Buzz* magazine or visit its website at www.buzzon.com to find out what's going on during your visit.

Nightlife

Theatre

North Cape

- Acadian Dinner Theatre, Centre Expo/Festival Centre, Abram-Village; 902-854-3300; www.regionevangeline.com. Acadian music and comedy. Reservations required. Group rates available.
- Feast Dinner Theatre, at Brothers Two, Water St. East, Summerside; 902-888-2200; 888-748-1010; www.brotherstwo.ca; www.feastdinnertheatres.ca. Dinner theatre, music and comedy. Seasonal. Mon–Sat, 6:30 pm Reservations recommended.
- Harbourfront Jubilee Theatre, 124 Harbour Dr., Summerside; 902-888-2500; 800-708-6505; www.jubileetheatre.com. Home of the popular musical "Anne &

Gilbert". Shows and musicals celebrate the culture and tradition of the Maritimes. Open year-round.

- La Cuisine a Mémé Dinner Theatre, Mont-Carmel Community Centre, Mont-Carmel.
- V'nez Chou Nous Acadian Dinner Theatre Productions, Palmer Road Community Centre, Rte. 2, Tignish; 902-882-0475; www.seperrey.org. Funny storyline based on local characters combines original and traditional Acadian song and dance. Mid-July–mid-Aug by reservation only.

Anne's Land

- Avonlea Village, Cavendish; 902-963-3050. Walk among the characters of *Anne of Green Gables* and see the story unfold around you. June–Sept.
- Eddie May Murder Mystery Dinner Theatre, Stanley Bridge Country Resort, Rte. 6, Stanley Bridge; 902-886-2882; 800-361-2882; www.eddiemay.ca. Murder mystery dinner theatre with audience participation. Mid-July to late Aug., Thurs at 7 pm.
- Montgomery Theatre, in Avonlea Village, Cavendish; 902-963-3847; www.themontgomerytheatre.com. Plays from the era of novelist L.M. Montgomery presented. July–Aug.

Charlotte's Shore

- Carrefour de l'Isle-Saint-Jean, Charlottetown; 902-368-1895; www.carrefourisj.org. Francophone theatre productions and concerts.

★ The Charlottetown Festival, Confederation Centre of the Arts, 145 Richmond St., Charlottetown; 902-566-1267; 800-565-0278; www.confederationcentre.com. Home of Canada's longest-running musical, "Anne of Green Gables — The Musical"™. The centre features two main-stage musicals (including "Anne") each year. As well, MacKenzie Theatre offers musical theatre in a cabaret-style setting and there are free outdoor performances by the Confederation Centre Young Company from July–late August. Festival runs late May–late Sept.

- Feast Dinner Theatre, Rodd Charlottetown, Charlottetown; 902-629-2321; www.feastdinnertheatres.ca. Actors serve a choice of entrée, salad, steamed mussels and dessert at the same time keeping up the plot line and lively music. Mid-June to early Sept., Tues–Sun, 6:30 pm Reservations recommended.
- The Guild, 111 Queen St., Charlottetown; 902-368-4413; 902-620-3333; www.theguildpei.com. Featuring a variety of local entertainment including sketch comedy, musical acts and plays. Open year-round.

★ Victoria Playhouse Festival, Victoria, off Rte. 1; 902-658-2025; 800-925-2025; www.victoriaplayhouse.com. A charming location for professional repertory theatre and musical concerts. Fine dining and café a few steps away. Late June–late Sept.

Points East Coastal Drive

- Kings Playhouse, Georgetown; 888-346-5666; www.kingsplayhouse.com. Featuring local performers in musical acts, plays, comedy and storytelling. Seasonal.
- St. Peters Bay Courthouse Theatre, Rte. 2, St. Peters Bay; 902-961-3636; www.courthousetheatre.com. Music, storytelling and dramatic productions with some of the best local talent. Open year-round.

Pubs and Taverns

Charlotte's Shore

- Baba's Lounge, 81 University Ave.; 902-892-7377; www.cedarseatery.com. Friendly bar featuring up-and-coming Island performers.
- Dundee Arms, 200 Pownal St.; 902-892-2496; 877-638-6333; www.dundeearms.com. Live entertainment in the Hearth and Cricket Lounge, Fridays, 6:30–10 pm Open year-round.
- Hunter's Ale House, corner of Kent and Prince Sts., Charlottetown; 902-367-4040; www.huntersalehouse.com. Bar features pub-style menu and live rock music.
- Olde Dublin Pub, 131 Sydney St.; 902-892-6992; www.oldedublinpub.com. A regular line-up of lively traditional music for an equally lively crowd. Live

music nightly mid-June–mid-Oct.

- Peake's Quay Restaurant and Bar, Charlottetown Waterfront; 902-368-1330; www.peakesquay.com. PEI's largest outdoor deck with bar. Live entertainment. May–Sept., Thurs–Sat.
- Ruthie's Pub & Eatery, 19 Water St., Victoria; 902-658-2200. Fresh seafood and steak dishes. View of beaches. Live entertainment and midnight swims. Open June–Sept.
- St. James Gate, 129 Kent St.; 902-892-4283. Restaurant and pub. Live entertainment Wed–Sat with local musicians. Open year-round.
- Victoria Row, Richmond St. A regular line-up of blues, jazz and local acts on an outdoor stage; dining on patios along the pedestrian mall. Seasonal.
- The Wave, 550 University Ave., Charlottetown; 902-566-0530; www.upeiwave.com. The campus bar for the University of Prince Edward Island. Student crowd and frequent live acts.

North Cape

- The Silver Fox Curling and Yacht Club, 110 Water St., Summerside; 902-436-2153. Live music, mostly country. Nice view of club boats.
- The Landing Oyster House and Pub, Tyne Valley; 902-831-2992. Live local music on Saturdays and many impromptu sessions.

Anne's Land

- Thirsty's Roadhouse, Rte. 6, Cavendish; 902-963-2441. Where the young and the restless congregate in the summertime. Eclectic mix of workers in the hospitality industry and those they're hospitable to. Top-40 music. Open mid-June to Sept.

Craft Shops

North Cape

- Abram-Village Handcraft Co-op, Abram-Village, at Rtes 124 and 165; 902-854-2096. Local crafts, weaving, quilts, rugs, pottery, mini-museum. Open mid-June to Sept, Mon–Sat 9:30 am–6 pm.
- Back Road Folk Art, Rte. 151, Lauretta; 902-853-3644; www.birchgate.ca/kerras. Folk art, antiques, birdhouses, carvings, rustic furniture, and studio. Open year-round, Mon–Sat, 9 am–5 pm; evenings and Sundays by chance or appointment.
- Boutique à Point, 597 Cannontown Rd., Rte. 165, Mont-Carmel; 902-854-2895. Handmade clothing, crafts, and souvenirs. Open year-round, Mon–Sat, 9 am–5 pm.
- Celtic Gift Shop, The College of Piping, 619 Water St., Summerside; 902-436-5377; 877-BAGPIPE; www.collegeofpiping.com. A wide selection of music, books, highland supplies, instruments, tartans and clan items. Open year-round.
- Basket Weavers of PEI Co-operative Ltd., Rte. 2 east of Richmond; 902-854-3063; 902-882-2247; www.basketweaverspei.com. Basket weaving and Island crafts. Workshops. Open June–Sept.
- ★ Indian Art and Craft of North America, Lennox Island, on Rte. 163, off Rte. 12; 902-831-2653; www.malpequebay.com. Contemporary and traditional First Nations' crafts from across North America. Specializing in Mi'kmaq ash-splint baskets and Micmac Productions pottery and figurines. Open mid-May–mid-Oct., Mon–Sat, 9 am–6 pm; Sun noon–6 pm.
- MacAusland's Woollen Mill, Bloomfield, on Rte. 2; 902-859-3005; www.macauslandswoollen mills.com. Watch while wool is carded, spun and woven. Shop on premises. Open year-round 8 am–5 pm Admission free.
- Malpeque Fine Iron, 1209 Barbara Weit Rd., Rte. 180, New Annan; 902-436-5006; 866-436-5006; www.malpequefineiron.com. One-of-a-kind fun pieces made from recycled metals. Hand-forged wrought-iron products. Open year-round. Mon–Fri 8 am–4 pm; Sat 8:30 am–1 pm.
- Spinnakers' Landing, Waterfront Properties, Summerside; 902-436-6692; www.summersidewaterfront.com/spinnakers. A boardwalk location on Summerside Harbour, featuring giftware, crafts, retail outlets and antiques. Food outlets, ice cream, free entertainment and free parking. Open early June–late Sept, daily.
- Tignish Treasures Gift Shop/Holiday

Island Productions, School St., Tignish; 902-882-2896; www.tignishtreasures.com. Handcrafted soaps and bath products made with PEI Irish Moss, Christmas ornaments and PEI souvenirs. Free studio tours. Open June–Sept.

- West Point Lighthouse Craft Shop, West Point, off Rte. 14, 364 Cedar Dunes Park Rd.; 902-859-3579. Locally made crafts and Atlantic giftware. Open June–Sept.; July and Aug, daily 9 am–9 pm; June and Sept, 10 am–6 pm.

Anne's Land

★ The Dunes, Brackley Beach, on Rte. 15; 902-672-2586; www.dunesgallery.com. Excellent selection of contemporary pottery designs by owner Peter Jansons, along with works by other Island artists and imports. Jewellery, glassware and other art items also on sale in gallery-restaurant. New annex features modern furniture fashions. Open May–Oct, daily 9 am–5 pm; evenings in summer.

★ Gaudreau Fine Woodworking, Rte. 6, South Rustico; 902-963-2273; www.woodmagic.ca. Fine crafts gallery features designer hardwood accessories, pottery, demos. Open daily May–Oct. Call for winter hours.

- New Glasgow Mercantile, 5626 Rte. 13, New Glasgow; 621-0973; Featuring Island made arts and crafts, "Anne" keepsakes, home and garden accents, kites, wind accessories and outdoor fun products, T-Shirts, sweatshirts and fleecewear. Open mid-May–mid-Oct.
- New London Village Pottery, Rte. 6, New London; 902-886-2473; www.pei.welcome.to. Pottery made on-site, Island crafts, jewellery, weavings and paintings. Open May–Oct., daily.
- North Shore Island Traditions Past & Present Rug Shop, 7176 Rustico Rd.; 902-963-2453; www.hookamat.com. Traditional rug-hooking supplies, a selection of smocking, folk art and beeswax candles. Open year-round, Mon–Sat, 10 am-6 pm Off-season, Tues–Thurs, 1-5 pm, Fri and Sat, 11 am-5 pm.
- Prince Edward Island Preserve Co. Ltd., junction of Rtes 224 and 258, New Glasgow; 902-964-4300; 800-565-5267; www.preservecompany.com. Craft and gift shop featuring fine preserves prepared on premises for market. On-site restaurant, ice cream take-out, and 12-acre New Glasgow Country Gardens. Open May to mid-Oct: July 1 to early Sept, 8 am–9:30 pm; reduced hours in the off-season.
- Quilt Eco-museum (Les Créations Louise Comeau), Abram-Village; 902-854-2614. Traditional patterned quilts, unique Anne of Green Gables quilt, demonstrations. Open seasonally.
- Sandscript, Rte. 8, New London; 902-886-3303. Handcrafted sand treasures, Island- and Canadian-made gifts. Open May to mid-Oct., 10 am–5 pm.
- Stanley Bridge Studios, Stanley Bridge, on Rte. 6; 902-886-2800; 902-621-0436; www.susanchristensenart.com. A large selection of pottery, reproduction tin lighting, fine jewellery, glass, quilts, collectibles. Open May–Oct., 10 am–5 pm daily; July–Aug., 9:30 am–8 pm.
- The Toy Factory, New Glasgow, on Rte. 13; 902-964-2299; www.toy-factory.ca. Unique wooden toys handcrafted while you watch. Lots of toys for play-testing too. Open mid-May–mid-Oct: June 15–Aug 31, Mon–Sat 9 am–9 pm, Sun 10 am–5 pm; reduced hours off-season.
- Trout River Pottery, Rte. 239, Millvale; 902-621-0498; www.peipottery.com. Off Rte. 254. Hand-thrown porcelain and stoneware pottery. Open mid-May–mid-Oct, Mon–Sat 9 am–6 pm, Sun in July and Aug.

Charlotte's Shore

★ Best of P.E.I., 156 Richmond St., Victoria Row, Charlottetown; www.bestofpei.com. Crafts, artwork, music, books. Every item in store made in PEI. Open year-round 9 am–9 pm.

- Cavendish Figurines Ltd, Gateway Village, Borden-Carleton; 902-437-2663; 800-558-1908; www.cavendishfigurines.com. Island souvenirs and giftware. Figurines made on premises, free bilingual tours. Open year-round.

- ★ Charlottetown Farmers' Market, 100 Belvedere Ave., Charlottetown; 902-626-3373. In addition to a vast array of locally grown produce, fresh meats, seafood, baked goods, pastries, international foods, fresh flowers and locally roasted coffees, a number of local craftspeople also market their products. Open year-round, Sat 9 am–2 pm; July–Aug., Wed and Sat.
- The Green Man Vintage and Vinyl, 48 University Ave., Charlottetown; 902-566-1361. Open daily year-round.
- Moonsnail Soapworks and Nature Store, 85 Water St., Charlottetown; 888-771-7627; www.moonsnailsoapworks.com. Special Island soaps and natural body treats, all handcrafted on site. Open year-round.
- Northern Watters Knitwear, 150 Richmond St., Victoria Row, Charlottetown; 902-566-5850; 800-565-9665; www.nwknitwear.com. Sweaters and accessories handcrafted on PEI using 100 percent British worsted oiled wool. Open year-round, Mon-Fri 8 am–8 pm, Sat 9 am–6 pm; Sun noon–5 pm.
- Peake's Wharf — Historic Waterfront Merchants, located at the foot of Great George and Prince Sts., Charlottetown; 902-629-1864; 800-955-1864; www.walkandseacharlottetown.com. Crafts, clothing, gifts, homemade ice cream, restaurants, bars and live entertainment. Open mid-May–mid-Oct.
- ★ The Showcase — Confederation Centre of the Arts, 145 Richmond St., Charlottetown; 902-628-6149; www.confederationcentre.com. Handcrafts from across Canada, books and Anne of Green Gables products. Contemporary art for rent or purchase. Open year-round.
- Stanley Pottery and Weaving Studio and Shop, Breadalbane, Rte. 246; 902-621-0316. Rural life and nature inspire the hand-painted scenes. Open May 1–Oct 31, daily 10 am–6 pm; off-season by chance or appointment.

Points East Coastal Drive

- Belfast Mini-Mills, 1829 Garfield St., Belfast; 902-659-2202. Fully operational mill, which specializes in exotic animal fibres, such as alpaca, angora rabbit, bison, llama. Wide range of yarns and rovings dyed and processed at the mill. Finished knitted and woven products, as well as felt and felted items.
- Ginger Snaps Treasures & Treats, Hillsborough River Eco-Centre, Mount Stewart; 902-731-3587. Handcrafted and unique gifts and sweets.
- Cardigan Craft Centre and Tea Room, Cardigan, off Rte. 5; 902-583-2930; www.cardigancrafts.com. A co-operative centre for handcrafts produced by its members, featuring rug hooking, quilting, weaving, soft-sculpture knitting, sheepskin products, free-hand pottery, ceramics. Open June–early Oct., Mon–Sat 10 am–5:30 pm.
- Fire & Water Creations, Bay Fortune, 690 Rte. 310; 902-687-3367; www.peiseaglass.com. Working studio gallery with handcrafted, genuine sea-glass jewellery. Open May to mid-Oct., 10 am–4 pm Off-season by chance or appointment.
- Koleszar Pottery, Rte. 204, Melville; 902-659-2570. Delicate porcelain pottery, decorated with an eye to beauty and the sweetness of nature. Open May 1–Nov. 15, 9 am–noon and 2–5 pm Closed Tues.
- Log Cabin Arts & Crafts, 30 Main St, Souris; 902-687-3046. Locally made crafts including souvenirs, quilts, paintings, ceramics, knitting, dried florals, weaving and books. Open May–Sept.
- Miss Elly's Genteel Gifts & Stuff, Main St., Murray Harbour by the wharf; 902-962-3555. Linens, lace, quilts, Island-wool blankets, hooked mats, Island pottery, prints, paintings and collectibles. Open mid-June to late Sept., Mon–Sat 10 am–5 pm, Sun 1–5 pm.
- Naturally Yours, 31 Beach Ave., Souris; 902-687-3301. Garden centre, PEI treasures, oil paintings of local landscapes, refinished antiques. Open June–Sept.,

Mon–Sat 9 am–5 pm.
- The Old General Store, Main St., Murray River; 902-962-2459. Turn-of-the-century general store featuring quality linens, quilts, clothing, jewellery, handcrafts, books, artwork and music. Open mid-June to late Sept. and Canadian Thanksgiving weekend, daily; other times by chance or appointment.
- Plough the Waves Centre, intersection of Rtes 1 and 4, Wood Islands; 902-962-3761. Gift shops, visitor information and liquor store on premises. Landscaped grounds with gazebo for relaxation and picnics. Open May–Oct.
- Serendipity Boutique, 500 Main Street, Down East Mall, Montague. Jewellery, painted *objects d'art*, handcrafted souvenirs and silk flower arrangements. Open year-round during mall hours.
- Shoreline Design, 40 Water St., Georgetown; 902-652-2240; www.shorelinedesignpei.com. Jewellery, one-of-a-kind Island sandstone and Brazilian soapstone carvings, pottery and ceramic pieces. Open daily 9 am-8 pm May-Sept. Off-season by chance or appointment.
- Spit'N Image — Creator of Fine Alpaca Knitwear, 649 Dover Rd., Murray River; 902- 962-2031; www3.pei.sympatico.ca/~micron. Sweaters and cardigans in a variety of styles, handcrafted from certified organic fibres. Meet alpacas "Carmen" and "Maple." Open year-round, daily.
- St. Peters Bay Craft and Giftware, 15465 Northside Rd., St. Peters Bay; 902-961-3223; www.stpetersbay.com. High quality pewter jewellery, pewter gifts, nature collectibles, leather figurines, books, photos and prints by local artists, and traditional music. Demonstrations in pewter casting. Open May–Oct., Mon–Fri 9 am–4 pm.

Product Tours

- Anne of Green Gables Chocolates, Avonlea Village, Cavendish; 902-963-2800; 902-963-3589. Premium chocolates and fudge. View chocolates being made on-site; feel free to sample. Seasonal.
- CheeseLady's Gouda, Rte. 223 off Rte. 2, Winsloe North; 902-628-6691; 902-368-1506. Come see how Gouda cheese is made. Sample herb, onion, peppercorn and garlic-flavoured cheeses. Farm with calves, sheep and llamas. Open year-round, Mon–Sat 9 am–6 pm; off-season Mon–Sat 10 am–5 pm; winter by appointment.
- Island Chocolates, Main St., Victoria; 902-658-2320. Chocolates handmade using Belgian chocolate and fresh PEI fruits. Hands-on workshops. Open June–Sept., daily: July and Aug., 10 am–8 pm; June and Sept., 10 am–5 pm.
- Prince Edward Island Preserve Company, corner of Rtes 224 and 258, New Glasgow; 902-964-4300; 800-565-5267; www.preservecompany.com. See, hear, smell and taste fine preserves being prepared for market in a 1913 butter factory in the scenic village of New Glasgow. Gift shop and café. Open May–early Oct.; July and Aug., 8 am–9:30 pm; reduced hours in the off-season.
- Rossignol Estate Winery, Rte. 4, Little Sands; 902-962-4193; www.rossignolwinery.com. Visit the farm winery and vineyard and sample fine wines. Open May–Oct., Mon–Sat 10 am–5 pm; Sun 1–5 pm.

Art Galleries

- Art Gallery of Tony Diodati, off Rte. 20 in Springbrook; 902-886-3009; www.tonydiodati.com. Featuring original art and limited-edition reproductions of Prince Edward Island scenes by owner/artist Tony Diodati. Open daily late May–late Sept.
- Barachois Inn & Fine Art Gallery, 2193 Church Rd., Rustico; 902-963-2194; www.barachoisinn.com. New gallery in restored heritage inn with Victorian gardens. Island artists. Open May–Oct, 1–5 pm

★ Confederation Centre Art Gallery, 145 Richmond St., Charlottetown; 902-628-6142; www.confederationcentre.com. Atlantic Canada's largest gallery featuring the works of Canadian artists. Open year-round.

★ The Dunes Studio Gallery, Brackley

Beach, on Rte. 15; 902-672-2586; www.dunesgallery.com. A good cross-section of Island contemporary art in a beautiful setting. Open June–Oct., daily 9 am–5 pm; evenings in summer.

- Ellen's Creek Gallery, 525 North River Rd., Charlottetown; 902-368-3494. Various Island artists. Open year-round, Mon–Sat 9 am–5:30 pm
- Eptek Centre, 130 Harbour Dr., Summerside; 902-888-8373; www.peimuseum.com. National exhibition centre with regular showings of Island artists. Open year-round.
- The Guild, 111 Queen St., Charlottetown; 902-368-4413; 866-774-0717; www.theguildpei.com. Exhibits by PEI Arts Guild members.
- Kensington Art Co-op, Freight Shed, Kensington Train Station. Works by local artists. Open mid-June–mid-Sept., Mon–Sat 10 am–4 pm.
- Lefurgey Cultural Centre, 205 Prince St., Summerside; 902-432-1327; www.wyattheritage.com. Small gallery of Island art. Open year-round; gift shop seasonal.
- Mermaid Art Gallery and Framing, 131 Grafton St., Charlottetown, in Confederation Court Mall; 902-626-3001; www.mermaidart.com. Featuring the works of Island and Atlantic Canadian artists. Open year-round.
- The Showcase Art Sales and Rentals, Confederation Centre of the Arts, 145 Richmond St., Charlottetown; 902-628-6129; 902-628-6149; www.confederationcentre.com. Fine Canadian art available for sale or rent. Open year-round.
- The Studio Gallery, 2 Howard St., Victoria-by-the-Sea; 902-658-2733; www.studiogallery.ca. The work of Island artists including artist-in-residence Doreen Foster. Open June–Oct., 10 am–5 pm or by appointment.

Outdoor Recreation

The variety of landscapes and activities offered by the Island's parks is astounding. Calm south shore beaches, rolling wooded hills, marshland full of wildlife, quiet meadows for picnicking — it's your choice. About half of PEI's 29 provincial parks have camping facilities. Many also have day programs providing guided nature walks, concerts, evening campfires and children's activities.

North Cape

- Belmont Provincial Park, off Rte. 123, Belmont. Camping, unsupervised beach, picnicking, showers, flush toilets, change house.
- Cedar Dunes Provincial Park, West Point, on Rte. 14. Camping, supervised beach, picnicking, showers, flush toilets, change house, nature trail, interpretive programs, wheelchair accessible washrooms.
- Green Park Provincial Park, on Rte. 12, Port Hill. Camping, unsupervised beach, picnicking, nature trails, showers, flush toilets, change house, floating dock.
- Jacques Cartier Provincial Park, Kildare Capes, on Rte. 12. Camping, supervised beach, picnicking, showers, change house, canteen, interpretation.
- Linkletter Provincial Park, on Rte. 11, Linkletter. Camping, unsupervised beach, picnicking, showers, change house, flush toilets.
- Mill River Provincial Park, on Rte. 136, just off Rte. 2. Camping, unsupervised beach, picnicking, showers, flush toilets, change house, wheelchair-accessible washrooms, marina.
- Miminegash Pond, off Rte. 14, south of the harbour. No facilities; interpretive program, camping, unsupervised beach.
- Nail Pond, off Rte. 12. No facilities, unsupervised beach.
- St. Chrysostome, off Rte. 11. No facilities, unsupervised beach.
- Union Corner Provincial Park, on Rte. 11, Union Corner. No facilities, unsupervised beach.

Anne's Land

In the Prince Edward Island National Park:

★ Brackley Beach. Group camping, supervised beach, information centre, flush toilets, change house, showers, canteen, wheelchair access.

- ★ Cavendish Beach. Camping, supervised beach, information centre, flush toilets, change house, showers, canteen, wheelchair access.
- ★ Dalvay Beach. Unsupervised beach, no on-site facilities, picnicking.
- • North Rustico Beach. Supervised beach, toilets, change house.
- • Stanhope Beach. Camping, supervised beach, flush toilets, change house, showers, canteen, wheelchair access.

Outside Prince Edward Island National Park:

- Blooming Point Beach. Off Rte. 218 at Blooming Point. No facilities, unsupervised.
- Cabot Beach Provincial Park, Malpeque, on Rte. 20. Camping, supervised beach, picnicking, showers, flush toilets, change house, interpretive program.
- Cousins Shore, off Rte. 20 at Darnley. No facilities, unsupervised beach.

Charlotte's Shore

- Argyle Shore Provincial Park, on Rte. 19, Argyle Shore. Unsupervised beach, picnicking, showers, flush toilets, change house.
- Brookvale Provincial Ski Park, Kelly's Cross. Walking trails.
- Chelton Beach Provincial Park, off Rte. 10. Supervised beach, picnicking, showers, flush toilets, change house, canteen.
- Port-La-Joye–Fort Amherst National Historic Site, Rocky Point. Information centre.
- Strathgartney Provincial Park, Strathgartney. Camping, picnicking, walking trails, showers, wheelchair-accessible washrooms.
- Tea Hill Beach, off Rte. 1, Tea Hill. Unsupervised beach, picnicking, showers, flush toilets, change house, canteen, recreation programs.
- Victoria Beach Provincial Park, off Rte. 1, Victoria. Unsupervised beach, picnicking, showers, flush toilets, change house.

Points East Coastal Drive

- ★ Basin Head Day Park, off Rte. 16, Basin Head. Outdoor showers, washroom facilities, gazebo, picnic tables, gift shop, canteen, ice cream, unsupervised beach.
- • Boughton Bay, off Rte. 310 near Little Pond. No facilities, unsupervised beach.
- • Brudenell River Provincial Park, on Rte. 3, Roseneath. Camping, supervised beach, picnicking, showers, change house, flush toilets, interpretive program, canteen, camping, nature trail.
- • Campbell's Cove Provincial Park, on Rte. 16, Campbells Cove. Camping, unsupervised beach, picnicking, showers, flush toilets, change house.
- ★ Greenwich, Prince Edward Island National Park, Rte. 313, Greenwich. Supervised beach, showers, change house, interpretive centre, walking trails.
- • Irvings Cape Beach, off Rte. 17 near Murray Harbour North. Unsupervised beach.
- • Kings Castle Provincial Park, on Rte. 348, Gladstone. Camping, unsupervised beach, picnicking, toilets.
- • Lord Selkirk Provincial Park, on Rte. 1, Eldon. Camping, unsupervised beach, picnicking, showers, flush toilets, change house, supervised swimming pool.
- • MacLeod's Beach, off Rte. 4, between White Sands and Little Sands. No facilities, unsupervised beach.
- • Northumberland Provincial Park, on Rte. 4, near Wood Islands. Camping, supervised beach, picnicking, flush toilets, showers, change house, recreational programs.
- ★ Panmure Island Provincial Park, Rte. 347, Panmure Island. Camping, supervised beach, picnicking, showers, change huts, flush toilets, canteen.
- • Pinette Provincial Park, on Rte. 1, Pinette. Unsupervised beach, picnicking, showers, flush toilets, change house.
- • Red Point Provincial Park, on Rte. 302, Red Point. Camping, supervised beach, picnicking, showers, flush toilets, change house.
- • Sally's Beach Provincial Park, off Rte. 310, near Inn at Spry Point, Spry Point. Facilities relating to resort, unsupervised beach, change house, picnicking.
- • Savage Harbour Beach, Rte. 218, Savage Harbour. No facilities,

unsupervised beach.
- Seal Cove, off Rte. 17, near Murray Harbour North. Unsupervised beach, nearby campground has picnicking facilities and toilets.
- Souris Provincial Park, on Rte. 2. Unsupervised beach, picnicking, showers, flush toilets, change house.
- Wood Islands Provincial Park, on Rte. 4. Unsupervised beach, picnicking, flush toilets, change house, canteen.

Golf

For more information on golf courses, visit www.golfpei.com, and for a tip-to-tip, week-long itinerary, visit www.peiplay.com/golf.

North Cape

- ★ Mill River Provincial Golf Course (18-hole, par 72), Mill River Provincial Park and Rodd Mill River Resort, off Rte. 2; 902-368-5761; 800-235-8909; www.golflinkspei.com. May–Oct.
- St. Felix Golf & Country Club (9-hole, par 36), Greenmount Rd., Rte. 153, St.-Felix; 902-882-2328; 877-311-2328; www.stfelixgolf.ca. May–Oct. Green fees: $30.
- Summerside Golf and Country Club (18-hole, par 72), Linkletter, Rte. 11 west of Summerside; 902-436-2505; 877-505-2505; www.summersidegolf.com. May–Oct. Green fees: $35–50.

Anne's Land

- Andersons Creek Golf Club (18-hole, par 72), Rte. 240, Stanley Bridge; 902-886-2222; 866-886-4422; www.andersonscreek.com. May–Oct. Green fees: $45–75.
- ★ The Eagles Glenn Golf Course (18-hole, par 72), Rte. 6, Cavendish; 902-963-3600; 866-963-3600; www.eaglesglenn.com. May–Oct.
- Forest Hills Golf Course (9-hole, par 36), Cavendish, on Rte. 6; 902-963-2887; 866-963-2887; www.foresthills.ca. May–Oct.
- French River Golf Course (18-hole, par 67), Rte. 263, French River; 902-886-2098. Apr.–Dec. Green fees: $14–20.
- Glasgow Hills Resort & Golf Club (18-hole, par 72), Rte. 13, New Glasgow; 902-621-2200; 866-621-2200; www.glasgowhills.com. May–Oct. Green fees: $50–80.
- ★ Green Gables Golf Course (18-hole, par 72), in the Prince Edward Island National Park, Cavendish, on Rte. 6; 902-963-2488; www.greengablesgolf.com. May–Oct. Green fees: $55–100.
- Line Road Triple Challenge (3-hole), Rte. 269, North Rustico. May–Nov. Green fees: $8 three holes; $15 six holes; $20 nine holes.
- Red Sands Golf Course (9-hole, par 32), Kerrytown Rd., Rte. 107 off Rte. 6, Clinton; 902-886-3344; 877-886-3344; www.golfredsands.com. May–Oct.
- Rustico Resort Golf and Country Club (18-hole, par 73), Rustico, off Rte. 6 on Rte. 242; 902-963-2909; 800-465-3734; www.rusticoresort.com. May–Oct. Green fees: $36. Reduced rates in afternoon.
- Serenity Valley Golf Course (9-hole, par 36), Howatt Rd., Rte. 263, French River; 902-886-2098. May–Oct. Green fees: $10–18; children half-price.
- Stanhope Golf and Country Club (18-hole, par 72), Stanhope, Black River Rd.,Rte. 25; 902-672-2842; www.stanhopegolfclub.com. May–Oct. Green fees: $49. Off-season rates.

Charlotte's Shore

- Belvedere Golf Club (18-hole, par 72), 1 Greensview Dr., Charlottetown; 902-368-7104; www.belvederegolf.com. May–Oct. Green fees: $55–75.
- Dog River Golf Links (9-hole, par 35), Clyde River, on Rte. 247; 902-675-2585; www.dogrivergolflinks.com. May–Oct. Green fees: $25–40.
- Countryview Golf Course (9-hole, par 36), Rte. 19, Cornwall; 902-675-2800; 866-464-2800; www.countryviewgolf.com. May–Oct. Green fees: $24.
- Fox Meadow Golf & Country Club (18-hole, par 72), 167 Kinlock Rd., Stratford; 902-569-4653; 877-569-8337; www.foxmeadow.pe.ca.
- Glen Afton Golf Course (18-hole, par 70), Nine Mile Creek, on Rte. 19; 902-675-3000; 866-675-3001; www.glenaftongolf.com. May–Oct. Green fees: $21–33.
- Vistabay Golf Course (9-hole, par

34), Rte. 1A, Alexandra; 902-569-2252; 866-209-8907; www.vistabay.ca. Mid-Apr. to Oct. Green fees: $12–44.

Points East Coastal Drive

- Avondale Golf Course (18-hole, par 72), Avondale; 902-651-4653; 866-651-2380; www.avondalegolf.com. Apr.–Oct.
- Beaver Valley Golf Club (18-hole, par 70), Martinvale; 902-583-3481; 877-351-4653; www.peisland.com/beavervalley. May–Oct. Green fees: $17–27.
- Belfast Highland Greens (9-hole, par 37), Eldon, off Trans-Canada Hwy; 902-659-2794; www.peisland.com/belfast. May–Oct.
- ★ Brudenell River Golf Course (18-hole, par 72), in Brudenell Provincial Park, Roseneath, off Rte. 3; 800-235-8909; www.golflinkspei.com.
- Callaway Golf Divine Nine (9-hole, par 30), at the Brudenell River Resort, Rte. 3; 800-235-8909. www.golflinkspei.com.
- Dundarave Golf Course (18-hole, par 72), in Brudenell River Resort, Roseneath, off Rte. 3; 800-235-8909; www.golflinkspei.com.
- Eagle's View Golf Course & Interpretive Centre (9-hole, par 36), Murray River; 902-962-4433; 866-962-4433; www.eaglesviewgolf.com. May–Oct.
- ★ The Links at Crowbush Cove (18-hole, par 72), Lakeside, on Rte. 350, off Rte. 2; 800-235-8909; www.golflinkspei.com.
- Peakes Tee (9-hole), Rte. 22, Peakes; 902-583-2632; www.peakestee.com. Open year-round.
- Rollo Bay Greens (9-hole, par 35), Rte. 2, Rollo Bay; 902-687-1586; www.rollobaygreens.com. May–Oct.

Boating and Sailing

- Cardigan Sailing Charters, Cardigan; 902-583-2020; www.cardiganlobstersuppers.com. Seasonal, 10 am–3 pm Lobster lunch.
- Cruise Manada, Montague; 902-838-3444; 800-986-3444; www.cruisemanada.com. Mid-May to Sept. Three departures daily during July and Aug (call to reserve). Interpretive river cruise.
- Marine Adventures Seal Watching, Murray River; 902-962-2494; 800-496-2494; www.sealwatching.com. June–Sept. Three departures daily. Murray River cruise.
- Peake's Wharf Boat Tours, foot of Great George St., Charlottetown; 800-955-1864. June to mid-Sept. Tours of Charlottetown Harbour. Four departures daily.
- Saga Sailing Adventures, Charlottetown Harbour; 902-672-1222; www.virtuo.com/sagasail. June–Sept. Three departures daily.

Mariners may launch their own boats at concrete-slab haul-out sites or at slipways. Boats may be docked at Quartermaster Marine and the Yacht Club in Charlottetown, and at the Silver Fox Yacht Club in Summerside. Floating dock facilities are available at the Municipal Marina in Montague, in Murray River, Georgetown, Cardigan, Brudenell and Murray Harbour. Wood Islands also offers a protected small-vessel harbour. Foreign pleasure craft are obliged to report to the nearest Canada Customs Office upon arrival. Charlottetown Customs: 94 Euston St.; 902-628-4287; 800-461-9999.

Canoeing and Kayaking

With so much water around, it seems a shame not to go boating while on the Island. Beginners can go out for a quick paddle, while adventurers can chart their way through scenic river systems. Some waterfront accommodations rent canoes, kayaks, and other vessels. Here are some other sources:

- By The Sea Kayaking, Victoria; 902-658-2572; 877-879-2572; www.bytheseakayaking.ca. June–Oct.
- Cascumpec Kayaking, Northport; 853-4095; www.cascumpeckayaking.com. July-Aug.
- Kingfisher Outdoors Inc., Leo F. Rossiter Angler's Park, Morell; 902-

961-2080. Kayak tours on Morell River. Bike rentals. July to mid-Sept.
- Malpeque Bay Sea Kayak Tours, Rte. 105 at Malpeque Bay; 902-432-0111; 866-582-3383; www.peikayak.ca. Tours and rentals. July-Aug.
- Outdoor Pursuits — Canoe Tours, Tracadie Harbour Wharf; 902-672-2000; www.pcpages.com/canoeing/travels.html. Explore the shoreline of Blooming Point in an eight-passenger replica of a Mi'kmaq open-water canoe. $20/paddler. June–Sept.
- Outside Expeditions, Brudenell and North Rustico Harbour; 800-207-3899; www.getoutside.com. Canoe and kayak rentals and excursions. Mid-June to early Sept.
- St. Catherine's Cove Canoe Rental Inc., St. Catherine's; 902-675-2035; www3.pei.sympatico.ca/~ajlucock/canoeskayaks/HomePage.html. Canoes and river kayaks. Phone ahead for best times and tides. May–Sept.

Cycling

There are few better ways to see Prince Edward Island than by bicycle. Sport PEI has information on cycling day tours and Nimbus Publishing of Halifax has published . Many inns, resorts and campgrounds rent bicycles. The following companies also rent bikes, sell package deals, and make other arrangements:

- Annandale Bicycle Rental & Repair Service, 274 Annandale Wharf Rd., Annandale; 902-583-2045; 902-969-3099 (cell); www.annandalepei.com. May–Oct.
- Freewheeling Adventures, Cathy and Philip Guest, RR 1, Hubbards, NS; 800-672-0775; www.freewheeling.ca. End-to-end van-supported multi-day trips with guides, or custom trip-planning, and bicycle rentals. Open year-round.
- Journey's End Bike Tours, Kensington Train Station Freight Shed; 902-836-4897. Guided tours. May–Oct.
- MacQueen's Island Tours — Bicycling Specialists, 430 Queen St., Charlottetown; 902-368-2453; 800-969-2822; www.macqueens.com. Independent and guided tours, bike and equipment rentals and repairs. Open year-round.
- Outside Expeditions, Brudenell and North Rustico; 800-207-3899; www.getoutside.com. Self-guided and custom tours and rentals. June–Sept.
- Paul's Bike Shop, 104 Chaisson Rd., St. Edward; 902-882-3750. Rentals and repair service available. Open year-round.
- The Pines Bicycle Rentals, 31 Riverside Dr., Montague; 902-838-3650; www.thepinesbb.ca.
- Plover Bike Rentals, St. Peters Bay; 902-961-3223. All sizes available. May–Oct.
- Smooth Cycle, 308 Queen St., Charlottetown; 800-310-6550; www.smoothcycle.com. Rentals, repairs and sales. Guided tours, route maps and shuttle service. Open year-round.
- Trailside Inn, Café and Adventures, 109 Main St., Mount Stewart; 902-676-3130; 888-704-6595; www.trailside.ca. Quality bike rentals, route maps, gourmet picnics and shuttle service, situated on the Confederation Trail. Open July and Aug., daily. Reduced hours in the off-season.

Sport Fishing

- Aiden's Deep-Sea Fishing, North Rustico; 902-963-3522; 902-963-2288; 866-510-3474; www.peifishing.com.
- Barry Doucette's Deep-Sea Fishing on Jason D 2000, Capts. Jamie and Jason Doucette, North Rustico; 902-963-2465; 902-963-2611.
- Bearded Skipper's Deep-Sea Fishing, Capt. Norman Peters, North Rustico Wharf. 902-963-2334; 902-963-2525.
- Ben's Lake, Ken and June Moyaert, Bellevue on Rte. 24; 902-838-2706; www.benslake.com. Trout fishing. Pay by the pound for catch or catch-and-release fly fishing. Tackle for rent.
- Bob's Deep-Sea Fishing, Capt. Bob Doucette, North Rustico; 902-963-2666; 902-963-2086; www3.pei.sympatico.ca/~bobsdeepsea.
- David McLellan's Canada Goose Hunting & Sea Trout Fishing, 476

Keppoch Rd., Stratford; 902-569-2579; www.waterfowlingpei.com. Waterfowling, trophy speckled trout and striped bass.

- Dale's Deep-Sea Adventures, Capt. Dale Wall, Kensington; 902-836-3393; 902-439-3693; www.kata.pe.ca/attract/dalesdeepsea.
- Graham's Deep-Sea Fishing, Capt. Marvin Graham, Stanley Bridge; 902-886-2491; 902-886-2077; 902-439-1742.
- Joey Gauthier's Deep-Sea Fishing, Capt. Jamie Gauthier, Rusticoville; 902-963-2295; 902-963-2191; www.joeysfishing.com.
- MacNeill's Tuna & Deep-Sea Fishing, Capt. Jeffrey L. MacNeill, North Lake; 902-357-2858; www.peitunacharters.com.
- New London Wharf Deep-Sea Fishing, Capt. Wade Graham, New London Wharf; 902-886-2647; 902-886-2124.
- Richard's Deep-Sea Fishing, Capt. Richard Watts, Covehead Harbour; 902-672-2376; 902-672-2260.
- Salty Seas Deep-Sea Fishing, Capt. Lonnie MacDonald, Covehead Harbour; 902-672-3246; 902-672-2681; www.virtuo.com/salty.
- Tony's Tuna & Deep-Sea Fishing, Capt. Tony MacDonald, North Lake; 902-357-2207; www.tonystunafishing.ca.
- Wade's Deep-Sea Fishing, Capt. Wade Gallant, North Rustico; 902-963-3604; www.wadesdeepseafishing.com.

Index

Photo Credits

Keith Vaughan is a Halifax-based photographer who has won many prizes and medals at home as well as in national and international competition. His other Formac publications include Lunenburg: Then and Now; The Nova Scotia Colourguide; and Maritime Flavours. All photographs are by Keith Vaughan; except where noted below.

T=top; M=middle; B=bottom
Adventure weddings, 144T; Andrew Dean, 18M; Andrew Penner, 1, 56M; Anne of Green Gables Museum: p29T; Arthur Kwiatkowski, 54B; Artis Rams, 8; 106T; Barrett MacKay, 64T; Blue Coconut Media: 63, 65T; Bobcatnorth, 166T; Brenda and Edward Dewar: 158M & B, 159B; Brent Matheson, 162; Brian Simpson: I18B, 121; Carter Jefferey, 141C, 142 2nd from B; Central Development Corporation: 142T; Dan Kennedy: 43B; Darrell Theriault, 89; Debra Wentzell-Hannams: 9B, 27, 110T, 120T; Denis Jr Tangney, 157B, 70T; Dylan Kereluk, 53T; Enterprise PEI: 48B (John Sylvester); 67T (Barrett and MacKay Photography); 69B (John Sylvester); Eric Michaud, 88T; Floortje, 117T; Full Frame Media, 91B; Henry Dunsmore, 151; Henry Dunsmore, 41T; Henry Dunsmore, 99B; James Ingram, 92T; James Noble, 120B; Jim Lorimer: 9T, 38B, 42B; John C. Watson: 132M; John Hebert, 61T; John Johnson, 66T; John Sylvester: 4B; 42T, 88M, 90M, 96B, 106B; Julian Beveridge: 2M, 49B, 52M, 55M, 103T, 143M; Keith Watson, 112B, 14T, 19B, 21; Kensington/Town of Kensington Staff: 107T; Kent MacDonald: 10T; Kevin Famsworth: 14M, 16B, 17B, 18C, 24, 25, 27T, 28T, 31B, 39, 40T & M, 43T, 44T, 45T, 46, 50T, 51B, 52 T, 56T, 57 M & B, 70B, 72T, 77, 87, 92B, 96T, 100 T & B, 101B, 104T, 105T, 1O7B,1O9, 110B, 111B, 112T, 115, U9B, 120M, 126, 127T& B, 133 M & B, 134, 139, 140T&M, 141T, 142B, 143 T, 145B, 152, 155M, 160, L, 164, 165, I67T&M 168T; Len Wagg: 26; Lena Arsenault, 135B; Lot 30, 117B; Louise Vessey, 65B Louise Vessey: 93; Macphail Woods, 59B, 155B; Marie Peters: 50B; 105B; 142 2nd from T; Seven Isleifson, 113; Mark Whitwright, 62, 66B; Martin Caird: 2B, 12B, 13B, 20T, 30T, 31T, 32T, 33T, 36T & M, 37B, 40B, I43T; Maxine Delaney, 118; Meredith Bangay, 138T, 143B, 99T; Mike Clarke, 140B; Morgie-39, 11T; MTLskyline, 18B; Old Home Week: 97T; Orwell Comer Historic Village: 111M, 154T, 155T; Patricia Hayes: 41B, 51T, 79; PEI Museum and Heritage Foundation: 108B; Prince Edward Island National Park/Parks Canada: 28B; Pro Photos: 64B; Reginald Porter: 81T & M; Richard Rodvold, 18T; Rick McCharles, 55T;Rob Hyndman, 38T, 114B; Samuel Burt, 122T; Sandi MacPherson, 13T, 58; Shane MacDougall: 83B; Shaun Lowe, 24B, 123, 125T; Sir Christopher Reynolds, 15B, 25T, 47T; Smudge_9000, 52B; Stanhope Bay and Beach Resort: 138B; Thomas Shortell, 61B; Tom England, 10B; Tourism PEI, 159T; Verena Matthew, 49T; Victoria Playhouse: 94B; Wax World of the Stars: 44B; Wendell Dennis: 94T; 95T; Wendy MacGregor: 2M; Wind Energy Institute of Canada/PEI Energy Corporation North Cape Wind Farm: 13 IT; Zach Vanwagner, 103B; ZMH, 11B, 153.

All maps courtesy of Tourism PEI, except for Charlottetown walking tour: courtesy of Image Works PEI Inc.

Formac Publishing Company
5502 Atlantic Street
Halifax, Nova Scotia
B3H 1G4
www.formac.ca

Distributed in the
United States by:
Casemate
2114 Darby Road, 2nd Floor
Havertown, PA 19083

Distributed in the
United Kingdom by:
Portfolio Books Ltd
Suite 3/4, Great West House,
Great West Road, Brentford,
Middlesex TW8 9DF

Printed and bound in China